942.1

LONDON.

By WALTER BESANT.

'What the late J. R. Green has done for England Mr. Besant has here attempted, with conspicuous success, for Cockaigne. The author of "A Short History of the English People" and the historian of the London citizen share together the true secret of popularity. Both have placed before the people of to-day a series of vivid and indelible pictures of the people of the past. . . . No one who loves his London but will love it the better for reading this book. He who loves it not has before him a clear duty and a manifest pleasure.'—GRAPHIC.

'The author has dealt with all sorts and conditions of men that have in successive well-marked generations trodden its streets and lived its life. For such a record the materials are abundant, and Mr. Besant has made good use of them. His work ought to be a welcome addition to every library. — DAILY TELEGRAPH.

'A charming volume, adorned with many exquisite illustrations. In a series of pictures Mr. Besant unrolls before our eyes the panorama of a living London in the ages that are past. We see the people at their daily toil and at their amusements. We are acquainted with their customs and their social habits. We walk about their streets and examine their houses. We watch the evolution and growth of their city. and the changes in their habits. Mr. Besant has clothed the dry bones of history with living and fascinating interest. . . . Written in a graphic style, there is not a dull page in Besant's "London."'—MORNING LEADER.

'A series of charming pictures of the City of London and its people from age to age. . . . The dry bones of ancient chroniclers, the forgotten learning of forgotten students, old tracts and stray household accounts, live again with valuable significance in the brightness and freshness of the pages of "London." . . . We shall have in vain exposed the nature of Mr. Besant's volume if our readers do not begin and finish it for themselves with avidity.'—DAILY CHRONICLE.

'"London" is as good as a novel—better than many. It is a romance in which the writer has found inspiration. His style marches with his narrative, his narrative is worthy of the events it records.'—YORKSHIRE POST.

'A book on London by Walter Besant must surely recommend itself sufficiently to all readers by its title and the name of its author. . . . It is a series of instantaneous photographs, taken from age to age, by an artist of rare skill in applying his camera and developing the latent details of his plate. . . . Altogether the book deserves a cordial welcome from all who take an intelligent interest in the London life of the past.'—TIMES.

'As everybody is aware, Mr. Besant knows and loves his London. He is as devoted a student of London as Dickens himself ever was. In historic knowledge of London Mr. Besant is, we imagine, equalled by few. . . . His book is a kind of London "At Home" during thirteen centuries. He has ransacked mediæval, Tudor, and subsequent literature and art for his materials. In his researches he has made some absolutely new discoveries, among which not the least interesting is a collection of household accounts.'—ECHO.

'Mr. Besant writes history as Thackeray wrote the chronicles of the Four Georges. The result is a series of charming sketches penned with all the picturesqueness of an author who has laid so many of his scenes in London town. . . . The book is a valuable as well as an eminently readable one.'—STANDARD.

'Mr. Besant could scarcely be dull if he tried, and in these pages he certainly has not made the attempt. The art of the novelist is conspicuous in the book, and the narrative at every turn conveys a realistic impression of places and people, manners and movements, which long ago waxed old and vanished away.'—LEEDS MERCURY.

'Mr. Besant has written a book in his sagest and brightest vein on the history of London. He goes up and down the centuries in a delightfully good humour, responding to Thackeray's famous appeal to the Muse of History not to take herself so seriously, but to show us the common life of every age. . . . Mr. Besant writes graphically and with good sense, and the volume deserves to be popular.'—MANCHESTER GUARDIAN.

'A brilliant series of pictures. . . . Nothing so vivid has ever before been done about old London. There does not seem to be a single false note, and the amount both of hard reading and of personal topographical observation necessary to its composition must have been enormous. Mr. Besant gives us just so much that we wish he had given us more. The novelist turned historian is delightful reading.'—SATURDAY REVIEW.

'Mr. Besant knows and loves his London thoroughly, and his beautifully illustrated book will call up in the minds of those who bow to the spell a thousand delights of memory and expectation. Mr. Besant contrives not merely to call back the old London, but to make the London of the present more living than before.'—SPECTATOR.

'Mr. Besant has given us a delightful book. . . . Here is a fascinating catalogue, and Mr. Besant comes up to his talogue with all the picturesque skill and conscientious learning which the public have learned to expect from him. No Londoner who takes an interest in his city can afford to be without it.'—SUN.

'A volume which every Londoner should read. It is at once instructive and entertaining. Mr. Besant has never written anything more absorbing and delightful than this description of London.'—GLOBE.

'Mr. Besant has invested all his chapters with the charm of a novel, and his seems to be the most successful attempt that has yet been made to picture old London in flesh and blood rather than in parchment and masonry.'—CITIZEN.

'Mr. Besant has given us in this delightful volume the romance of London—with an accuracy and a care for truthful detail as conspicuous as they are in Maitland or in Stow himself.'—NATIONAL OBSERVER.

⁎ *A few copies of the LIBRARY EDITION may still be had, demy 8vo. cloth gilt, gilt top, price 18s.*

London : CHATTO & WINDUS, 214 Piccadilly, W.

The Towers of Westminster

WESTMINSTER

BY

WALTER BESANT, M.A. F.S.A.

AUTHOR OF 'LONDON' ETC.

WITH AN ETCHING BY FRANCIS S. WALKER, R.P.E.
AND 130 ILLUSTRATIONS BY WILLIAM PATTEN AND OTHERS

LONDON

CHATTO & WINDUS, PICCADILLY
1895

TO

MRS WILLIAM PATTEN

IN MEMORY OF HER

MANY WANDERINGS IN WESTMINSTER WITH HER HUSBAND

WHILE HE WAS ADORNING THESE PAGES

AND IN MEMORY OF

A STAY IN ENGLAND FAR TOO SHORT FOR HER MANY FRIENDS

THIS VOLUME IS DEDICATED

BY ONE OF THOSE FRIENDS

THE AUTHOR

PREFACE

THESE papers in their original form first appeared in the Pall Mall Magazine. Additions have been made in some of the chapters, especially in the three chapters entitled 'The Abbey.' As in the book entitled 'London,' of which this is the successor, I do not pretend to offer a History of Westminster. The story of the Abbey Buildings; of the Great Functions held in the Abbey; of the Monuments in the Abbey; may be found in the pages of Stanley, Loftie, Dart, and Widmore. The History of the Houses of Parliament belongs to the history of the country, not to that of Westminster. It has been my endeavour, in these pages, (1) to show, contrary to received opinion, that the Isle of Bramble was a busy place of trade long before London existed at all. (2) To restore the vanished Palaces of Westminster and Whitehall. (3) To portray the life of the Abbey, with its Services, its Rule, its Anchorites, and its Sanctuary. (4) To show the connection of Westminster with the first of English printers. And, lastly, to present the place as a town and borough, with its streets and its people.

I hope that, with those who have made my 'London' a companion, my 'Westminster' may be so fortunate as to find equal favour.

I must not omit my acknowledgments to the Editors of the Pall Mall Magazine *for the costly manner in which they presented these pages. Nor must I forget to record my sense of the pains and thoroughness brought to the work of its illustration by my friend Mr. William Patten; nor my sense of the assistance rendered me by Mr. Loftie in many consultations and suggestions; nor my thanks to the Benedictine Fathers of Downside, near Bath, who kindly received Mr. Patten and myself as their guests and showed us what a modern Benedictine House really means, and how the House at Westminster may have been during its five centuries of existence, even such as their own, a Home of Religion and Learning.*

W. B.

United University Club,
September 1895.

CONTENTS

LIST OF ILLUSTRATIONS

CHAPTER I

THE BEGINNINGS

HE who considers the history of Westminster presently observes with surprise that he is reading about a city which has no citizens. In this respect Westminster is alone among cities and towns of the English-speaking race : she has had no citizens. Residents she has had—tenants, lodgers, subjects, sojourners within her boundaries—but no citizens. The sister city within sight, and almost within hearing, can show an unequalled roll of civic worthies, animated from the beginning by an unparalleled tenacity of purpose, clearly seeing and understanding what they wanted and why, and how they could obtain their desire. This knowledge had been handed down from father to son. Freedom, self-government, corporations, guilds, brotherhoods, privileges, safety, and order—all have been achieved and assured by means of this tenacity and this clear understanding of what was wanted.

B

Westminster has never possessed any of these things. For the City of London these achievements were rendered possible by the existence of one single institution : the Folk's Mote— the Parliament of the People. Westminster never possessed that institution. The history of London is a long and dramatic panorama, full of *tableaux*, animated scenes, dramatic episodes, tragedies, and victories. In every generation there stands out one great citizen, strong and clear-eyed, whom the people follow : he is a picturesque figure, lifted high above the roaring, turbulent, surging crowd, whom he alone can govern. In Westminster there is no such citizen, and there is no such crowd. Only once in its history, until the eighteenth century, do we light upon the Westminster folk. Perhaps there have been, here and there, among them some mute inglorious Whittington—some unknown Gresham. Alas! there was no Folk's Mote—without a Folk's Mote nothing could be done—and so their possible leaders sank into the grave in silence and oblivion. Why was there no Folk's Mote ? Because the land on which Westminster stood, the land all around, north, west, south—how broad a domain we shall presently discover—belonged to the Church, and was ruled by the Abbot. Where the Abbot was king there was no room for the rule of the people.

Nor could there be any demand in Westminster for free institutions, because there were no trades and no industries. A wool staple there was, certainly, which fluctuated in importance, but was never to be compared with any of the great City trades. And Westminster was not a port, she had no quays or warehouses : neither exports nor imports—save only the wool—passed through her hands. There was no necessity at any time for the people who might at that time be her tenants to demand corporate action. Westminster has never attracted or invited immigrants or settlers.

Again, a considerable portion of those who lived in Westminster were criminals or debtors taking advantage of sanctuary. The privilege of sanctuary plays an important part in the history of Westminster. It is not, however, from sanctuary birds that one would expect a desire for order and free institutions. Better the rule of the Abbot with safety than freedom of government and the certainty of gallows and whipping-post therewith.

We may consider that for five hundred years the Court and the Church, the Palace and the Abbey, divided between them the whole of Thorney Island. Until, therefore, the swamps were drained, there was no place — or a very narrow place—for houses and inhabitants on the south and west. Towards the north, between New Palace Yard and Charing Cross, houses began and grew, but quite slowly. Even so recently as the year 1755 the parish of St. Margaret's had extended westward no farther than to include the streets called Pye Street, Orchard Street, Tothill Street, and Petty France, now York Street. King Street was the main street connecting Westminster with London by way of Charing Cross ; and east and west of King Street, at the Westminster or southern end, was a network of narrow streets, courts, and slums, a few of which still exist to show what Westminster of the Tudors and the Stuarts used to be.

After the Dissolution—though the Dean succeeded the Abbot—there was some concession in the direction of popular government. The Dean still continued to be the over-lord. He appointed a High Sheriff, who in his turn appointed a Deputy ; the city was divided into wards, in imitation of London, with a burgess to represent each ward. The court thus formed possessed considerable powers of police ; but neither in authority, nor in power, nor in dignity, could such a chamber be compared with the Court of Aldermen of London. Edward VI. granted two members of Parliament to the City of Westminster.

Another reason which hindered the advance of the city in the last century was that the Dean and Chapter would neither sell their lands nor grant long leases. Therefore no one would build good houses, and the vicinity of the Abbey remained covered with mean tenements and populated by the scum and refuse.

For these reasons Westminster has had residents of all conditions—from king and noble to criminal and debtor. But it has had no citizens, no corporate life, no united action, no purpose. The City of London is a living whole : one would call its history the life of a man—the progress of a soul ; the multitudinous crowd of separate lives rolls together and forms but one as the corporation grows greater, stronger, more free, with every century. But Westminster is an inert, lifeless form. Round the stately Abbey, below the noble halls, the people lie like sheep—but sheep without a leader. They have no voice ; if they suffer, they have no cry ; they have no aims ; they have no ambition ; without crafts, trades, mysteries, enterprise, distinctions, posts of honour, times of danger, liberties to defend, privileges to maintain, there may be thousands of men living in a collection of houses, but they are not citizens. In the pages that follow, therefore, we shall have little to do with the people of Westminster.

The following is Bardwell's account of the original site of Westminster (' Westminster Improvements,' p. 8) :

'Thorney Island is about 470 yards long and 370 yards broad, washed on the east side by the Thames, on the south by a rivulet running down College-street, on the north by another stream wending its way to the Thames down Gardener's-lane : this and the College-street rivulet were joined by a moat called Long-ditch, forming the western boundary of Thorney Island, along the present line of Prince's and De la Hay streets. This Island was the Abbey and Palace precinct, which, in addition to the water surrounding it, was further defended by lofty stone walls (part of which still remain in the Abbey gardens) : in these walls were four noble gates, one in King-street, one near New Palace-yard (the foundations of which I observed in this month, Dec. 1838, in excavating for a new sewer), one opening into Tothill, or as it was called by William the First Touthull-street, and one at the mill by College-street. The precinct was entered by a bridge, erected by the Empress Maud, at the end of Gardener's-lane in King-street, and by another bridge, still existing, though deep below the present pavement, at the east end of College-street.'

The beginning of city and abbey is an oft-told tale, but, as I shall try to show, a tale never truly and properly told. Antiquaries, or rather historians who have to depend on antiquaries, are apt to follow each other blindly. Thus, we are informed by every one who has treated of this beginning, that the place on which Westminster Abbey stands was chosen deliberately as a fitting place for a monastic foundation, because of its seclusion, silence, and remoteness. 'This spot,' writes the most illustrious among all the historians of the Abbey, when he has described the position of Thorney, 'thus entrenched, marsh within marsh, forest within forest, was indeed *locus terribilis*—the terrible place, as it was called, in the first notices of its existence ; yet, even thus early, it presented several points of attraction to the founder of whatever was the original building which was to redeem it from the wilderness. It had the advantages of a Thebaid as contrasted with the stir and tumult of the neighbouring forest of London.' [1] And the same theory is adopted by Freeman, when he speaks of the site as 'so near to the great city, and yet removed from its immediate throng and turmoil.' There is no doubt as to the meaning of both writers. The idea in their minds was of a place deliberately chosen by the founders of the first abbey, and adopted by Edward the Confessor as a wild, deserted, secluded place, difficult of access, remote from the ways of men, where in silence and peace the holy men might work and meditate. Let us examine into this assumption. The result, I venture to think, will upset many cherished opinions.

In the examination of ancient sites there are five principal things to ascertain before any conclusion is attempted—that is to say, before we attempt to restore the place as it was, or to identify it. The method which I began to learn twenty years ago, while following day by day Major Conder's Survey of Palestine, and studying day by day his plans and drawings, his arguments and identifications, of a land which is one great field of ruins, I propose to apply to Thorney Island and the site of Westminster Abbey. These five points are : (1) the evidence of situation ; (2) the evidence of excavation ; (3) the evidence of ancient monuments, ruins, foundations, fragments ; (4) the evidence of tradition ; and (5) the evidence of history.

Let us take these several points in order.

[1] Stanley, *Westminster Abbey*, p. 7.

1. *Evidence of Situation.*

The river Thames, which narrowed at London Bridge, began to widen out west of the mouth of the stream called the Fleet. There was a cliff or rising bank along the Strand, which confined the stream on its north bank as far as Charing. At this village the course of the river turned south, and, after half a mile, south-west. Here it formerly broadened into a vast marsh or lagoon, quite shallow to east and west, in parts only covered with water at high tide, and in parts rising above even the highest tides. This great marsh covered all the land known later as St. James's Park, Tothill Fields, the Five Fields, Victoria, Earl's Court, and part of Chelsea : on the other bank the marsh extended from Rotherhithe over Bermondsey, Southwark, Lambeth, Vauxhall, and part of Battersea. The places which here and there rose above the reach of flood were called islands : Bermond's-ea—the Isle of Bermond ; Chels-ea—the Isle of Shingle (Chesil) ; Thorn-ea— the Isle of Bramble ; Batters-ea the Isle of Peter. You may find little islands (eyots—aits) just like these higher up the river, such as Monkey Island, Eelpie Island, and so many others. No doubt, in very remote times, these little river islets were secluded places indeed ; if any people lived upon them, they lived like the lake dwellers of Glastonbury, each family in its cottage planted down in the sedge and mud of the foreshore, resting on piles, with its floor of hard clay pressed down on timber, its walls of clay and wattle, its roof of rushes, its boat floating before the door. They trapped elk and deer and boar, they shot the wild fowl with their slings, they caught the salmon that swarmed in the river. Thorney, then, the site of the future abbey, the Isle of Bramble, was an islet entirely surrounded by the waters of a broad and shallow river. It was so broad that the backwater extended as far as the present site of Buckingham Palace. It was so shallow that at low tide a man would wade across from the rising ground of the west to the island and from the

island to the opposite shore, where is now St. Thomas's
Hospital.

This is the evidence of the natural situation, and so far all
would be agreed.

2. *Evidence of Excavation.*

The kindly earth covers up and preserves many precious
secrets—'underground,' says Rabelais, 'are all great treasures
and wonderful things'—to be revealed at some fitting time,
when men's minds shall be prepared to receive them. The
earth preserves, for instance, the history of the ancient world
—witness the revelations in our own time of the cuneiform

SARCOPHAGUS OF VALERIUS AMANDINUS

tablets and the vast extension of the historic age : the arts of
the ancient world, and their houses, and their manner of life—
witness the revelations of Pompeii.   Applied to Thorney,
excavation has shown—what we certainly never could have
known otherwise—that here, of all places in the world, in this
little secluded islet in the midst of marshes (this most unlikely
spot, one would think, in the whole of Britannia), there was a
Roman station, and one of considerable importance.   The
first hint of this fact was suggested when there was dug up in
the North Green of the Abbey, in the year 1869, a fine
Roman sarcophagus inscribed with the name of Valerius
Amandinus.   The lid has a cross upon it, from which it has

been conjectured that the sarcophagus was used twice, its second occupant having been a Christian. What reason, however, is there for supposing that Valerius Amandinus himself was not a Christian ?—for at least a century before the withdrawing of the Legions Roman Britain was wholly Christian. For more than two centuries Christians had been numerous. During the fourth century the country was covered with monastic foundations for monks and nuns. Christian or not, there stands the sarcophagus of Valerius Amandinus, for all the world to see, at the entrance of the Chapter-house ; and why a Roman cemetery should be established in Thorney no one could guess. But some ten years ago there was a second discovery. In digging a grave under the pavement of the nave, there was found a mosaic floor in very fair condition. This must have belonged to a Roman villa. But, if one villa, why not more ? The question has been settled by the discovery, of late years, wherever the ground on Thorney has been opened, of Roman bricks and fragments of Roman buildings. It is now impossible to doubt the existence here of a Roman station.

That is, so far, the (unfinished) evidence of excavation.

But why did the Romans place a station, an important station, on this bit of a bramble-covered eyot, with a shallow river in front and a marshy backwater behind ? What strategic importance could be attached to such a spot ? The next branch of evidence will serve to answer the question.

3. *Evidence of Ancient Monuments.*

There are here none of those shapeless mounds of ancient ruins which are found elsewhere—as in Egypt. Nor are there any foundations above ground, as at Silchester. Yet there is one fact of capital importance, which not only serves to explain why the Romans established a station on Thorney, but also illustrates, as we shall see, many other facts in the history of the island. It is this.

The river from Thorney to the opposite shore, as we have

seen, was fordable at low tide. The marsh from Thorney to the rising ground on the west was fordable probably at all tides—certainly at low tide.

This ford, the only one across the river for many miles up stream, belonged from time immemorial to the highway, a road or beaten track leading from the north of England to the south, and 'tapping' the midland country on the way. The road which the Saxons called Watling Street, when it reached this neighbourhood, ran straight down Park Lane, or Tyburn Lane as it was formerly called, to the edge of the marsh. There it ended abruptly. If you will draw this line on any map, you will find that it ended at the western extremity of St. James's Park, just about Buckingham Palace, where the marsh began. At this point the traveller plunged into the shallow waters, and guided by stakes, waded—at low tide there were, haply, stepping-stones—across the swamp to Thorney. Here, if the tide served, he again trusted himself to the guidance of stakes ; and so, breast high, it may be, waded through the river till he reached the opposite shore, where another high road, 'Dover Street,' which also broke off abruptly at this point, awaited him. Later on, when London Bridge was built, Watling Street was diverted at the spot where now stands the Marble Arch, was carried along the present Oxford Street and Holborn, and passed through the City to the Bridge. This alternative route probably took away a great deal of the traffic : but for those who had business in the south or the south-west, or for those who were bound for the port of Dover, the ford was still preferred as the shorter way. A bridge was convenient, but the traveller of the fourth century was accustomed to a ford. Those who had no business in London were not likely to be turned out of their way by another ford, after they had crossed so many.

The high road between the north and the south, the great highway into which were poured streams from all the other

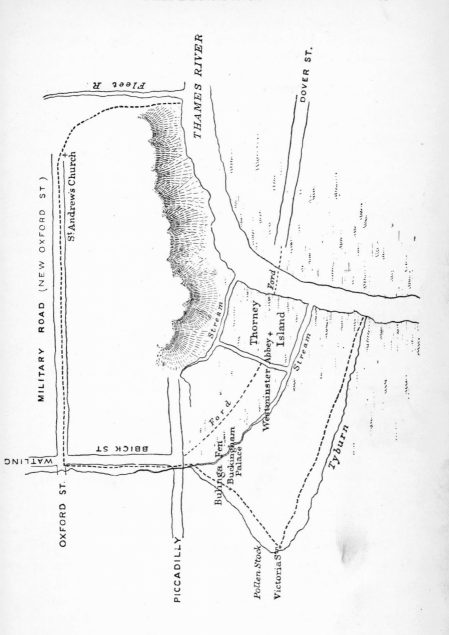

ways, passed through this double ford, and over the Isle of Bramble. This was not a highway passing through a wild and savage country ; on the contrary, Britain was a country, in the two latter centuries of the Roman occupation, thickly populated, covered with great cities and busy towns. No one who has stood within the walls of Silchester, and has marked the foundations of its great hall, larger that Westminster Abbey, the remains of its corridors and courts and shops, the indications of wealth and luxury furnished by its villas, the extent of its walls, can fail to understand that the vanished civilisation of Roman Britain was very far superior to anything that followed for a good deal more than a thousand years. It was more artistic, more luxurious, than the Saxon or the Norman life. But it was essentially Roman. Civilised Rome could not be understood by Western Europe until the fifteenth century. Roman Britain is only beginning to be understood by ourselves. We have not as yet realised how much was swept away and lost when, after two centuries of fighting, the Britons were driven to their mountains, with the loss of the old arts and learning. All over the country were the great houses, the stately villas, of a rich, cultured and artistic class ; all over the country were rich cities, filled with people who desired, and had, all the things that made life tolerable in Rome herself. The condition of Bordeaux in the fourth century, her schools, her professors, her poets, her orators, her lawyers, may suggest the condition of London, and in a less degree that of many smaller cities.

If we bear these things in mind, I think we shall understand that the roads must have been everywhere crowded and thronged by the long processions of packhorses and mules engaged in supplying the various wants of this people, bringing food supplies to the cities, wines and foreign luxuries to the unwarlike people who were doomed before long to fall before the ruder and stronger folk of the Frisian speech. For our purpose it is sufficient to note that it was a country where the wants of the better sort created, by themselves, a vast trade, where, in addition, the exports were large and valuable, and where the traffic of the highways was very great and never-ending.

In other words, this wild and desolate spot, chosen, we are told, as a fitting site for a monastery because of its remoteness and its seclusion, was, long before a monastery was built here, the scene of a continual procession of those who journeyed south and those who journeyed north. It was a halting- and resting-place for a stream of travellers who never stopped all the year round. By way of Thorney passed the merchants, with their hides bestowed upon their packhorses, going to embark them at Dover : London had not yet gathered in all the trade of the country. By way of Thorney they drove the long strings of slaves to be sold in Gaul. By way of Thorney passed the legions on their way north ; craftsmen, traders, mimes, actors, musicians, dancers, jugglers, on their way to the towns of Glevum, Corinium, Eboracum, and the rest. Always, day after day, even night after night, there was the clamour of those who came and those who went : such a clamour as used to belong, for instance, to the courtyard of an old-fashioned inn, in and out of which there lumbered the loaded waggon, grinding heavily over the stones ; the stage-coach, the post-chaise, the merchant's rider on his nag—all with noise. The Isle of Bramble was like that courtyard : outside the Abbey it was a great inn, a halting-place, a bustling, noisy, frequented place ; the centre, before London, the mart of Britannia ; no 'Thebaid' at all ; no quiet, secluded, desolate place, but the centre of the traffic of the whole island. And it remained a busy place long after London Bridge was built, long after the Port of London had swallowed up all the other ports in the country. When the river, by means of embankments, was forced into narrower and deeper channels, the ford disappeared.

By this time the backwater and the marsh had been dried, and the traveller could walk dry-shod from the end of Watling Street to the Isle of Bramble. Perhaps, it may be objected, solitude descended upon the island, and the silence of desertion, with the deepening of the channel. Not so ; for now another highway had been created—the highway up the river. The growth of London created the necessity for this highway. From the western country all the exports came down the river to the Port of London : from the Port of London all the import trade went up the river to the west of England. At the flow of the tide the deeply-laden barges, like our own, but narrower, went up the river ; at the ebb they went down. Going up, the barges carried spices, wines, silks, glass, candles, lamps, hangings, pictures, statuary, books, church furniture, and all the foreign luxuries that were now necessary in the British city : going down they were laden with pelts and wool. The slaves, which formed so large a part of British export, not only at this period, but later, under the Saxons, were marched along the highway. There were also the barges laden with fruit, vegetables, grain, poultry, wild birds, carcases, for that wide London mouth which continually devoured and daily called for more. And there were the fishermen casting their nets for the salmon in the season, and for the other fish with which the river, its waters clean and wholesome, teemed all the year round. Full and various was the life upon the river. Always there was traffic, always movement, always activity, and always noise—much noise. A great noise : where boatmen are there is always noise ; they exchange the joke Fescennine, they laugh, they quarrel, they fight, they sing. To the Benedictine monks the river presented the spectacle of a procession as noisy and as animated as that which in the old days had made a stepping-stone of the island from one ford to the other. In short, there was never any time, from the beginning of the Roman occupation to the present day, when the Isle of Bramble was a quiet, secluded, desolate spot. Always crowded, bustling, and noisy. Why should not a Benedictine monastery be planted in the midst of the people? The Rule of Benedict was not the Rule of Robert of Citeaux.

Two hundred years later, when the Priory of the Holy Trinity was founded, did they place the monastery in the wilds of Sheppey, or in the marshes of the Isle of Dogs, or on lonely Canvey? Not at all: they placed it within London Wall— at Aldgate, the busiest place in the City. And the Franciscans, were they exiled to some remote quarter? Not at all: they were established within the walls. So were the Austin Friars and the Crutched Friars; while White Friars and Black Friars were close to the City wall. And even the austere Carthusians were within hearing of the horse fairs, the races, the

SHIELD OF CELTIC WORK, FOUND IN THE THAMES 1857

tournaments, and the sports of the citizens upon the field called Smooth. Nor does it ever appear that the monks were dissatisfied with their position, and craved for solitude: they preferred the din and roar of the noisiest city in the habitable world.

So that, by the evidence of natural situation, by the evidence of excavation, and by the evidence of ancient monuments, we understand that the Isle of Bramble was a Roman station, the point where the highway of the north met the highway of the south—the very heart of Britannia, the centre of all internal communication, the place by which, until London gathered all into her lap, the whole traffic of the island must pass. Before London existed, Thorney had become a place of the greatest importance ; long after London had become a rich and busy port, Thorney, the stepping-stone in the middle of the ford, continued its old importance and its activity. Never a place of trade, but always a place of passing traffic, its population was great,

A ROMAN ROAD

but as ephemeral as the May-fly : its people came, rested a night, a day, an hour, and were gone again.

4. We have next the *Evidence of Tradition.*

According to this authority we learn that the first Christian king was one Lucius, who in the year 178 addressed a letter to the then Pope, Eleutherius, begging for missionaries to instruct his people and himself in the Christian faith. The Pope sent two priests named Ffagan and Dyfan, who converted the whole island. Bede tells this story ; the old Welsh chroniclers also tell it, giving the British name of the king, Lleurwg ap Coel ap Cyllin. He it was who erected a church on the Isle of Bramble, in place of a temple of Apollo formerly standing there. We remember also that St. Paul's was said to have been built on the site of a temple of Diana.

This church continued in prosperity until the arrival, two hundred and fifty years later, of the murderous Saxons. First, news came up the river that the invader was on the Isle of Rum, which we call Thanet; next, that he held the river—that he had overrun Essex—that he had overrun Kent. And then the procession of merchandise stopped suddenly. The ports of Kent were in the hands of the enemy. There was no more traffic on Watling Street. The travellers grew fewer daily; till one day a troop of wild Saxons came across the ford, surprised the priests and the fisher-folk who remained, and left the island as desolate and silent as could

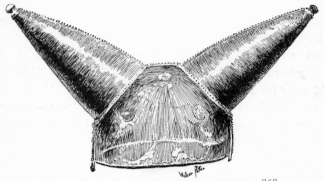

BRITISH HELMET, FOUND IN THE THAMES 1868

be desired for the meditation of holy men. This done, the Saxons went on their way. They overran the midland country; they drove the Britons back—still farther back— till they reached the mountains. No more news came to Thorney, for, though the ford continued, the island, like so many of the Roman stations, remained a waste Chester.

In fulness of time the Saxon king himself settled down, became a man of peace, obeyed the order of the convert king to be baptized and to enter the Christian faith; and when King Sebert had been persuaded to build a church to St. Paul on the highest ground of London, he was further convinced that it was his duty to restore the ruined church of St. Peter

C

on the Isle of Thorney beside the ford.   Scandal indeed
would it be, were the throng that daily passed through the
ford and over the island to see in a Christian country, the
neglected ruins of this Christian church.   Accordingly the
builders soon set to work, and before long the church rose
tall and stately.   The Miracle of the Hallowing, often told,
may be repeated here.   On the eve of the day fixed by the
Bishop of London for the hallowing and dedication of the new
St. Peter's, one Edric, a fisherman, who lived in Thorney, was
awakened by a loud voice calling him by name.   It was midnight.   He arose and went forth.   The voice called him
again from the opposite side of the river, which is now
Lambeth, bidding him put out his boat to ferry a man across
the river.   He obeyed.   He found on the shore a venerable
person whose face and habiliments he knew not.   The
stranger bore in his hands certain vessels which Edric knew
could only be intended for church purposes.   However, he
said nothing, but received this mysterious visitor into his boat
and rowed him across the river.   Arrived in Thorney, the
stranger directed his steps to the church, and entered the
portal.   Straightway—lo! a marvel!—the church was lit up
as by a thousand wax tapers, and voices arose chanting
psalms—sweet voices such as no man, save this rude fisherman, had ever heard before.   He stood and listened.   The
voices, he perceived, could be none other than those of angels
come down from heaven itself to sing the first service in the
new church.   Then the voices fell, and he heard one voice
loud and solemn : and then the heavenly choir uplifted their
voices again.   Presently all was still : the service was over,
the lights went out as suddenly as they had appeared, and
the stranger came forth.

'Know, O Edric,' he said, while the fisherman's heart
glowed within him, 'know that I am Peter.   I have hallowed
the church myself.   To-morrow I charge thee that thou tell
these things to the Bishop, who will find a sign and token in

the church of my hallowing. And for another token, put forth again upon the river, cast thy nets, and thou shalt receive so great a draught of fishes that there will be no doubt left in thy mind. But give one-tenth to this my holy church.'

So he vanished ; and the fisherman was left alone upon the river bank. But he put forth as directed, and cast his net, and presently brought ashore a draught miraculous.

In the morning the Bishop with his clergy, and the King with his following, came up from London in their ships to hallow the church. They were received by Edric, who told them this strange story. And within the church the Bishop found the lingering fragrance of incense far more precious than any that he could offer ; on the altar were the drippings of wax candles (long preserved as holy relics, being none other than the wax candles of heaven), and written in the dust certain words in Greek character. He doubted no longer. He proclaimed the joyous news, he held a service of thanksgiving instead of a hallowing. Who would not hold a service of praise and humble gratitude for such a mark of heavenly favour ? And after service they returned to London and held a banquet, with Edric's finest salmon lying on a lordly dish in the midst.

How it was that Peter, who came from heaven direct could not cross the river except in a boat, was never explained or asked. Perhaps we have here a little confusion between Rome and Heaven. Dover Street, we know, broke off at the edge of the marsh, and Dover Street led to Dover, and Dover to Rome.

5. We are now prepared for the *Evidence of History*, which is not perhaps so interesting as that of tradition. Clio, it must be confessed, is sometimes dull. One misses the imagination and the daring flights of her sister, the tenth Muse—the Muse of Fiction. The earliest document which refers to the Abbey is a conveyance by Offa, King of Mercia,

of a manor called Aldenham, to ' St. Peter and the people of the Lord dwelling in Thorney, that " terrible "—i.e. sacred— place which is called at Westminster.' The date of this ancient document is A.D. 785 ; but Bede, who died in 736, does not mention the foundation. Either, therefore, Bede passed it over purposely, or it was not thought of importance enough to be mentioned. He does relate the building of St. Paul's ; but, on the other hand, he does not mention the hundreds of churches which sprang up all over the country. So that we need not attach any importance to the omission. My own opinion is that the church—a rude country church, perhaps—a building like that of Greenstead, Essex, the walls of split trees and the roof of rushes, was restored early in the seventh century, and that it did succeed an earlier church still. The traditional connection of King Sebert with the church is as ancient as anything we know about it, and the legend of Lucius and his church is at least supported by the recent discoveries of Roman remains and the certainty that the place was always of the greatest importance.

There is another argument—or an illustration—in favour of the antiquity of some church, rude or not, upon this place. I advance it as an illustration, though to myself it appears to be an argument : I mean the long list of relics possessed by the Abbey at the Dedication of the year 1065. We are not concerned with the question whether the relics were genuine or not, but merely with the fact that they were preserved by the monks as having been the gifts of various benefactors— Sebert, Offa, Athelstan, Edgar, Ethelred, Cnut, Queen Emma, and Edward himself. A church of small importance and of recent building would not dare to parade such pretensions. It takes time even for forgeries to gain credence and for legends to grow. The relics ascribed to Sebert and Offa could easily have been carried away on occasion of attack. As for the nature of these sacred fragments, it is pleasant to read of sand and earth brought from Mount Sinai and Olivet, of the beam which supported the holy manger, of a piece of the holy manger, of frankincense presented by the Magi, of the seat on which our Lord was presented at the Temple, of portions of the holy cross presented by four kings at different times, of bones and vestments belonging to apostles and martyrs and the Virgin Mary and saints without number, whose very names are now forgotten. In the cathedral of

TOMB OF KING SEBERT, WESTMINSTER ABBEY

Aix you may see just such a collection as that which the monks of St. Peter displayed before the reverent eyes of the Confessor. We may remember that in the ninth and tenth centuries the rage for pilgrimising extended over the whole of Western Europe: pilgrims crowded every road, they marched in armies, and they returned laden with treasures— water from the Jordan, sand from Sinai, clods of earth from Gethsemane, and bones and bits of sacred wood without number.

When Peter the Hermit arose to preach it was but putting a match to a pile ready to be fired. But for such a list as that preserved by history, there was need of time as well as credulity.

Then the same thing happened to the Saxon church which had been done by Saxon arms to the British church. It was destroyed, or at least plundered, by the Danes. The priests, who perhaps took refuge in London, saved their relics. After a hundred years of fighting, the Dane, too, came into the Christian fold. As soon as circumstances permitted, King Edgar, stimulated by Dunstan, rebuilt or restored the church, and brought twelve monks from Glastonbury. He also erected the monastic buildings after the Benedictine Rule ; and, as Stanley has pointed out, since in the monastery the church or chapel is built for the monks, the monastic buildings would be finished before the church.

Next, Edgar gave the monks a charter in which these lands are described and the boundaries laid down. You shall

THE FUNERAL PROCESSION OF KING EDWARD THE CONFE

see what a goodly foundation—on paper—was this Abbey of
St. Peter when it left the King's hands. Take the map of
London : run a line from Marble Arch along Oxford Street
and Holborn—the line of the new Watling Street—till you
reach the church of St. Andrew's, Holborn ; then follow the
Fleet river to its mouth—you have the north and east boundaries. The Thames is a third boundary. For the fourth,
draw a line from the spot where the Tyburn falls into the
Thames, to Victoria Station—thence to Buckingham Palace
—thence north to Marble Arch. The whole of the land
included belonged to the Abbey. A little later the Abbey
acquired the greater part of Chelsea, the manor of Paddington, the manor of Kilburn, including Hampstead and Battersea,—in fact, what is now the wealthier half of modern
London formerly belonged to the Benedictines of Westminster. At the time of Edgar's charter, however, they had the
area marked out above. More than half of it was marsh land.
In Doomsday Book there are but twenty-five houses on the

MINSTER ABBEY.   FROM THE BAYEUX TAPESTRY

whole estate.   Waste land, lying in shallow ponds, sometimes flooded by high tides, only the rising ground between what is now St. James's Park and Oxford Street could then be farmed.   The ground was reclaimed and settled very slowly ; still more slowly was it built upon.   Almost within the memory of man snipe were shot over South Kensington : a hundred years ago the whole of that thickly populated district west and south-west of Mayfair was a land of open fields.

So that, notwithstanding the great extent of their possessions, the monks were by no means rich, nor were Edgar's buildings, one imagines, very stately.   Yet the later buildings replaced the older on the same sites.   A plan of the Abbey of Edgar and Dunstan would show the Chapter-house and the Church where they are now ; the common dormitory over the common hall, as it was afterwards ; the refectory where it was afterwards ; the cloisters, without which no Benedictine monastery was complete, also where are those of Henry III. But the buildings were insignificant compared with what followed.

Roman Britain, we have said, was Christian for at least a hundred and fifty years ; the country was also covered with monasteries and nunneries.   Therefore it would be nothing out of the way or unusual to find monastic buildings on Thorney in the fourth century.   There was as yet no Benedictine Rule.   St. Martin of Tours introduced the Egyptian Rule into Gaul—whence it was taken over to England and to Ireland.   It was a simple Rule, resembling that of the Essenes. No one had any property ; all things were in common ; the only art allowed to be practised was that of writing ; the older monks devoted their whole time to prayer ; they took their meals together—bread and herbs, with salt—and, except for common prayer and common meals, they rarely left their cells : these were at first simple huts constructed of clay and bunches of reeds ; their churches were of wood ;

they shaved their heads to the line of the ears ; they wore
leather jerkins, probably because these lasted longer than
cloth of any kind ; many of them wore hair shirts. The
wooden church became a stone church ; the huts became
cells built about a cloister ; the cells themselves were abolished,
and a common dormitory was substituted. Then came the
Saxons, and the monks were dispersed or fled into Wales,
where they formed immense monasteries, as that of Bangor,
with its three thousand monks. All had to be done over again,
from the beginning. But monasticism, once introduced,
flourished exceedingly among the Saxons, until the long war
with the Danes destroyed the safety of the convent and
demanded the service of every man able to carry a sword,
and there were no more monks left in the land. All of which
is necessary to explain why Dunstan had to people his Abbey
with monks brought from Glastonbury. For Glastonbury
and Abingdon, into which the Benedictine Rule had been
introduced, were then the only monasteries surviving the long
Danish troubles.

These are the beginnings of the Abbey and the Church,
and of life upon the Island of Bramble. This is the foundation of the history that follows. A busy place before London
Bridge was built ; a place of throng and turmoil far back in
the centuries before the coming of the Roman ; a church
built in the midst of the throng ; monks in leather jerkins
living beside the church ; a ruined church, lying in ruins for
two hundred years while the Saxon infidel daily passed
beside it across the double ford ; then a rebuilding—why not
by Sebert ? Another destruction, and another rebuilding.

This view is also taken by Loftie in his 'Westminster
Abbey.' He does not, however, defend it and insist upon it
so strongly. He says, to quote his exact words, ' The hillock
on which we stand is called Thorn-Ey. There are some
Roman remains on it, and there may have been the ruins of
a little monastery and chapel, of which floating traditions

were afterwards gathered and exaggerated. The paved causeway to the westward is the Watling Street. On both sides of it runs the Tyburn, of which Thorn-Ey is a kind of delta. The road rises to Tot Hill, which is a conspicuous landmark here, and goes straight on over the "Bulunga Fen" till it reaches another, the "road to Reading," which has just crossed the Tyburn at Cowford, where Brick Street is now in Piccadilly. From Thorney, then, looking northward and westward, we see what remains of the great Middlesex forest, if the Danes have not burnt it all, and the paved Watling Street running straight on toward the distant Chester, keeping to the left of the lofty hill which is now crowned by the town of Hampstead. It is interesting to trace this ancient road through the modern streets, the more so as its existence determined the site and early importance of Westminster. When it emerged from the wild woods of northern Middlesex and came down towards the ford of the Thames, it followed what we call the Edgeware Road, Edgeware being the name of the first stopping place on the road, near the edge of the forest. Passing down the Edgeware Road in a straight line it is interrupted at the Marble Arch by a corner of the Park, which crosses the direct road towards Westminster. We know, however, that this corner is a comparatively recent addition to the Park, and the Watling Street soon resumes its course in Park Lane, which, keeping well on the high ground above the brook, nevertheless derived the name it was known by for many centuries from the Tyburn. Tyburn Lane reached the road to Reading at what we call Hyde Park Corner, and then ran straight through what was once called "Brookshott"—a little wood, where now is the Green Park and the gardens of Buckingham Palace—and on, right through the site of the palace itself, where the brook approached it very closely. So it descended to Tothill, the name of which has been plausibly explained to mean a place where the traveller "touted" for a guide or a boat, as the case might be, for the dangerous ford of the Thames below. This is rather conjectural, but is not to be rejected until a better explanation has been offered. One thing more has to be stated about this ancient highway—the Watling Street. How is it that we find the same name in the City? To answer this question we must look back to a period so remote that we cannot accurately date it, yet so definite, in one way, that there can be no mistake about it. This is the time at which London Bridge was built. When that great event took place Watling Street was diverted from Tyburn Lane, and instead of going to Westminster in order to ford the Thames, it turned to the left, along the modern Oxford Street and Holborn, and, entering the City at Newgate, went on to the bridge. Only a small part of the road still bears the ancient name, but that any of it does so is a most interesting and significant fact.

' We may conclude, therefore, if we wish to do so, that in a sense Westminster is older than London itself. What name it was called by we know not ; but the Romans certainly had a station here, as I have said, and the importance of the place before the making of London Bridge may have been considerable.'

In course of time the river was embanked, and ran in a deeper channel ; then the ford, as has been stated above, vanished, and the marshes were partly reclaimed, only pools remaining on both sides of the river—the Southwark pools remained till the beginning of this century. But Thorney after the drying of the marsh continued to be an island. On the north, the west, and the south sides it was bounded by streams ; on the east by the Thames. If you will take the map, and draw a line through Gardiner's Lane across King Street to the river, you will be tracing the exact course of the rivulet which ran into the Thames and formed the northern boundary of the island ; another line, down Great College Street, marks the course of a second stream ; while a third

line, down De la Hay and Princes Streets, joining the other
two, marks the lie of a connecting canal called Long Ditch.
It is interesting to walk along the narrow Gardiner's Lane,
one of the few remaining old streets of Westminster, and to
mark how the road presents a certain unmistakable look of
having been the bed of a stream : it bends and curves exactly
like a stream. The same thing may be imagined—by a
person of imagination—concerning Great College Street.

The island thus formed covered an area of four hundred
and seventy yards long from north to south, and three
hundred and seventy yards broad from east to west. At
some time or other—after the disappearance of the ford—the
Abbey precinct was surrounded by a wall. In the same way
St. Paul's, in the midst of the City, was surrounded by a wall
with embattled gates. A portion of this wall is perhaps still
standing. The wall was pierced by four gates. One of these
was in King Street, where the rivulet crossed ; one was at the
east end of Tothill Street ; a third was in Great College
Street, and its modern successor still stands on the spot with
no ancient work in it ; the last was in New Palace Yard. In
front of the riverside wall lived the population of Thorney—
the town of Westminster, such as it was—decayed indeed
since the deepening of the river : fisher-folk mostly, who
plied their trade on the river. But of town or village, in the
time of Edward the Confessor, there was little or none.

When the old Palace of Westminster was founded another
wall was erected round its buildings. Then the island was
completely surrounded by a fortification ; the fisher-folk
removed northward and settled somewhere lower down the
river, where afterwards arose the New Palace and Whitehall :
not higher up, where the ground continued to be a marsh for
many centuries to come. We have seen the beginnings of
the Church and of the Abbey. What were the beginnings of
the Palace ? When did a king begin to live on Thorney
Island ? And why ?

Since neither tradition nor history speaks to the contrary, we may suppose that Cnut was the first to build some kind of palace or residence in this place. His buildings are said to have been burned in the time of Edward ; therefore he must have built something. His residence on Thorney was neither continuous nor at any time of long duration. The court of the kings for many generations to come was a Court Itinerant. King Cnut travelled perpetually from place to place, followed by his regiment of house carles, though one knows not how many accompanied him. He stayed at Thorney because he loved the conversation of the Abbot Wolfstan. It was at Thorney that, according to the familiar story, he rebuked the courtiers in the matter of the rising tide ; and it was in the concluding years of his reign, when that marvellous change, graphically described by Freeman, fell upon him, and he became exactly the opposite of what he had before shown himself ; when he founded and endowed and augmented churches and monasteries. His heart was changed : the stately services of the minster, the rolling of the organ, the chanting of the monks, the splendour of the altar, the story of the Gospel, the legends and the acts of the Saints, the pilgrimage to Rome,—these things pleased him more than the clash of steel on shield, the war cry, and the glorious madness of the fight. The beginner of the old Palace was the great King Cnut the Dane.

We write under the shadow of the Abbey : the bells peal out over our heads ; the organ swells and dies ; within the walls are the coffins and the bones of dead kings and princes and nobles. The air is ecclesiastic : we may talk of changed hearts and repentant age. The age of civil wars, intestine wars—the worst wars of all, the wars of those who speak the same language—lasted for five hundred years after the death of King Cnut. We who belong to a generation which has learned some self-control, cannot realise the intensity, the strength of the passions which devoured and maddened the kings of old. The things which make history dreadful : the murders, the cry to arms at the least provocation ; the cruel disregard of innocent suffering ; the wasting, pillaging, destroying of lands and fields, and villages and towns, in blind revenge ; the blinding and torturing and maiming of which every page is full,—these things mean the rage of kings, the revenge of kings upon their enemies. Cnut in his last years had no enemies ; he had killed them all. Then there were no more rages ; he suffered his head to dwell upon nobler things : in modern language, he 'got religion.' And so, at the end of this Prologue to the Westminster Play, we see the King taking off his blood-stained ermine, laying down the sword which has set free so many unwilling souls, and walking, in meditation and godly discourse, under the quiet cloisters of the Abbey. Outside, the noisy court and camp ; within, the calm and peace of the religious life. The picture strikes a note of what is to follow when we pass into the period of history written from day to day, and draw up the curtain for the Pageant, Mystery, or Play of Westminster.

CHAPTER II

THE KING'S PALACE OF WESTMINSTER

THE kings of England held their Court in the Old Palace, the Palace of Westminster, for five hundred years. Of all the buildings which formed that Palace, there remain at this day nothing but a Hall, greatly altered, a Crypt, and a single Tower. Sixty years ago, before the last of the many fires which attacked the Palace, there was left, much disfigured, a single group of buildings which formerly contained the heart of the Palace, the king's House. This group, however, was so much shut in and surrounded with modern houses, courts, offices, taverns and stores, that the ancient parts could be with difficulty detached. Fortunately this task was accomplished before the fire : one can therefore restore one part, at least, of the Palace.

In considering the Palace of Westminster, we have the choice, as regards time, of any year we please between the accession of Edward the Confessor and the removal of Henry VIII. to York House. Let us take the close of the fourteenth century : let us attempt to restore the Palace as it was in the reign of Richard II. It was a time when that shadowy, intangible force called Chivalry was most active. Yet at best it was never stronger than its successor, which we now call Honour. Chivalry taught loyalty, even unto death ; protection of the weak ; respect for women ; fidelity in love ; mercy to the conquered ; charity to the poor ; obedience to the Church ; fidelity to the spoken word : you may find these teachings in the pages of Froissart. Knights who obey these

precepts are greatly extolled by poets ; yet the opposites of
these things are continually reported by historians. I think
that we may roughly, but certainly, ascertain the chief besetting sins of any age by looking for the contraries, which
will be the things which preachers and poets do mostly extol.

It has been remarked that antiquarians are prone to fall
into the incurable vice of looking at the past through the
wrong end of the telescope. This comes from constantly
endeavouring to reconstruct the past out of an insufficient
number of fragments. Of course the result is that everything
is reduced in size. Thus, many antiquarians, being afflicted
with this disease, have found themselves unable to see
anything but a collection of miserable hovels in that London
of the fourteenth century which was a city of nobles' palaces,
merchants' stately houses, splendid churches, monastic buildings, beautiful and lofty, side by side with warehouses,
wharves, ships riding at anchor, crowded streets and rich
shops. No antiquary, however, is wrong in showing that
Westminster was, at this time, nothing more than a City—as
yet not called a City—gathered round the Church and the
Court. To those who journeyed thither from London by the
river highway, a line of noble houses faced the river, each
with its stairs, its barges, and its water gate. Thus, taking
boat at Queenhithe, the traveller passed, among others,
Baynard's Castle, Blackfriars' Abbey, Bridewell Palace,
Whitefriars, the Temple, Durham House, the Savoy, York
House, before he reached the King's Stairs at Westminster.
At the back of these houses, where is now Fleet Street and
the Strand, there were no houses, in the fourteenth century,
except just outside Ludgate. As late as 1543, according to
the map of Anthony van den Wyngreede, the houses of Westminster were all gathered together in that little triangle opposite Westminster Hall, whose northern boundary was the stream
running down Gardiner's Lane and cutting off Thorney.
All beyond was open country lying in fields and meadows.

It is impossible to ascertain what, and of what kind, were the buildings of Edward the Confessor : tradition always assigned to him the Painted Chamber and the group of buildings which survived to the year 1835. Let us, however, consider what were the actual requirements of a Royal Palace under the Plantagenets. It will be seen very soon that this group of buildings could have formed only a very small

EAST END OF THE PRINCE'S CHAMBER

portion of the whole Palace. It will also be found that the Palace grows in the mind as we consider it. At first the Court was itinerant. Edward the Confessor was constantly travelling into different parts of his realm : he kept every Christmas, except his last, at Gloucester ; his Easter he kept at Winchester ; he resided a good deal at Westminster ; we hear of him at Worcester ; at Sandwich ; he hunted in Wiltshire. Henry II., whose actual itinerary has been re-

D

covered and published, seldom remained more than a few days in one place ; he was sometimes in France for three or four years at a time ; during the whole of his long reign he was only in Westminster on seventeen occasions, and then often for a night or two only.   Until the Tudors began a stationary Court, the kings of England travelled a great deal, and, in case of war, always went out with the army.   Whether they travelled or whether they stayed in one place, there was always with them a following greater than that of any baron. Warwick rode into London with seven hundred knights and men at arms ; that was but a slender force compared with the company which rode after the king.   Cnut, who perhaps began this first standing army, had three thousand 'hus-carles' ; Richard II. had four thousand archers always with him.

First, then, for the people, the service, the officers, necessary for the Court.   There were, to begin with, the artificers and craftsmen.   Everything wanted for the Court had to be done or made within the precincts of the Palace. There were no Court tradesmen ; no outside shops.   The king's craftsmen were the king's servants ; they had quarters of some kind, houses or chambers, allotted to them in the Palace ; they received wages, rations, and liveries.   Thus, in Richard II.'s Palace of Westminster there were retained for the king's service a little army of three hundred and forty-six artificers—viz., carpenters, coopers, blacksmiths, whitesmiths, goldsmiths, jewellers, 'engineers,' pavilioners, armourers, 'artillers,' gunners, masons, tilers, bowyers and fletchers, furriers, 'heaumers,' spurriers, brewers, every kind of 'making' trade : everything that was wanted for the king's service was made in the king's Palace—except, of course, the fruits and harvest of the year, the wine, spices and silks, and costly things that came from the far East through the markets of Bruges and Ghent.   These craftsmen were all married—we are not, remember, in a monastery.

Give them an average of each five children, and we have, to begin with, a little population of about two thousand five hundred. Take next the commissariat branch : one begins already to realise the stupendous task of feeding so many, and the order and system which must have grown up to

SOUTH SIDE OF THE PRINCE'S CHAMBER

meet these wants with certainty and regularity. Thus we find that every branch of the commissariat had its officers—clerks, ushers, and serjeants—a responsible service, with individual and clearly defined duties—for pantry, buttery, spicery, bakehouse, chandlery, brewery, cellars, and kitchen. Of these officers there were two hundred and ten. How many servants they had it is impossible to tell. But if we multiply the number of officers by three only for the servants, we get a total of six hundred. If these men were also married, they with their wives and children would give us another company of four thousand. But some of the servants in the kitchen might be women. Then we have the gardeners, the barbers, who were also blood-letters, the bonesetters (a very necessary body), the trumpeters, messengers, bedesmen, grooms and stable-boys—no one can reckon up their number. Add to these the lavenders or laundry-women : the women who embroidered, did fine needlework, made and mended, weaved and span—many of these were doubtless the wives and daughters of the servants. A step higher brings us to the chaplains, the College of St. Stephen, the minstrels, the clerks and accountants, the scribes and illuminators, the heralds and pursuivants. Another step, and we come to the judges and the head officers, with all their staff, clerks and servants. Next the archbishops, bishops and abbots, some of whom were always with the king. Then we come to the great officers of state : viz., the Grand Seneschal *Dapifer Angliæ* or Lord High Steward, who was head and chief of every department, next to the king : the High Justiciary or Lord Chief Justice ; the Seneschal, *Dapifer Regis*, or Steward of the Household : the Constable, the Marshal, the Chamberlain, the Chancellor, and the Treasurer.[1] Lastly, there was the royal household with its officers : the Clerks of the Wardrobe, the King's Remembrancer, the Keeper of the Palace, the Queen's Treasurer, the Maids of Honour (*domicellæ*), the Gentlemen Ushers and the pages, and (which we must again set down) the King's regiment of four thousand archers.

I think it is now made plain that the people attached to

[1] Edward the Confessor's officers were named respectively the Marshal ; the Stallere (*Comes stabuli*, or Constable) ; the Bower-Thane (Chamberlain) ; the Dish-Thane (Seneschal) ; the Hordere (Treasurer); with, of lower rank, Carver, Cup-bearer, Butler, Seal-bearer, Wardrobe-Thane, Harper, and Headsman.

a stationary Court numbered not hundreds, but many thousands ; it is not too much to estimate the number of inhabitants within the walls of Westminster Palace in the reign of Richard II. at twenty thousand—all of whom had 'bouche of court' (i.e. rations, pay, arms, lodging and living).   It was, therefore, a crowded city, complete in itself, though it produced nothing and carried on no trade ; there were workshops and forges and the hammering of armourers and blacksmiths, but there were no stalls, no chepe, no clamour of those who shouted their goods and invited the passengers to 'buy, buy, buy.' This city produced nothing for the country ; it received and devoured everything : it was not an idle city, because the people earned their daily bread ; but for all their labour they never increased the wealth of the country.   Listen to the voice of the poet—it is Harding who speaks of King Richard's Court :

> Truly I herd Robert Ireliffe say,
>   Clerk of the Green Cloth, that to the household
> Came every daye, for moost partie alwaye,
>   Ten thousand folke by his messe is told,
>   That followed the hous, aye, as thei would ;
> And in the kechin three hundred servitours,
> And in eche office many occupiours.
> And ladies faire, with their gentilwomen,
>   Chamberers also and lavenders,
> Three hundred of them were occupied there :
>   Ther was greate pride among the officers,
>   And of all menne far passing their compeers,
> Of riche arraye, and muche more costious
>   Than was before or sith, and more precious.

The ten thousand do not include the women and children.

We have ceased to desire a Court magnificent with outward splendour and lavish expenditure.   There has been, in fact, no such Court among us since that of Charles II. ; and the splendour of his Court was but a poor thing compared with the splendour of the Third Edward, who was

magnificent—or of Richard II., who was profuse. Let us
remember that in our time we cannot make any show, or
festival, or pageant—we have lost the art of pageantry—
which can compare with the shows which our forefathers saw
daily : the shows of magnificent trains, queens and princesses
in such raiment as the greatest lady of these times would be
afraid to put on, lords and knights and gentlemen of the
livery, streets with their gabled houses hung with crimson
and scarlet cloth ; minstrels and music everywhere ; mysteries
and pageants and allegories, with fair maidens and giants,
angels and devils ; lavish feasts at which conduits ran with
wine for long hours and all the world could get drunk if it
pleased.   And there was never anything more splendid than
Richard II. himself.   The time of great shows vanished, like
the spirit of Chivalry, during the Wars of the Roses.

What kind of quarters were given to the king's courtiers
and his army and his servants ? This is a question to which
one can give no satisfactory answer. We hear of many
rooms and buildings, but there does not exist any description
or plan of the Palace as it was.   It must certainly have contained a vast number of buildings for the accommodation of
so many thousands.   The fact that these buildings existed
was proved after the fire of 1834, when a most extensive
range of cellars and vaults was found to exist under the
burned buildings round St. Stephen's. The old buildings
had long before been destroyed and modern houses had taken
their places ; but the vaults and cellars remained, showing by
their strength and solidity the importance of the halls and
chambers that had been built upon them.

It was the first duty of the mediæval builder to provide a
wall of defence.   This was done at Westminster : the wall, as
indicated on the plan, entirely surrounded the Palace ; it was
provided with a water gate at the King's Bridge or King's
Stairs : a postern at the Queen's Stairs ; a gate leading into
the Abbey precinct east of St. Margaret's Church ; a subway

by which the king could enter the Abbey, at Poet's Corner ;
and a gate opposite the Great Hall leading into the Wool
Staple.

Thus fortified, the Palace assumed something of the usual
plan of a Norman castle. The Outer Bailly was represented
by the New Palace Yard, with its Clock Tower and place

A BIT OF THE OLD WALL FROM BLACK DOG ALLEY

for martial exercises, ridings and tournaments ; Westminster
Hall faced the Outer Bailly; to right and to left, to
east and to west, stood buildings ; on the south were other
buildings which enclosed the Inner Bailly, now Old Palace
Yard ; south of these were gardens and stables with less important houses, offices and barracks. The great mass of

the Palace buildings was between Westminster Hall and the river.

Of the old Palace there survived, long after the removal of the Court to Whitehall, and until the fatal fire of sixty years ago, a group of its most interesting and most historical buildings. Changes had been made in them ; their roofs were taken down and replaced, their windows were altered, the very walls in some had been rebuilt ; yet they were the rooms in which Edward the Confessor and all the kings and queens of England lived up to the time of the Eighth Henry.

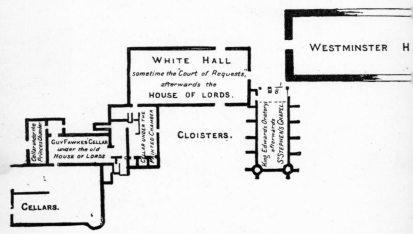

PLAN OF WESTMINSTER PALACE IN 1834

Beneath them the solid substructures of the Confessor remained after the fire, and, for all I know, remain to this day.

The plan shows the position of these buildings. Beginning with the south, there is first of all the Prince's Chamber, afterwards the Robing Room of the old House of Lords. It was forty-five feet long and twenty feet wide ; it ran east and west. The chamber had five beautiful lancet windows on the south side and three each on the east and west. On the north side it opened into the old House of Lords. It was in this room that Queen Elizabeth hung up the tapestry celebrating the defeat of the Spanish Armada. This excellent piece of work was afterwards transferred to the Court of Requests, where it was burned in the last fire.

The hall adjoining the old House of Lords formed, with the Painted Chamber and the Court of Requests, Edward the Confessor's living-rooms. Under the House of Lords was the King's kitchen, afterwards the cellar where Guy Fawkes and his friends placed the barrels of gunpowder. After the Lords removed to the Court of Requests this room was called the Royal Gallery.

The third room, perhaps the most beautiful, was the Painted Chamber. This hall, certainly that in which the Confessor breathed his last, was eighty feet long, twenty broad and fifty high—a lofty and narrow room, perhaps too narrow for its length. The meaning of its name had long been forgotten until the year 1800, when, on taking down the tapestry, which had hung there for centuries, the walls were found to be covered with paintings, representing on one side of the room the wars of the Maccabees, and on the other side scenes from the life of Edward the Confessor. It was then remembered, or discovered, that in an itinerary of two Franciscan pilgrims in the year 1322, preserved among the manuscripts of Corpus Christi, Cambridge, these paintings are mentioned. In the year 1477 the hall was called St. Edward's Chamber ; Sir Edward Coke calls it the Chamber Depeint or St. Edward's Chamber.

The fourth of these groups of ancient buildings was the Council Room of King Edward, called afterwards the Whitehall, the Little Hall, the Court of Requests, and the House of Lords.

In the midst of this stately group of noble buildings rose the most stately and most noble chapel of St. Stephen. It was founded, according to tradition, by King Stephen, on the site, it has been sometimes said, of the Confessor's oratory ; but this seems not true, for the oratory was on the east of the Painted Chamber. The chapel was rebuilt as a thank-offering for his victories by Edward I., who then endowed it with large revenues. His foundation was large enough to maintain a college, consisting of dean, twelve secular canons and twelve vicars ; it was, in fact, a rich foundation planted in the middle of the Palace, over against the Abbey. Was

COLLEGIATE SEAL OF ST. STEPHEN'S

there any desire on the part of the King to separate the Court from the Abbey ? Perhaps not ; but there arose perpetual quarrels between the College and the Abbey. The masses said in St. Stephen's for the past and present kings might just as well have been said, one supposes, in the Abbey. So rich was the foundation that at the Dissolution its revenues were a third of those of St Peter's. By that time the College buildings con-

tained residences or chambers for thirty-eight persons. These buildings consisted, first, of the exquisite Chapel, which afterwards became the House of Commons ; the Chapel of our Lady de la Pieu, standing somewhere to the south of St. Stephen's (in this Chapel Richard heard mass before going out to meet Wat Tyler) ; the Crypt, which happily still remains ; the exquisite cloisters long since vanished ; with the Chantry Chapel, and the said residences of the dean,

INTERIOR OF THE CRYPT CALLED THE 'POWDER PLOT CELLAR,' BENEATH THE OLD PALACE OF WESTMINSTER, LOOKING TOWARDS CHARING CROSS. TAKEN DOWN IN JUNE 1883

canons and vicars, and King Richard's Belfry. The Chapel
was smaller than some other royal Chapels—Windsor, for
instance, and King's, Cambridge—but it was beautiful exceedingly, and in its carved work and decorations perhaps

WEST END OF THE PAINTED CHAMBER AS IT APPEARED AFTER
THE FIRE OF 1834

more finished than any other Church or Chapel in the country.
Details of the Chapel have been preserved for us by J. T. Smith
(' Antiquities of Westminster '), and by Brayley and Britton's
' Houses of Parliament.' The beauty of the cloisters of the
Chantry Chapel, and of the Chapel itself, makes the fire of

1834 on this account alone a great national disaster. Such work can never again be equalled. At the same time, the Chapel had been so much altered and cut about for the accommodation of the Commons that it was irretrievably spoiled.

The next of this group of ancient buildings was Westminster Hall. On this monument and its historical associations many have enlarged. Let it suffice in this place to remind ourselves that William Rufus built it, Richard II. enlarged it and strengthened it, and that George IV. repaired and new-fronted it.

On the east side of the Hall was the Court of Exchequer, built by Edward II. This hall was seventy-four feet long and forty-five broad. The traditions of the chamber are full of curious stories. It was the breakfast-room, it was said (one knows not why), of Queen Elizabeth : a chamber adjoining was her bedchamber. She at least reformed the Court of Exchequer. There

CURIOUS NEWELL STAIRCASE AT THE SOUTH-EAST ANGLE OF PAINTED CHAMBER

were two cellars under the Court of Exchequer, called 'Hell' and 'Purgatory.' As their names denote, they were prisons. The former name was also applied to a tavern in the Palace precinct.

The notorious Star Chamber was on the east side of New Palace Yard. The room was probably rebuilt in the time of Queen Elizabeth. It was used afterwards as the Lottery office.

One more ' bit ' of the Palace still remains. If you turn to the left on reaching the eastern end of Great College Street, after passing through stables and mews, you will light upon a most venerable old Tower hidden away in this corner. It is the last of the many Towers which formed part of the Westminster Palace. It was always ascribed to the Confessor as part of his Abbey buildings. When antiquaries first considered it, they found that Edward I. bought the piece of ground on which it stands of the Abbey ; so it was concluded that he bought the Tower upon the ground. Later antiquaries, however, on fresh investigations, made up their minds that there was no Tower when Edward took the ground ; therefore—the logic of the antiquary is never his strongest point—Edward built this Tower. Again, other antiquaries examined further : and they have now decided that the Tower was built by Richard II. One would

GUY FAWKES' DOOR

have preferred the Confessor as architect, but the end of the fourteenth century gives us a respectable antiquity.

Certain accounts of repairs—carpenters', masons', painters' work—still preserved enable us to get a clearer understanding of the buildings that, in addition to the central group, which can be so exactly described and figured, made up the old Palace of Westminster. There must have been work for builders going on continually, but in the years 1307 to 1310 there were very extensive repairs, in consequence of a fire ; the bills for these repairs have been preserved. They speak of the following buildings : of the Little Hall, of which mention has been already made ; of the water-conduit—the

VAULT UNDER THE PAINTED CHAMBER

pipes of which were repaired or restored ; of the Queen's Hall ; the Nursery ; the Mayden Hall, the private hall of the *domicellæ*, maids of honour,—all these halls had their chambers, wardrobes and galleries ; of the chambers and cloisters round the Inner Hall—was this the old House of

Lords ?—of the King's Wardrobe : of Marculf's Chamber ; of the Chandlery ; of the Lord Edmund's Palace ; of the Almonry ; of the Gaol ; of the houses and chambers of the chaplains, clerks and officers of Court and Palace ; of houses standing in the Inner Bailly—i.e. Old Palace Yard ; of herbaries, vineries, gardens, galleries, aqueducts and stew ponds.

It is impossible to assign these buildings and places to their original site. Take the plan of Thorney, with its Palace, Abbey and City. Remember that there was an open space for the Inner Bailly—Old Palace Yard ; and another for the Outer Bailly—New Palace Yard. In this respect the Palace followed the practice of every castle and great house in the country—even in a college the first court is a survival of the Outer Bailly. Leave, also, an open space east of the wall from the Jewel House to the outer wall for the gardens and herbaries—perhaps, like the Abbey, the Palace had gardens in the reclaimed meadows outside. Then fill in the area between the King's House and the river with other halls, houses, offices, galleries, wardrobes and cloisters. Let barracks, stables, shops of all kinds run under the river wall ; let there be narrow lanes winding about among these courts, connecting one with the other and all with the Inner and the Outer Bailly and the Palace stairs. This done, you will begin to understand something of the extent and nature of the King's Palace in the fourteenth century. Add to this that the buildings were infinitely more picturesque than anything we can show of our own design, our own construction, our own grouping. The gabled houses turned to the courts and lanes their carved timber and plaster fronts ; the cloisters glowed in the sunshine with their lace-like tracery and the gold and crimson of their painted roofs and walls ; grey old towers looked down upon the clustered and crowded little city ; everywhere there were stately halls, lofty roofs, tourelles with rich carvings—gables, painted windows, windows of tracery most beautiful, archways, gates, battlements ; granaries, storehouses, barns, chantry chapels, oratories, courts of justice, and interiors bright with splendid tapestry, the colours of which had not yet faded, with canopies of scarlet and cloth of gold, and the sunlight reflected from

EAST FRONT OF ST. STEPHEN'S CHAPEL AS IT APPEARED AFTER
THE FIRE OF 1834

many a shining helm and breastplate, from many a jewelled hilt and golden scabbard, from many a trophy hanging on the walls, from many a coat of arms bright with colour— azure, or, gules and argent. It is the colour in everything that makes the time so picturesque and bright. We see

E

how small their chambers were, how narrow were the lanes
how close the houses stood ; but we forget the bright colours
of everything, the hangings and the arras, the painted
shields, the robes and dresses, the windows and the walls, the
chambers, halls and refectories, the galleries and the cloisters
When Time brings in another age of colour—it is surely due
—we shall understand better the centuries of the Plantage
nets.

When the fire destroyed these buildings how much we
lost that connected us with the past! True it is that in
Westminster Abbey and in Westminster Hall we seem to
stand face to face with the history of the country. In the
Hall were done such and such things ; before us lies the
effigy of a king to remind us that he was a living reality—
to most of us the past is as unreal as the future ; we need
these reminders lest the voice of our ancestors should fall
upon our ears with no more meaning than the lapping of the
tide or the babble of the brook or the whisper of the stream
among the rushes. But we have nothing to remind us of the
Palace where the Princes lived ; the things that were done in
them are not in the Book of Kings, but in that of the Things
Left out—the Book of Chronicles—mostly as yet unedited.

Princes were born here, and played here, and grew here
to the age when they could ride the great horse and practise
exercises in the New Palace Yard. Kings' Daughters were
born here, and were kept here till they were sent away to
marry : strange lot of the King's Daughter, that she never
knew until she married what her country was to be ! Queens
prayed here for the safety of their husbands and their sons ;
here was all the home life, the private life of the Kings and
Queens ; in these chambers were held the King's feasts ; here
he received ambassadors ; here he held his council ; here he
looked on with the Queen at the mummeries and masques ;
here he held Christmas revelry ; here he received and entertained—or else admonished—my Lord Mayor and Aldermen

of London ; here were his Parliaments ; here were executed
many nobles ; here God Himself was invited to give judgment on the ordeal of battle. In the Painted Chamber, for
instance, died King Edward the Confessor ; this was the
council-chamber of the Normans ; here Edward III. received
the embassy of Pope Benedict XII. ; here Charles's judges
signed his death warrant ; here
Chatham lay in state. In the Court
of Requests, close by, Richard I.
heard cases as a judge ; here Edward IV. kept his Christmas in
1472, and entertained the Mayor
and Aldermen. In the old House
of Lords Bacon was sentenced and
disgraced, Somers was acquitted,
Chatham was struck down. Under
this hall the conspirators of the
Gunpowder Plot piled the barrels
which were to destroy the Lords
sitting in council. In Old Palace
Yard died Raleigh ; on the north
side of Old Palace Yard lived
Geoffrey Chaucer, clerk of the
works. From the Confessor and
Harold through five hundred years
of kings and princes, for the whole
history of England's Parliament,
for the whole history of English law and justice, the things
that belonged to these chronicles passed in this succession of
halls and chambers.

PASSAGE FROM ST. STEPHEN'S
CHAPEL TO THE CLOISTER

Thus, then, presented to you, was the Palace. You have
restored the Palace of Westminster. It stands before you,
plain and clear. But as yet it is a silent city—a city of the
cold daybreak, a city of the sleeping. Fill it again with the
living multitude—the thousands who thronged its courts—

when it was the Palace of the Second Richard. Look : the
men-at-arms and esquires and knights bear the cognisance—
a fatal cognisance it proved to many—of the White Hart
It is the Palace of the Second Richard, whose court was the
most splendid and his expenditure the most prodigal that the
country had ever witnessed.

It is the third day of May, 1389. The sun rises before
five and the day breaks at three at this season ; long before
sunrise, before daybreak, the silence of the night is broken
by the rolling of the organ and the voices of the monks at
Lauds ; long before sunrise, even so early as this, there are
signs of life about the Court. Stable-boys and grooms are
up already, carrying buckets of water ; dogs are leaping and
barking ; when the sun lifts his head above the low Surrey
hills and falls upon the wall and towers of the Palace, the
narrow lanes are full of men slowly addressing themselves to
the work of the day. Clear and bright against the sky stand
the buildings ; huddled together they are, certainly : it is not
yet a time for architectural grouping, except in the design of
an abbey, which is generally placed where there is room
enough and to spare. Where there is the King there is an
army ; there is also a place which may be attacked : therefore the smaller the circumference of the wall, the better for
the defence. Besides, a Palace is like a walled city : it grows,
but it cannot spread ; it fills up. This hall needs another
beside it ; that chamber must have a gallery ; this chapel
must have cloisters ; here let us put up a clock tower ; if
there are council chambers, there must also be guest
chambers ; the Court becomes more splendid, the Palace
precinct becomes more crowded.

The place is more like a camp than a Palace. The
grooms lead out the horses—there are thousands of horses in
the place ; in both Outer and Inner Bailly the pages—wards
of the King—boys of eight or nine to sixteen, are exercising
already, riding, leaping, fencing, running. In the long

chambers where the archers lie upon beds of rushes and of straw the men are gathered about the doors passing round the blackjack with the morning draught. At the water gate are crowding already the boats laden with fish caught in the river and brought here daily. The servants are running to and fro ; the fires are lit in kitchen and in bakery ; the clerks,

CLOISTER COURT AS IT APPEARED AFTER THE FIRE

pen in hand and ink-bottle hanging from their belts, go round to the offices. Listen to the baying of the hounds ; see the falconers bringing out their birds ; here are the chained bears rolling on the ground ; there go the young nobles hasting to the King's chamber,—it is the time of gorgeous raiment : half a manor is in the blue silk jacket of that young lord, one of the King's favourites. There is already, from this side or that, the tinkling of a mandoline, the scraping of a crowd ; yonder fantastic group, the first to enter when the Palace gates are thrown open, are mummers, jugglers and minstrels, who come to make sport for the archers and for the Court if the King's Highness or the Queen's most excellent Grace so wills. These people can play a mystery if needs be ; or they can dress like fearful wild beasts, or dance like wild men of the woods ; they have songs from France—love songs, songs for ladies—rougher songs in English for the soldiers ; they can dance upon the tight-rope ; they can eat fire : they can juggle and play strange tricks which they have brought hither all the way from Constantinople—at sight of them you cross yourself and whisper that it is sorcery. As for the music of the King's chamber, that is made by the King's minstrels, who wear his colours and have bouche of court. See yonder gaily dressed young man : he is a minstrel ; none other can touch the harp and sing with skill so sweet ; he looks on with contempt at the fantastic crew as they sweep past to the soldiers' quarters ; they, too, carry their minstrel instruments with them, but their music is not his music. In the evening the minstrel will join in the crowd to see the dancing of the girls—the almond-eyed, dark-skinned girls of Syria—who follow the fortunes of the mummers and toss their round arms as they dance with strange gestures and wanton looks, at sight of which the senses swim and the brain reels and the soul yearns for things impossible.

The noise of the Palace grows ; it is wide awake : the day has begun.

Outside the Palace, the road—there is now a road where there was once a marsh or shallow with a ford—is covered with an endless procession of those who make their way to the Palace and the Abbey with supplies. Here are drivers with herds of cattle and flocks of sheep ; here are long lines of packhorses laden with things ; here are men-at-arms, the

following of some great lord : this is a procession which never
ceases all the year round. And on the river barges are
coming down with the stream piled up, laden to the level of
the water, with farm produce ; and at flood-tide barges come
up the stream from the Port of London, sent by the merchants
whom the King despoils—yet they have their revenge—
boats laden with the things for which this magnificent Court
is insatiable—cloth of gold, velvet and silk ; wines of France

THE STAR CHAMBER. DEMOLISHED IN 1834

and Spain and Cyprus and Gaza ; spices, perfumes, inlaid
armour and arms, jewels and glass and plate, and wares
ecclesiastic for the outer glory of St. Peter and St. Stephen—
golden cross and chalice silver gilt, and vestments such
as can only be matched in the Church of St. Peter at
Rome.

Also, along the Dover road, and up and down the road
called Watling, and up the river and down the river, there
ride day and night the King's messengers. Was there a

special service of messengers? I think not: men were despatched with letters and enjoined to ride swiftly. There were neither telegraphs nor railways nor postal service, yet was the Court of every great king fully supplied with news. If it came a month after the event, so it came to all. We of to-day act on news of the moment: the statesmen of old acted on news of yesterday or yesterday fortnight. But communications with the outer world never ceased; news poured in daily from all quarters: from the Low Countries; from France and Spain; from Rome; from the Holy Land. Whatever happened was carried swiftly over Western Europe. If the king of Scotland crossed the border, in three days it was known in Westminster; if there was a rebellion in Ireland, four days brought the news to Westminster; if the Welsh harried the March, three days sufficed to bring the news to Westminster. Besides the messengers and bearers of despatches there were pilgrims who learned and carried about a vast quantity of information; there were the merchants whose ships arrived every day from Antwerp and from Sluys; and there were the foreign ships which came to London Port from the Levant and the Mediterranean.

The messengers as they arrived at the Palace of Westminster carried their letters not to the King, but to the Archbishop of Canterbury and to the Duke of Gloucester, the King's uncle.

As for what follows, it is related by Francis de Winchelsea, scribe or clerk to the King's Council, the same who went always limp or halt by reason of a knee stiffened by kneeling at his work; for before the Council the clerk who writes what he is commanded must neither sit nor stand. He kneels on his left knee and writes on the other knee. Many things were secretly written by Francis which are kept in the Abbey hard by, not to see the light for many years—perhaps never— because things said and done in secret council must not be spread abroad, as the cleric Froissart spread abroad all he

knew and could learn, to the injury of many reputations.
Thus sayeth Francis :—

'On the morning of that day—the Induction of the
Cross—it chanced that I was standing in the Cloisters of
Saint Stephen, whither I often repaired for meditation. The
King came forth, and with him one—I name him not—who
was his companion and friend. They walked in the cloisters,
I retiring to a far corner ; they were deep in conversation,
and they marked me not. They talked in whispers for half
an hour. Then the King said aloud, " Have no fear : this
day will I reward my friends."

'" Beau Sire," replied the other, " your friends have mostly
lost their heads thus far. Yet to die as your Highness's
friend should be reward enough."

'" Thou shalt not die. By St. Edward's bones—when it
comes to dying—— But wait."

'Then I knew that something great was going to happen.
And since whatever happens to Princes affects their subjects,
I began to tremble. "This day," said the King. Now, there
was not any Prince in the world more comely to look upon
than King Richard. Since the time of David there had never
been a Prince of more lovely aspect. He was then in early
manhood : his chin and cheek were lightly fringed with down
rather than with a beard ; his face was long ; his flowing
hair was of a light brown ; his eyes were large—I have
noticed that the eyes of those who sit apart and dream are
often large—yet could the King's eyes become suddenly
and swiftly terrible to meet : never yet was English King
who was not terrible in his wrath. His nose was long and
thin, his mouth was small and delicately shaped, his chin was
not long but round and firm ; his shoulders were sloping, his
fingers were long. He loved, as no other great Lord ever
loved, rich apparel : he commonly wore a doublet or jerkin of
green embroidered with flowers, crowns, and the letters of his
name. He was already twenty-three years of age, yet he took

no part in the affairs of his own kingdom, which was managed by his uncles, the Dukes of Lancaster and Gloucester ; so that, if it be permitted thus to speak of a King, he was fast falling into contempt as a Roy Fainéant, one who would do nothing ; and there were whispers, even in the Palace, that a king who can do nothing must, soon or late, give place to one who can. Yet I marked that the King looked ever to his archers, of whom he had four thousand, and that he entertained them royally and kept them to their loyalty. Doubtless Richard remembered the fate of this great-grandfather, Edward the Second.

'At the hour of nine, mass said and breakfast despatched, the King's Council met in Marculf's Chamber. There were present the Archbishop of Canterbury, the Bishop of Hereford, the Duke of Gloucester and the Earl of Arundel. And I also was there, on my knee, pen in hand, ready to write.

'My Lords of the Council discoursed pleasantly of this and of that : they had no suspicion of what would happen. Nor had I guessed the King's purpose. Now learn what the Roy Fainéant did.

'While the Archbishop was speaking, without a word of warning the council door was suddenly flung open wide and the usher called out, "My Lords—the King !"

'Then Richard stood in the doorway : upon his head he wore a crown ; in his hand he carried his sceptre ; on his shoulders hung the mantle of ermine, borne below by two pages ; and through the door I saw a throng of armed men and heard the clink of steel. Then I understood what was about to happen.

'The Council rose and stood up. White were their cheeks and astonied were their faces.

'" Good my Lord," began the Duke of Gloucester.

'The King strode across the room and took his seat upon the throne. Let no one say that Richard's eyes were soft. This morning they were like the eyes of a falcon ; and the look which he cast upon his uncle betrayed the hatred in his heart and foretold the revenge that he would take. Afterwards, when I heard of the King's visit to Pleshy, I remembered that look.

' " Fair uncle," he said : " tell me how old am I ? "

' " Your Highness," replied the Duke, " is now in your twenty-fourth year."

' " Say you so ? Then, fair uncle, I am now old enough to manage mine own affairs."

' So saying, he took the Great Seal from the Archbishop, and the keys of the Exchequer from the Bishop of Hereford ; from the Duke of Gloucester he took his office ; he appointed new Judges ; he created a new Council.

' Look you,' said Francis of Winchelsea, ' how secret are the counsels of the mighty ! They keep their designs secret because they cannot trust their courtiers. The King made no sign when his uncles took the management of the realm into their own hands ; he was not yet strong enough : he amused himself. They drove away his favourites and beheaded them ; the King still made no sign : he amused himself. When the moment came he sprang up and delivered his blow. 'Twas a gallant Prince. Alas ! that he was not always strong. That he compassed the death of the Duke of Gloucester no one doubts ; but then the Duke had compassed the death of his friends. Twice in his life Richard was strong : on that day and another ; twice was he strong.

' That night there was high revelry in the Palace : the mummers and the minstrels and the music made the Court merry ; and the dancing girls moved the hearts of the young men. And the King's Fool made the courtiers laugh when he jested about the Duke's amazement and the Archbishop's discomfiture. And as for me, plain Francis the scribe, I am inclined, seeing the miseries that have since fallen upon that most puissant Prince and upon this country, to humble myself and to acknowledge the mercy of Heaven in refusing me a higher place than this of scribe. The Kings succeed ; the council changes ; the axe and the block are always doing their work ; but the scribe remains, and were it not for the stiffness of this right knee and a growing deafness, I should have but little cause for complaint.'

Here ends the manuscript of Francis de Winchelsea.

When the King's House was removed from Westminster to Whitehall the importance of the old Palace suffered little diminution. St. Stephen's was dissolved, but the chapel was not destroyed nor were the cloisters broken down. The Commons came across the road leaving the Chapter House and exchanging one lovely building for another. They proceeded so to alter and to rebuild and add and subtract that by the time of the Fire there was not much left of the old St. Stephen's. The other buildings of the Palace were gradually modernised, so that in the end little was left of the old Palace except the nest of chambers that belonged in the first instance to Edward the Confessor, with the Hall of Rufus. As for this mediæval Palace with its narrow lanes, its close courts, its corridors and cloisters, its lancet windows, its tourelles, its carved work —all that was gone, never to be replaced. But a good deal of history, a great many events, had to take place on this site before the building of the present House of Parliament, which is the greatest change of all. I set out in these chapters with the desire not to repeat, more than was necessary, stories that have been told over and over again. It is not always possible to avoid this repetition, since things must be related if only to avoid a probable charge of ignorance. Some things can be avoided as belonging rather to the History of the Nation than the History of Westminster. Among such things are the rise and development of the House of Commons. Some things again may be avoided as having been told so often that no one is ignorant of them ; such as the death of Henry IV. in the Jerusalem Chamber. In what follows, chiefly concerning the Palace after its desertion by the King, there will be found some things well known to everybody, some things half known, some things not known at all.

In the Old Palace Yard, the open court belonging to the first Palace, many functions took place : tournaments, executions, trials by battle.   At one of these tournaments, that of 1348, two Scottish knights, the Earl Douglas and Sir William Douglas, prisoners of war, acquitted themselves so valiantly that the King sent them home free.   Of executions in Old Palace Yard there is recorded the hanging of a man for slaying another within the Palace ; his body, for an example, remained hanging for two days.   Of trial by battle, many are recorded in Tothill Fields and elsewhere, and those of Old Palace Yard.   One of these was held in the presence of King Edward III., between Thomas de la Marche and John de Visconti to prove that the former had not been guilty of treachery against the King of Sicily.   De la Marche unhorsed his opponent and struck him in the face as he fell.   It is not stated what became of the wounded man.

On the south side of the Old Palace Yard were certain fish ponds or stew ponds which were kept stocked with eels and pike.   On the east side Geoffrey Chaucer for a very short time—less than a year—occupied a house.   It stood nigh to the White Rose tavern abutting on the old Lady Chapel.   King Henry VII.'s Chapel now occupies the site. And there was a gateway or passage from the Abbey churchyard to Old Palace Yard over which was a house sacred to the memory of Ben Jonson who lived there.

In the south-east corner of Old Palace Yard stood the house which was hired by Percy, one of the conspirators of the Gunpowder Plot, through which the barrels of powder were conveyed to the vaults.   In Palace Yard four of the conspirators, Guy Fawkes, Thomas Winter, Ambrose Rokewood and Robert Keyes were executed fifteen years later, to the shame and dishonour of the English nation.   Raleigh was brought to Old Palace Yard to die. The day chosen for his execution was Lord Mayor's Day so that the crowd should be drawn to the pageant rather than the execution. It is curious to read how Lady Raleigh attended at the execution and carried away the head in a bag. She kept it during the rest of her life, and after her death it was kept by her son Carew. The body lies buried in the Chancel of St. Margaret's.

The memory of these great mobs closes the history of Old Palace Yard. One of these was in 1641 when 6,000 citizens, armed with swords and clubs, seized on the entrance to the House of Lords and called for justice against Lord Strafford. The second in 1773, when the Sheriff and Aldermen and Common Council of London in a procession of two hundred carriages, attended by a huge mob, went to Westminster to petition against the Excise scheme of Sir Robert Walpole. The third is the mob that followed Lord George Gordon. On this occasion both Lords and Commons found it necessary to adjourn.

New Palace Yard has been the scene of many eventful episodes in history. Take, for instance, the history of the fight between the men of London and the men of Westminster. From this story may be learned the difficulty of controlling a mob, and that a London mob—and a mob fired with a sense of wrong—that kind of wrong that always fires an Englishman's blood — where the game is played against the rules. Sport of all kinds must be played by rule. Here were the men of Westminster fairly and honestly beaten. That they should seek to revenge themselves in so mean and treacherous a fashion—oh ! it was intolerable ! How would the men of Yorkshire be fired with rage if, after a football match, the conquerors should be treacherously assailed and murdered ? Yet this is exactly what happened. Let Stow tell the tale.

On Saint Iames **day, the Citizens of** *London* **kept games of defence and wrestling, neere vnto the Hospital of**

Matild, where they got the maisterie of the menne of the Suburbes. The Baylife of *Westminster* deuising to be reuenged, proclaymed a game to be at *Westminster* vppon Lammas daye, wherevnto the Citizens of *London* repayred, and when they had played a while, the Baylie with the men of the suburbs harnised themselues and fell to fighting, that the Citizens being foully wounded, were forced to runne into the Citie, where they rang the common Bel, and assembled the Citizens in gret number, and when the matter was declared, euery man wished to reuenge the fact. The Maior of the Citie being a wise man and a quiet, willed them sirste to moue the Abbot of *Westminster* of the matter, and if he wold promise to see amendes made, it were sufficient: but a certaine Citizen named Constantine Fitz Arnulfe, willed that all houses of the Abbot and Baylie should be pulled downe, whiche word being once spoken, the common people issued out of the Citie without anye order, and fought a ciuil battaile: for Constantine the sirste pulled downe many houses, and ofttimes with a loude voyce cryed in prayse of the sayd Constantine, the ioye of the mountaine, the ioy of the mountaine, God helpe and the Lord Lodowike.

A fewe dayes after this tumult, the Abbot of *Westminster* came to *London* to Phillip Dawbney, one of the kings counsel, to complaine of the iniuries done to him, which the *Londoners* perceyuing, beset the house aboute, and tooke by violence twelue of the Abbots horsses away, cruelly beating of his men, &c. But whiles the foresayde Daubney, laboured to pacifie the vprore, the Abbot gotte out at a backe dore of the house, and so by a boate on the *Thamis* hardlye escaped, the Citizens throwing stones after him in great aboundāce. These things being thus done, Hubert de Burgo, Iusticiar of *England*, with a great armye of men came to the Tower of *London*, and sent for the Maior and Aldermē, of whom he enquired for the principal aucthours of this faction. Then Constantine, who was constaunt in the sedition, was more constante in the aunsweare, affirming, that he had done it, and that he hadde done muche lesse than he ought to haue done. The Justiciar tooke him and two other with him, and in ꝑ morning earely sent them to Falcatius by water with a gret number of armed men, who brought Constantine to the gallowes, and when he sawe the rop about his necke, he offered for his life 15000. marks but that would not saue him: so he was hanged with Constantine his nephew, & Galfride, that proclaymed his proclamation on the sixteenth of August.

Then the Justiciar entring the City with a great army, caused to be apprehended as many as he could learne to be culpable, whose feet and hands he caused to be cut off, which crueltie caused many to flee the Citie.

The King toke of the Citizens 60 pledges, which he set to diuers Castelles: he deposed the Maior, appointing a Gardien or keeper ouer the Citie, and caused a greate gybet to be made, and after heauie threatnings the Citizens were reconciled, paying to the king many thousande markes.

The bawling for the Lord Lodowicke was a very foolish thing to do. It showed, first, that the Londoners associated the men of Westminster with the Court ; it showed also that the memory of Prince Louis of France, who had taken up his residence for a time in London, still survived. But it was ill advised because it set the King against the citizens.

The pillory of New Palace Yard has held some notable persons in its embrace : Perkin Warbeck, for instance, who had to read his own confession. The same ceremony was performed in Cheapside 'with many a curse and much wondering,' says Stow. In this pillory stood Alexander Leighton for a fanatical libel. Here stood William Prynne for writing the 'Histrio Mastix.' Here stood Titus Oates, and here stood the printer of Wilkes's famous ' No. 45.'

New Palace Yard was formerly an enclosed area, surrounded by buildings picturesquely grouped. I do not think we have anything to show more picturesque than New

NORTH PORCH

Palace Yard in the fifteenth century. On the North side stood the Clock Tower, just where Parliament Street now begins. It was a very handsome Clock Tower, erected against his will by Chief Justice Ralph Hingham in the reign of Edward I. He was amerced in the sum of 800 marks for altering a court roll in favour of a poor man. His charity cost him dear. There was a warden of the Clochier and the bell, called Tom, was the heaviest in London. In the year 1698 the Clock Tower was given to the Vestry of St Margaret's. They proceeded to pull it down—one knows not why: the materials were sold for 200*l.*: the bell for 385*l.* 17*s.* 6*d.*: it weighed 82 cwt. 2 qrs. 21 lbs. The bell was recast and taken to St. Paul's.

On either side of the Clock Tower ran houses belonging to the merchants of the Wool Staple, the market place of which was at the back of the houses: an archway opened into King Street at the north-west corner: the west side was occupied by houses, the gate into the Abbey and St. Margaret's: on the south side was Westminster Hall with the Courts of the Exchequer: on the east was the Star Chamber ending in what was called the Bridge, and a pier running out into the river. Under the Courts of the Exchequer were two prisons called 'Hell' and 'Purgatory.' There was also 'Heaven,' and all these places became taverns.

When one speaks of Westminster Hall it seems as if the whole of English history rolls through that ancient and venerable building. Historians have exhausted their eloquence in speaking of these grey old walls. What things have they not seen? The coronation banquets: the entertainments of kings: the proclamations: the solemn oaths the State trials:—we cannot if we would keep out of Westminster Hall. It was once the High Court of Justice: three Judges sat here in different parts of the Hall, hearing as many cases.

The State trials may be left to Macaulay and the historians.

I think that we are here most concerned in that curious trial of the 'prentices which followed ' Evil May Day,' 1517.

Everybody knows that the Church of St. Andrew Undershaft is so called because a tall May-pole, the highest in London, was laid along, under a pentise, the side of the church and a row of houses called Shaft Alley. Every May Day the pole was taken off its iron hooks and set up on the south side of the church in the street, being higher than the steeple itself. Now as to the connection of the steeple with Westminster Hall, it shall be told in the words of Maitland :—

' About two Years after this, an Accident happened, which occasioned the Epithet of *Evil* to be added to this Day of Rejoicing, and that Day was afterwards noted by the Name of *Evil May-Day*. In the ninth Year of the Reign of King *Henry* VIII. A great Heart-burning, and malicious Grudge, grew amongst the *Englishmen* of the City of *London*, against Strangers ; and namely, the Artificers found themselves much aggrieved, because such Number of Strangers were permitted to resort hither with their Wares, and to exercise Handicrafts, to the great Hindrance and Impoverishing of the King's Liege People : Which Malice grew to such a Point, that one *John Lincolne*, a Broker, busied himself so far in the Matter, that about *Palm-Sunday*, or the fifth of *April*, he came to one Dr. *Standish*, with these Words ; " Sir, I understand that you shall preach at the *Spital* on *Monday* in *Easter* Week ; and so it is, that *Englishmen*, both Merchants and others, are undone by Strangers, who have more Liberty in this Land, than they, which is against Reason, and also against the Commonweal of this Realm. I beseech you, therefore, to declare this in your Sermon, and in so doing you shall deserve great Thanks cf my Lord-Mayor, and of all his Brethren." And herewith he offered unto the said Doctor a Bill containing the Matter more at large : But Doctor *Standish*, wisely considering, that there might more Inconvenience arise from it, than he would wish, if he should deal in such Sort, both refused the Bill, and told *Lincolne* plainly, that he meant not to meddle with any such Matter in his Sermon.

'Whereupon the said *Lincoln*, went unto one Dr. *Bell*, or *Bele*, a Canon of the aforesaid *Spital*, that was appointed likewise to preach upon *Tuesday* in *Easter* Week, at the same *Spital*, whom he persuaded to read his said Bill in his Pulpit.   Which Bill contained (in effect) the Grievances that many found from Strangers, for taking the Livings away from Artificers and the Intercourse from Merchants, the Redress whereof must come from the Commons united together; for, as the Hurt touched all Men, so must all set to their helping Hands: Which Letter he read, or the chief Part thereof, comprehending much seditious Matter, and then he began with this Sentence; *Cœlum Cœli Domino, Terram autem dedit Filiis Hominum*, i.e. *The Heavens to the Lord of Heaven, but the Earth he hath given to the children of Men:* And upon this Text he shewed how this Land was given to *Englishmen*, and, as Birds defend their Nests, so ought *Englishmen* to cherish and maintain themselves, and to hurt and grieve Aliens for Respect of their Commonwealth : And on this Text, *Pugna pro Patria*, i.e. *Fight for your Country*, he brought in, how (by God's Law) it was lawful to fight for their Country, and thus he subtilly moved the People to oppose Strangers.   By this Sermon, many a light-headed Person took Courage, and spoke openly against them : And by chance there had been divers ill Things of late done by Strangers, in and about the City of *London*, which kindled the People's Rancour the more furiously against them.

'The twenty-eighth Day of *April*, divers young Men of the City picked Quarrels with certain Strangers, as they passed along the Streets : Some they smote and buffeted, and some they threw into the Channel ; for which the Lord-Mayor sent some of the *Englishmen* to Prison, as *Stephen Studley*, Skinner, *Stevenson Betts*, and others.

'Then suddenly rose a secret Rumour, and no Man could tell how it began, that on *May-Day*, next following, the City would slay all the Aliens, insomuch that divers Strangers fled out of the City.

'This Rumour came to the Knowledge of the King's Council ; whereupon the Lord Cardinal sent for the Mayor, and other of the Council of the City, giving them to understand what he had heard.

'The Lord-Mayor, as one ignorant of the Matter, told the Cardinal, that he doubted not so to govern the City, but that Peace should be obtained.

'The Cardinal willed him so to do, and to take heed, that, if any riotous Attempt were intended, he should by good Policy prevent it.

'The Mayor coming from the Cardinal's House, about four o'Clock in the Afternoon, on *May-Eve*, sent for his Brethren to the *Guildhall* ; yet was it almost seven o'Clock before the Assembly was set. Upon Conference had of the Matter, some thought it necessary, that a substantial Watch should be set of honest Citizens, which might withstand the Evil-Doers, if they went about any Misrule : Others were of contrary Opinion, as rather thinking it best, that every Man should be commanded to shut up his Doors, and to keep his Servants within. Before eight o'Clock, the Recorder was sent to the Cardinal with these Opinions, who, hearing the same, allowed the latter : And then the Recorder, and Sir *Thomas More*, late Under-Sheriff of *London*, and of the King's Council, came back again to the *Guildhall*, half an Hour before nine o'Clock, and there shewed the Pleasure of the King's Council ; whereupon every Alderman sent to his Ward, that no Man, after nine o'Clock, should stir out of his House, but keep his Doors shut, and his Servants within, until nine o'Clock in the Morning.

'After this Command was given in the Evening, as Sir *John Mundy*, Alderman, came from his Ward, he found two young Men in *Cheap*, playing at the Bucklers, and a great many young Men looking on them ; for the Command seemed to be scarcely published : He ordered them to leave off ; and, because one of them asked, Why ? he would have them sent to the *Compter* : But the 'Prentices resisted the Alderman, taking the young Man from him, and cried, *'Prentices, 'Prentices ! Clubs, Clubs !* then out of every Door came Clubs, and other Weapons, so that the Alderman was put to Flight. Then more People arose out of every Quarter, and forth came Serving-men, Watermen, Courtiers, and others, so that by eleven o'Clock there were in *Cheap* six or seven hundred ; and out of St. *Paul's* Church-yard came about three hundred. From all Places they gathered together, and broke open the *Compter*, took out the Prisoners committed thither by the Lord-Mayor for hurting the Strangers ; they went also to *Newgate*, and took out *Studley* and *Betts*, committed for the like Cause. The Mayor and Sheriffs were present, and made Proclamation in the King's Name, but were not obeyed.

'Being thus gathered in crowds, they ran thro' St. *Nicholas's Shambles* ; and at St. *Martin's* Gate Sir *Thomas More*, and others, met them, desiring them to return to their Homes, which they had almost persuaded them to do ; when some within St. *Martin's*, throwing Sticks and Stones, hurt several who were with Sir *Thomas More*, particularly one *Nicholas Dennis*, a Serjeant at Arms, who, being much wounded, cried out, *Down with them* ; and then all the unruly Persons ran to the Doors and Windows of the Houses within St. *Martin's*, and spoiled all they found. After that they ran into *Cornhill*, and so on to a House East of *Leadenhall*, called the *Green-Gate*, where dwelt one *Mewtas*, a *Picard*, or *Frenchman*, with whom dwelt several other *Frenchmen*. These they plundered ; and, if they had found *Mewtas*, they would have struck off his Head.

'They ran to other Places, and broke open and plundered

the Houses of Strangers, and continued thus till three o'Clock in the Morning, at which Time they began to withdraw ; but by the Way they were taken by the Mayor and others, and sent to the *Tower, Newgate,* and the *Compters,* to the Number of three hundred.

'The Cardinal, being advertised of this by Sir *Thomas Parre,* sent him immediately to inform the King of it at *Richmond* ; and he forthwith sent to learn what Condition the City was in. Sir *Roger Cholmeley,* Lieutenant of the Tower, during the Time of this Business, shot off certain Pieces of Ordnance against the City, but did no great Hurt. About five o'Clock in the Morning the Earls of *Shrewsbury* and *Surrey, Thomas Dockery,* Lord Prior of St. *John's, George Nevil,* Lord *Abergavenny,* and others, came to *London,* with what Forces they could get together ; so did the Inns of Court : But, before they came, the Business was all over.

'Then were the Prisoners examined, and the Sermon of Doctor *Bell* called in Question, and he sent to the *Tower.* A Commission of *Oyer* and *Terminer* was directed to the Duke of *Norfolk,* and other Lords, for the Punishment of this Insurrection. The second of *May,* the Commissioners, with the Lord-Mayor, Aldermen, and Justices, went to *Guildhall,* where many of the Offenders were indicted ; whereupon they were arraigned, and pleaded *Not Guilty,* having one Day given them, 'till the fourth of *May.*

'On which Day, the Lord-Mayor, the Duke of *Norfolk,* the Earl of *Surrey,* and others, came to sit in the *Guildhall.* The Duke of *Norfolk* entered the City with one thousand three hundred Men, and the Prisoners were brought thro' the Streets tied with Ropes ; some Men, some Lads but of thirteen or fourteen Years old, to the Number of two hundred seventy-eight Persons. That Day *John Lincolne,* and divers others were indicted ; and the next Day thirteen were adjudged to be drawn, hanged and quartered ; for Execution whereof ten Pair of Gallows were set up in divers Places of the City, as at *Aldgate, Blanchapleton, Grass-Street, Leaden-hall,* before each of the *Compters,* at *Newgate,* St. *Martin's,* at *Aldersgate,* and *Bishopsgate :* And these Gallows were set upon Wheels to be removed from Street to Street, and from Door to Door, as the Prisoners were to be executed.'

On the seventh of *May, Lincolne, Sherwin,* and the two Brothers named *Betts,* with several of their Confederates, were found guilty, and received Sentence as the former ; when, within a short Time after, they were drawn upon Hurdles to the Standard in Cheapside ; where *Lincolne* was first executed ; but, as the rest were about to be turned off, a Reprieve came from the King to stay the Execution ; upon which the People shouted, crying, *God save the King ;* and thereupon the Prisoners were carried back to Prison, there to attend the King's farther Pleasure.

'After this, all the Armed Men, which before had kept Watch in the City, were withdrawn ; which gave the Citizens Hope that the King's Displeasure towards them was not so great as themselves conceived : Whereupon, on the eleventh of *May,* the King residing at his Manor of *Green-wich,* the Mayor, Recorder, and divers Aldermen, went in Mourning Gowns to wait upon him ; and having Admittance to the *Privy-Chamber* Door, after they had attended there for some Time, the King, attended with several of his Nobles, came forth ; whereupon they falling upon their Knees, the Recorder in the Name of the rest spake as followeth :

'" Most Natural, Benign, and our Sovereign Lord, We well know that your Grace is highly displeased with us of your City of *London,* for the great Riot done and committed there ; wherefore we assure your Grace, that none of us, nor no honest Person, were condescending to that Enormity ; yet we, our Wives and Children, every Hour lament that your Favour should be taken from us ; and forasmuch as light and idle Persons were the Doers of the same, we most humbly beseech your Grace to have Mercy on us for our Negligence, and Compassion on the Offenders for their Offences and Trespasses."

'To which the King replied; "Truly you have highly displeased and offended us, and therefore you ought to wail and be sorry for the same ; and whereas you say that *you the substantial Citizens were not consenting to what happened*, it appeareth to the contrary ; for you never moved to let them, nor stirred to fight with those whom you say were so small a Number of light Persons ; wherefore we must think, and you cannot deny, but that you did wink at the Matter : Therefore at this Time we will neither grant you our Favour nor Goodwill, nor to the Offenders Mercy ; but resort to our Lord *Chancellor*, and he shall make you an Answer, and declare to you our Pleasure."

'At this Speech of the King's, the Citizens departed very sorrowful ; but, having Notice that the King intended to be at his Palace of *Westminster* on the twenty-second of *May*, they resolved to repair thither, which they did accordingly, though not without the Appointment of Cardinal *Wolsey*, who was then Lord *Chancellor* ; when as a Cloth of Estate being placed at the upper End of *Westminster-Hall*, the King took his Place, and after him the Cardinal, the Dukes of *Norfolk* and *Suffolk*, the Earls of *Wiltshire*, *Surry*, *Shrewsbury*, and *Essex*, with several others ; the Lord-Mayor, Recorder, and Aldermen, together with many of the Commons, attending in their Liveries ; when, about nine o'Clock, Order was given for the bringing forth the Prisoners, which was accordingly done ; so that in they came in their Shirts, bound together with Ropes, and Halters about their Necks, to the Number of four hundred Men, and eleven Women, one after another ; which Sight so moved several of the Nobility, that they became earnest Intercessors to the King for their Pardon.

'When Silence was made, and they were all come into the King's Presence, the Cardinal sharply rebuked the

Mayor, Aldermen, and Commonalty, for their negligence ; and then, addressing his Speech to the Prisoners, he told them, That for their Offences against the Laws of the Realm, and against his Majesty's Crown and Dignity, they had deserved Death : Whereupon they all set up a piteous Cry, saying, *Mercy, Gracious Lord, Mercy* ; which so moved the King, that, at the earnest Intreaty of the Lords, he pronounced them pardoned ; upon which giving a great Shout, they threw up their Halters towards the Roof of the Hall, crying, *God save the King.* When this News was bruited abroad, several that had been in the Insurrection, and had escaped, came in upon their own accords with Ropes about their Necks, and received the Benefit of the King's Pardon ; after which the Cardinal gave them several good Exhortations tending to Loyalty and Obedience ; and so dismissed them, to their no small Joy ; and within a while after the Gallowses that were set in the several Parts of the City, were taken down, which so far pleased the Citizens, that they expressed infinite Thanks to the King for his Clemency.

' This Company was called the *Black Waggon* ; and the Day whereon this Riot and Insurrection happened, bears the Name of *Evil May-Day* to these our present Times. And thus have you heard how the Citizens escaped the King's Displeasure, and were again received into Favour ; though, as it is thought, not without paying a considerable Sum of Money to the Cardinal to stand their Friend, for at that Time he was in such Power, that he did all with the King.

' These great *Mayings* and *May-Games*, with the triumphant Setting-up the great Shaft, a principal May-pole in *Leadenhall-Street* before the Parish Church of St. *Andrew,* thence called *Undershaft*, were not so commonly used after this Insurrection on *May-Day*, 1517, as before.'

The story must be finished, though this part of it does not belong to Westminster, by showing the end of the shaft.

After the Evil May Day it was never raised again. This proves the growing dread, in the minds of the officials, of the mob when they came together. The after history of London is full of this dread, which experience fully justifies. The famous May-pole hung upon its hooks from the year 1517 to the year 1549, the third of Edward VI. There flourished at that time a certain person named Sir Stephen, a curate of St. Katharine Cree, a fanatic of the most abominable kind. He wanted to turn the Reformation into a Revolution : all the ancient ways were to be abandoned or turned upside down : he wanted the names of the churches to be altered : the names of the days in the week to be altered—'Saturday' is sheer pagan, and so is Friday, for we all know who Freya was : he wanted fishdays to be any days except Friday and Saturday : and Lent to be observed at any time of year except the time between Shrove Tuesday and Easter Sunday. ' I have often,' says Stow, ' seen this man forsaking the pulpit of his said parish church, preach out of a high elm tree in the midst of the churchyard, and then entering the church, forsaking the altar, to have sung his high mass in English upon a tomb of the dead towards the north.' Now on one occasion Sir Stephen preached at Paul's Cross, and he told the people that by naming the church St. Andrew Under-shaft they made an idol of a May-pole. ' I heard his sermon,' says Stow, ' and I saw the effect that followed : for in the afternoon of that present Sunday, the neighbours and tenants to the said bridge over whose doors the said shaft then leaned, after they had well dined, to make themselves strong, gathered more help and with great labour rending the shaft from the hooks, whereon it had rested two and thirty years, they sawed it in pieces, every man taking for his share so much as had lain over his door and stall, the length of his house : and they of the alley divided among them so much as had lain over their alley gate. Thus was this idol, as he, poor man, termed it, mangled and after burned.'

Many great and memorable events took place in the Hall, apart from the grand functions of State, or beside them. For instance, here began the massacre of the Jews at the coronation of Richard I. Here, in the same reign, the Archbishop and the Lords sat to pronounce sentence upon William Longbeard, who came with thousands of followers, so that they dared not pronounce sentence upon him. Here they brought the prisoners of Lincoln, a hundred and two Jews charged with crucifying a child, Hugh of Lincoln. That must have been a strange sight, this company of aliens who could never blend with the people among whom they lived : different in face, different in ideas, different in religion. They are dragged into the Hall, roped together : the prospect of death is before them : they are accused of a crime which they would not dare to commit, even at the very worst time of oppression ; even when the wrongs and injustices and hatred of the people had driven them well-nigh mad. At the end of the Hall sit their judges : the men-at-arms are at their side to let none escape : the Hall is filled with people eager for their blood : the witnesses are called : they have heard this said and that said : it is all hearsay : there is nothing but hearsay : and at the close eighteen of them are sentenced to be hanged, and the rest are driven back to prison, lucky if, after many years, they live to receive the King's release.

Stalls and shops for books, ribbons, and other things, were set up along the sides of the Hall ; and it was always a great place for lawyers. Lydgate says, speaking of the Hall :—

> Within this Hall, neither riche nor yet poore,
>> Wolde do for aught, althogh I sholde dye :
> Which seeing I gat me out of the doore,
>> Where Flemynge on me began for to cry,
> Master, what will you require or by ?
>> Fyne felt hatts or spectacles to rede,
> Lay down your sylver and here you may spede.

And so enough of Westminster Hall and the History of England.

CHAPTER III

THE ABBEY—I

ASL LAVRENTIUS

I LEAVE to courtly hands, to ecclesiastics of rank, to those who understand the pomp and dignity of history, the Abbey Church, with its royal memories and national associations. It is for Deans to dwell at length upon this stately shrine of England's story. Those whose place is duly assigned and reserved for them at Coronations, Functions and Funerals in this Church—those whose office brings them into personal relations with Kings and Queens, Princes and Princesses, those who belong to the Palace as much as to the Abbey —are the fittest persons to write on the events and episodes belonging to the Church, and to enumerate the chapels, altars, tombs and monuments within its walls. Again, there is the building itself : this has been described over and over again by architects and the students of architecture ; stone by stone the structure has been examined ; hardly one that has not been assigned to its builder and its date : we have been taught all that remains of Edward the Confessor ; all that Henry III. began and his son continued ; what Richard II. raised ; what is due to Henry VII., and what to Wren. We may leave aside, for the most part, the ceremonies of state, Coronations, Weddings, Funerals, the monuments, and the architecture. Are they not written in the book of the Dean ? Some of us, when we read of these great Functions, fall into the reflection that in that time, as in this, the place of the scholar, the poet or the story-teller would have been outside among the crowd: the man of letters would have been distinguished beyond expectation had he been invited to stand somewhere far back in the nave,—if he had secured a point of vantage near the North Porch, or anywhere in the Abbey Precinct where he could stand and see the Procession sweep past, the Procession of Heralds, Trumpets, Knights and Barons, and rich Lords, Bishops, and Mitred Abbots, Pursuivants and more Trumpets, splendid banners and canopies and shields borne by Nobles, Esquires and the King's Vallets: lastly, their Highnesses the King and the Queen themselves. If he should happily stand near the Porch, he would hear the

ARMS OF THE ABBEY OF
WESTMINSTER

rolling of the organ and the voices of those who sing. When the soldiers rushed out of the church at William's crowning to hack and cut down the people in suspicion of a tumult, the poet was among them and was glad to escape with a broken head; when King Richard's men-at-arms slew the Jews, the poet who was then outside among them thought himself happy that he was not mistaken for one of those unfortunates; the poet was standing outside the Abbey Church—in a very good place too—when with Pageant, songs and flowers, the whole world turned out to welcome Good Queen Bess. At every Coronation before and since that festival he has formed part of the outside throng. When the Rejoicing and the Thanksgiving for the happy closing of Fifty Years were solemnly celebrated, seven years ago, the poets and the men of letters occupied their old, old place: it was the kerb. All that was really noble and great and worthy of honour in the nation was invited within the walls. For literature was left, according to immemorial custom, the usual struggle

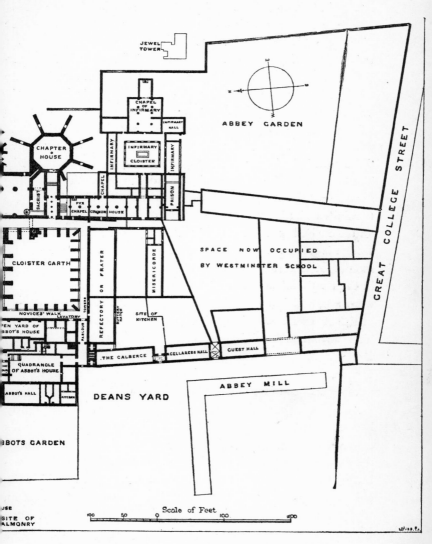

PLAN OF THE BENEDICTINE ABBEY OF WESTMINSTER
(By kind permission of Professor Henry Middleton)

for a place upon the kerb. The proper place for the man of letters in this country has always been, and is still, the kerb.

Here let us stand, then, happy at least in hearing the discourse of the people. When the Procession has been reformed and has swept past us again, we will betake ourselves to coffee-house or tavern, there to talk about it, while the great folk—the Quality—sit down to their banquet in Westminster Hall. If we take from Westminster Abbey its Kings and Princes, its Abbots, its Coronations, its Funerals, what remains? Exactly that which remains when you have taken out of history the Kings, Barons and great Lords. There remain the people—in this case the monks, with the servants of the Abbey. If we consider the daily life of one monk, we shall understand pretty well the daily life of all; and we shall presently realise that our old friend Barnaby Googe is not an authority to be altogether trusted; that the monks of Thorney were not all gross sensualists, wallowing in their animalism; and that on the other hand most of them were not, and in the nature of things could not be, followers of the austere and saintly life, great scholars or great divines. The unremembered life of Hugh de Steyninge, in Religion Brother Ambrosius, sometime monk in this Benedictine House, may be chosen to illustrate the Rule, as it was practised in the fifteenth century, just before the Dissolution.

Hugh de Steyninge was the younger son of a knightly house; the family originally, as the name shows, held lands in Steyninge, east of Chichester; at the time of his father's death—he was killed fighting for the Red Rose at Tewkesbury—there was still a small estate in Sussex, to which the eldest son succeeded; the second son was sent to London, where he was articled to Sir Ralph Jocelyne, Draper, Lord Mayor in the year 1476. (This son afterwards rose to be Sheriff, and would have been Mayor but that he died of the sweating sickness.) A third son went abroad and entered the service of the Duke of Tuscany. What became of him is not known. Hugh, the youngest, for whom there seemed nothing but the poor lot of becoming bailiff or steward to his brother, was so fortunate as to receive admission to the most wealthy Monastery in the kingdom. He was thus assured of

HABIT OF A NOVICE OF THE ORDER OF ST. BENEDICT

an easy life, with the chance of rising, should he show ability, to a position of very considerable dignity and authority.

It was now extremely difficult to enter one of the richer Abbeys ; a lad of humble origin had no chance of admission. Sometimes Founders' or Benefactors' kin possessed the right of nomination : sometimes admission was bought by money

G

or the gift of land : sometimes it was obtained by the private interest of some great man.

At this time, however,—about the year 1472—the monastic life, owing to many causes, had lost some of its attractions. First, there was coming on a long and exhausting civil war, in which many noble houses were doomed to destruction, and the flower of English youth had to perish. Men had become too valuable to be shut up in a cloister. Again, the spread of Lollard opinions made all classes of people question the advantages of the monastic life. Thirdly, the wars had greatly damaged the value of the monastic property, so that an Abbey no longer supported so many monks as formerly. Thus the number of monks decreased steadily : at Westminster there had been eighty : before the Dissolution this number sank below thirty ; at Canterbury a hundred and fifty became fifty-four ; at Gloucester a hundred went down to thirty-six. Probably those who remained had no desire to return to the former and longer roll, which would involve a diminution in the splendour of their establishment. We must remember that the external splendour of the Abbey, which does not necessarily involve luxury and gluttony, was a thing always greatly regarded by the Brethren : it magnified the Order ; it glorified the religious life. Even the most ascetic desired a splendid service, rich robes, vessels of gold and silver, gorgeous tapers, a fine organ, a well-trained choir of glorious voices, troops of servants, and stately buildings. So that this remarkable diminution of numbers may have been due, in some measure, to the increase of this kind of luxury.

However, there is no doubt that when little Hugh de Steyninge was admitted to the Abbey of St. Peter the House was at its highest point of splendour. It was the richest of all the English Houses : its manors had partly recovered from the losses caused by the civil wars ; the Abbot was greater than any bishop ; he lived in a palace ; he entertained kings : the Brethren were surrounded by lay brothers and servants ; the early austerities of the Rule had long been relaxed ; the buildings of the Abbey, Church, Cloisters, Chapter House were more stately than those of any other House ; the situation, close to the Palace and within easy reach of the Port and Markets of London, was most desirable. Nobody asked the boy if he would like to be a

ENTRANCE TO CHAPTER HOUSE

monk : nobody in those days ever consulted boys on such subjects ; the child was told that he would be a monk, and he obeyed.

They offered little Hugh in the Church as a Novice. First they cut his long curls round, offering the hair to the

Abbey—an act which symbolised something, but I know not what,—only a Brother learned in the Rule could interpret all the symbols in the ritual ; he was then, carrying in his hand the host and chalice, presented to the priest at the altar. The parents, or their representative, then wrapped the boy's hands in the pall of the altar, and read a written promise that they would not induce him to leave the Monastery or the Order. After this the Abbot consecrated a hood for the boy and laid it upon him. He was then taken out, shaved after the fashion of the Order, robed and brought back, when he was received with prayers. This done, he was a Novice, and was supposed to belong to the House for life, provided he entered upon full vows in due course.

It took many years to make a perfect monk. The rules under which Hugh was now brought up were more voluminous than those of the Talmudic Law. Long hours of silence, sitting with eyes downcast, never being left alone, allowed to play only once a day ; the performance of every action, even to the lifting of a cup to the lips, to be done according to the Rule ; the separation of the boys from each other,—all these minute regulations, all these vexatious and petty precautions, learned after frequent floggings, and fully observed only after the habit of long years, gradually transformed the boy from possible manhood to certain monkhood. Gradually the old free look vanished ; he became silent, timid, obedient. The House was all his world ; the things of the House were the only things of importance in the whole world. He was not cruelly treated ; on the contrary, he was most kindly treated,—well fed, well clothed, well cared for. He quickly understood, as children do, that these things, so irksome at first, were necessary ; that all the elders, even the Abbot and the Prior, had gone through the same discipline. All the time the boy's education in other things besides the Rule was going on. He was taught a great deal,—grammar, for instance, logic, Latin, philosophy, writing and illumi-

nating, music, singing, the history of the Order. The Benedictines always rejoiced in a liberal education. The schoolhouse
was the west cloister. Here, the arches being glazed, desks
were placed one behind the other, and the boys sat in this single
file, with their books before them. There were rules of
silence, rules of talking French only, rules how to sit, how to

WALL OF THE REFECTORY, FROM ASHBURNHAM HOUSE

carry the hands, rules here and rules there, regulations everywhere. If they had all been enforced, imbecility must have
followed. As Hugh did not become imbecile, the regulations
were certainly interpreted in a kindly spirit. The Brethren,
for instance, except the teachers, were not allowed to converse with the boys; but we may be very certain that they

did converse with them, and that they were kind to them, because St. Benedict could never wish to drive out of human nature that best part of it which prompts man to be tender towards the young. What happened to Hugh was that he acquired, little by little, the habit of living according to Rule, that by continual iteration he gradually learned the whole of the Litanies and Psalms, and that he obtained, before he became a full monk, some knowledge of the various branches of learning in which he had been grounded at his desk in the west cloister.

I pass over the ceremony of Profession. To give it in detail would take up too much space ; to quote extracts might convey a false impression. Let it suffice that nothing was wanting to make the ceremony the most solemn occasion possible. It is true that children were brought to the Abbey quite young and without regard to vocation : but might not the practice be defended on the grounds (1) that nothing, from the mediæval point of view, could be better for a man than the Benedictine Rule, so that every one, even though he might yearn for the outer world, ought to be grateful for this seclusion ; and (2) that by the long years of preparation and education the calling to Religion, which ought to be in every mind, was cultivated and developed ? And really, when we consider how many of our own clergy are in the same way set apart from youth, without question as to their vocation we need not throw stones at the mediæval Benedictines.

Hugh, therefore, at the age of eighteen made his profession and became Brother Ambrosius, a Junior in the House. His was the duty of reading the Gospel and the Epistle ; he carried a taper in processions ; he read the martyrology in the Chapter. And he now entered upon the daily round, which was to continue until the end of his life or till old age demanded indulgence.

It consisted mainly of services. They began at 2 in the morning with Matins. These finished, the choir went back to bed ; the rest remained to sing Lauds for the dead. They then went to bed again until daybreak or 5 in the morning, when they rose for Prime ; at 9 a.m. there was Tierce ; at 11 a m. there was Sext ; Nones were held at 2 p.m., and Vespers at 6 p.m. The day's services ended with Complines. There were thus eight stated services, requiring certainly as much as eight hours out of the twenty-four. They went to bed at 8 p.m.,

THE ABBOT'S DINING-HALL AT WESTMINSTER ; NOW USED AS THE
DINING-ROOM OF THE SCHOOL

getting six hours of sleep before Matins and two or three after Lauds. This accounts for sixteen hours. Then there was the daily gathering in the Chapter House, taking perhaps one hour. This leaves only seven hours for meals, rest and work. We are told that a Benedictine House was to be self-supporting as far as possible ; everything wanted by the Brethren was to be made in the place, if possible ; every

Brother was to be working when he was not in the Church, in the Refectory, or in the Dormitory. We know that there have been many learned works produced by Benedictines. Not, as I understand it, that learning or art or handicraft was ordered by the Founder, save as a means of keeping the hands of the Brethren out of mischief. Dean Stanley wonders mildly why, in the long history of Westminster Abbey, there was found no scholar in the Brotherhood, and there was produced no learned work. One would rather be surprised if any good work had been produced ; nor can we readily believe that good work could be produced by men wearied by seventeen hours of services and ceremonies.[1]

The situation of St. Peter's exposed the younger Brethren to temptations from which the monks of such retired spots as Glastonbury, Tintern, or Fountains were happily free. These temptations assailed the young Brother Ambrosius with great violence during the earlier years of his profession. It was, indeed, on account of these temptations that he was more than once, in the Chapter House, flogged in the presence of the whole fraternity. Eight years of drill and discipline although they made him a monk, had yet left in him the possibility of becoming a man.

Consider the dangers of the situation for a young man. On the other side of the wall which formed the eastern boundary of the Abbey was the Palace, the court and camp of the King, a place filled with noisy, racketing, even uproarious life. There were taverns without the Palace precincts where the noise of singing never ceased. There was the clashing of weapons ; there were the profane oaths of the soldiers ; there was the blare of trumpets ; there were the pipe and tabor of the minstrels and the jesters ; the monks in their cloister, which should have been so quiet, could never escape the clamour of the barrack. The world, in fact, was always

---

[1] The rules, it is true, were relaxed in the case of scholars engaged upon any learned work, and there must have been some such scholars at Westminster.

with these good monks: they could not escape it; invisible,
but audible, the temptations of the world, the flesh and the
devil were continually presented to them through the medium
of ears unwilling, yet constrained to hear. Only a low wall
between a world of action and the world of prayer; between
a world rushing headlong down the flowery path, gathering
roses with both hands, committing sins all day long, heedless
of repentance, and a world of Rule, where even the holy

TOWEL AUMBRIES IN THE SOUTH WALK

brethren had to step heedfully along the narrow walk prescribed by the wisdom or the inspiration of St. Benedict.

In the cloisters the Brother Ambrosius sat before his books,
eyes down-dropped. What did he read on the illuminated
page? I know not; what he heard—and it filled his heart
with yearnings indescribable—was the sound of pipe and
tabor, the merry squeak of crowd and the jangled bells of
tambourine; was the lusty song trolled out by soldier; and
—ah, Heaven! why is everything that the natural man longs
for sinful?—the singing, like the voice of a bird for silver

sweetness—it sank into the soul, and blurred the page of the Psalter, and made him giddy—the singing to the tinkling of the mandoline—the singing of girls. All that life, that

CHAPEL OF THE PYX

worldly life, the life of those who feasted and drank, sang, made love, and died on the battle-field, going headlong— there was no doubt whither—might be heard all day long in the cloister of the Abbey. Did no young man ever leap to his feet, tear off hood, gown and robe, and rush out of the Abbey gate (that which led into King Street), and so into the outer life, there to wallow in the transitory joys of this sinful world ?

DOOR TO THE CHAPEL OF EDWARD THE CONFESSOR ; NOW PYX OFFICE

There are no chronicles of the House left to tell if this lamentable lapse ever happened. So, on the other side, did the chanting of the monks, the rolling of the organ, awaken no thought of repentance in the rude soldiers? We know not; for, again, no chronicles survive of the men who followed the King and had bouche of Court. In the course of time even these temptations ceased to assail the young monk. Brother Ambrosius became like his brethren; he mechanically chanted the Psalms and the responses; his chief joy was in Refectory; he sat in the cloisters and whispered the small talk of the day; he went to Misericorde for indulgence permitted; as for scholarship, he had no turn for it. His whole life was worked out according to formula and by repetition. Just as the labourer goes forth every day with his spade for twelve hours' digging without a murmur or any discontent, so did Brother Ambrosius every morning rise at two to begin the many hours spent in the services of the day. They were his work. And for the ordinary monk, of no more than average intellect, it was quite enough work for the day.

Brother Ambrosius was never advanced to any post of honour or dignity in the House. A certain rusticity, perhaps a certain dulness produced by the discipline acting on a mind of only ordinary intelligence, prevented his advance. But he presently became not only learned in the minor points of the Rule, but also a great stickler for forms. He knew everything: the exact time and manner of changing clothes, putting on shoes, taking knife in hand, lifting the cup to drink, holding the hands in the Chapter, and other important points. He knew them all: he watched his Brethren; he insisted on observance; he was so jealous for these things that the Sub-Prior once rebuked him, saying that the Rule must be obeyed indeed, but that he who thinks too much of his brother's obedience in small things is apt to forget his own obedience in great things.

Perhaps this Brother at one time may have entertained ambitions. There were many offices of honour in the House. Might not he, too, aspire to rise? Who would not wish to be an Abbot, and especially a mitred Abbot? Besides ruling

the House and the Brethren, the mitred Abbot had the rank
of a peer : he rode abroad, hawk in hand, his mule equipped
with cloth of gold, followed by a retinue of a hundred persons ;
he created knights ; he could coin money ; he received the
children of noble families among his pages ; he administered
enormous estates.   Or, if he could not be Abbot, he might be
Prior.   The privileges and duties and powers of the Prior are
bewildering to read : to go first after the Abbot ; to sit in a

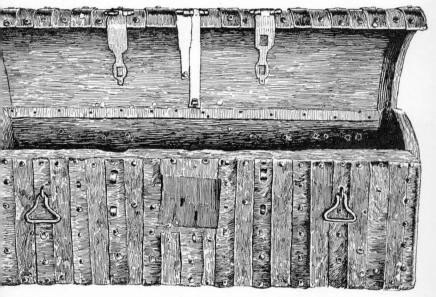

TREASURE CHEST IN THE CHAPEL OF PYX, USED IN THE
TRANSPORTATION OF THE KING'S EXCHEQUER

certain stall ; to put on his hood before the others,—in the
cloister as well as out precedence was the chief thing sought.
Or there was the office of Sub-Prior, who sat among the
monks at meat, said grace, saw that every one behaved properly, and, at five o'clock in the evening, shut up the House.
    There were next the offices of administration.   The
importance of the Altarer could not be denied.   He had the
care of refectory, kitchen and cellar.   The interest naturally

taken in the proper administration of kitchen and cellar caused the officer exemption from at least half the daily services. There was the Precentor (*cantor*), a functionary who knew the exact order of everything in church, refectory, cloister and dormitory. He was the Director of Ceremonies : so complicated were the rules, so exact and minute were the prescribed ceremonies, robes and gestures, that no one except those who had been brought up from childhood in the House could hope to learn or to remember them all. There were, besides, the Kitchener, who ordered and arranged the food, and looked after the sick in the infirmary ; the Seneschal, who was a kind of bailiff and held the courts ; the Bursar, who received the rents and paid the bills and the wages ; the Sacrist, who had charge of the Church plate and vestments and candles, and, with the sub-Sacrist, slept in the church ; the Almoner, who did a great deal more than administer alms, for he provided the mats and the rushes for the cloister, chapter house, and dormitory, he distributed broken victuals to the poor, and he was to seek out cases deserving of help and relief in the town or nearest villages—*e.g.*, St. Thomas's Hospital was originally the almonry of Bermondsey Abbey, and it was in the town of Southwark that the Almoner sought for deserving cases. Next, there was the Master of the Novices. There were other offices ; but these were chiefly held by lay brothers and by servants, of whom in Westminster Abbey there were some two hundred, following every conceivable trade that was wanted for the maintenance of the Abbey.[1]

Brother Ambrosius held no office, and presently lost whatever ambitions he might have had. But the life, which seems to us so monotonous, was to him full of variety. There

---

[1] Here are some of the lesser offices. Infirmarer, Porter, Refectioner, Hospitaller, Chamberlain, Keeper of the Granary, Master of the Common House, Orcharder, Operarius, Registrar, Auditor, Secretary, Butler, Keeper of Baskets, Keeper of the Larder, Baker, Brewer, Carpenter, Carver, Sculptor, Bookbinder, Copyist, Conveyancer, etc.

was always something to expect, just as children are always looking forward to holidays, to a birthday, to a change. For instance, here are some of the incidents which saved him from falling into lethargy. On certain days the Brethren shaved each other in the cloister. On an appointed day, two days

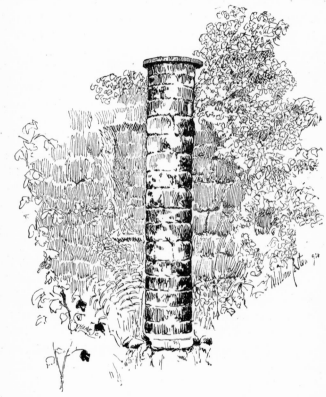

A PILLAR NOW STANDING IN MR. THYNNE'S GARDEN AND FORMING
PART OF THE RUINED CHAPEL OF ST. CATHERINE

before Christmas, the whole Brotherhood bathed. On Christmas Day there were rules about combing the hair. At the same season they celebrated the Office of the Shepherds, acted by boys for the angels and the Brethren for the shepherds. They also enacted a Feast of Asses, for which there was to be prepared a furnace made of cotton and linen ready to be fired ; there was a procession of prophets, including Balaam on his ass, the angel represented by one of the boys. This drama finished with the appearance of Nebuchadnezzar with an idol : three youths were called upon to worship the idol ; they refused and were instantly thrown upon the lighted furnace, and as instantly taken out again by a supposed miracle. At this juncture the Sibyl appeared, but her reason for joining in the drama is not apparent.

At this season there was also the Liberty of December, with its Feast of Fools, the Abbot of Fools, the burlesque services, the bawling, drinking and misrule permitted at that season.

On the Epiphany they performed another miracle-play called the Office of the Three Kings. Another Feast of Asses represented the Flight into Egypt. On Shrove Tuesday there was feasting. At Easter there was a succession of offices, plays, shows and processions. At Whitsuntide the Descent of the Holy Spirit was represented by the flight of a white pigeon.

This multiplication of rules, this attention to trifles, these childish diversions, prove, if any proof were wanted, the deadly dulness of the monastic life, unless it was lit up by spiritual fervour. The ordinary mind cannot dwell continually upon things spiritual, yet it must be occupied with something ; therefore, when the monks were not engaged in services or in the Refectory, although they were ordered to work at some bodily or intellectual pursuit, most of them occupied themselves with trifles ; they amused themselves with childish shows ; they admonished and corrected each other with boyish discipline. We need not ask why Westminster produced no great scholars : it was not the real business of the Abbey to produce scholars, but to sanctify the life of the monk, and to sing so many services a day for the good of the Brethren first and of those outside afterwards. Now comes the question—how much of the Rule was obeyed in the latter days, just before the Dissolution? The discipline varied from House to House. It is very certain that the Carthusian Rule was strictly observed at the Charter House, and that the Benedictine Rule was observed with laxity at the Priory of the Holy Trinity. Chaucer's jolly monk has

JERUSALEM CHAMBER. ABBOT'S RESIDENCE, WESTMINSTER

horses in the stable; he can go abroad as he pleases; he is not dressed as a monk. Again, there is one of the stories concerning Long Meg of Westminster which seems to show that the monks went about in the taverns outside the Abbey. Yet the holding of certain offices gave permission to go outside the Abbey. There is every kind of evidence to prove that luxury and pride and laziness had become a common

II

charge against the monks long before the Dissolution. Was
there a voice or a hand raised in London or Westminster to
save the Houses? Why, had there been even a small minority
in London by whom the Houses were respected, Henry had
not dared to touch them. He beheaded those who opposed
his will. True, the great nobles he beheaded, but not the
crowd, who, had they cared for the Houses, could have
defended them against all the power of the King. But the
scanty memoir of Hugh de Steyninge, which has been
collected painfully from various sources, does not enable
me to state with any exactness how far the Rule was still
observed.

There exists no portrait of this, or any other, Brother.
He lived in the Abbey, whose walls he never left till he died,
full of years, and with the reputation of having been a good
monk. He was buried in the cemetery close to St. Margaret's
Church with his brethren of a thousand years : of them, and of
their works, the name and the memory have long since perished.
Although no portrait remains of Hugh, in Religion Brother
Ambrosius, we can discern his face after the manner of the
photographer who produces a type by superposition. There
are thirty generations of Westminster monks passing in
procession before us. Here and there one perceives the
keen eye and the aquiline nose of the administrator. Such a
brother will become Abbot in due course. One observes
here and there the face of a scholar : such a brother is moody
and irritable ; he cannot even after forty years reconcile
himself to the wearisome iteration of services. Here and
there one observes an ascetic, thin, pale, fiery-eyed ; here and
there the face of a saint—the kind of face which you may see
on the marble tomb of Westminster's greatest and noblest
Dean. The rest are like our friend Hugh de Steyninge :
they are dull and heavy-eyed ; their faces express the
narrowness of their lives ; they are not alert, like other men ;
they have no craft or guile in their eyes ; in worldly things

they are ignorant ; you have only to look at them to discover
this. But Hugh de Steyninge never became a hypocrite, nor
was he ever a sensualist ; at the worst he was a man checked
in his growth, stunted in mind, ignorant, incapable of the

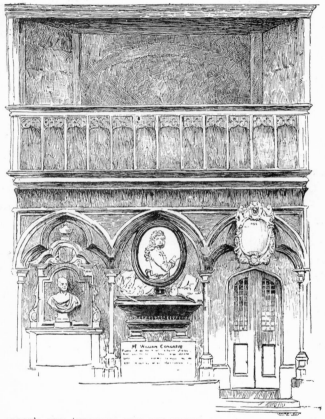

ABBOT'S PEW (SHOWING THE MEDALLION OF CONGREVE BELOW)

finer emotions because he was thus stunted, an imperfect man
because he was cut off from the things which made the real
man in the Palace Yard beyond the wall : viz., the dangers
and perils and chances of life ; the struggle for life ; the
natural affections ; the madness of battle, victory or defeat.

What compensation could there be for a life so stunted ? Alas ! poor Hugh ! One of his brothers, I believe, was killed in battle, and another was hanged for alleged conspiracy ; he was quite safe all his life, his eternal future even was assured. And yet—yet . . . Besides, there are sins in the cloister as well as without. No man, even among the Trappists, oan escape from himself, from the wanderings of his thoughts, from his instincts and his heredities. He has buried the half of himself—is it the nobler part ? For the other half, besetting devils still contend.

Some of us can remember how under the old system at Cambridge the Senior Fellows remained in College all their lives, their interests centred in the Society, dining in hall every day, sitting over the College port in Combination Room every day. Few among the Seniors, as one remembers them, were any longer capable of intellectual work ; they had never had any ambitions ; they played bowls in the garden ; they walked every day the customary round ; they were in Orders ; they were regular at chapel, and they led decorous lives ; when they grew very old they fell into the hands of their bedmaker. Of other women they knew little. Such as were these aged dons, so were, I believe, the monks of Westminster—dull and respectable, decorous, obedient to so much of the Rule as they could not escape, and stupid and ignorant —since they had been locked up within those walls from childhood. Just as those old dons had long since lost any enthusiasm for learning which might once have possessed them, so our friend Hugh de Steyninge, plodding through the monotonous days, with the iteration of the same services till he knew every line by heart, had long ceased to connect their words with any meaning.

There is one exception to the general charge of worldliness and luxury. It is an officer—rather a resident—of the Abbey concerning whom historians are mostly silent. Of him alone it can be said that he was most certainly neither

luxurious nor sensual nor a hypocrite. This man was the
Solitary, the Recluse, the Anchorite or Ankret, of the Abbey.

The Ankret must not be confused with the Hermit, who
was another variety of the Recluse. The latter chose his
own place of residence : sometimes it was a cave, sometimes
a hollow tree, sometimes a cell on or near a bridge, sometimes
a wood ; he was a law to himself ; he owed obedience to no

SQUARE WINDOW, A (NOW WALLED UP), USED BY THE ABBOT TO
MAINTAIN SURVEILLANCE OF THE MONKS AT NIGHT

one ; all he had to do was to impress the people with the
belief that he was a real hermit in order to live by their
charity. The Ankret, on the other hand, was set apart and
consecrated by a solemn service ; there was generally one at
least attached to every great religious House, there was an
Ankret or an Ankress belonging to many parish churches.
On the other hand, no church was allowed the distinction of

a Recluse without the special permission of the Bishop. Thus in 1361 the Bishop granted permission to the parish church of Whalley to maintain two Ankresses in the church-yard, with two women as their servants, on an endowment provided by Henry, Duke of Lancaster. These two Ankresses were apparently immured in their cells, the attendants bringing them their food. In many cases the Ankress slept in the church, which she swept and kept clean. This office might appear desirable for many a poor woman, and probably such an Ankress was never wanting. But to be actually immured ; to sit for the rest of life in a narrow cell with a narrow grating for light and air and conversation ; without fire or candle ; alone day and night, in good or bad weather, without hearing a voice or speaking with any one ; unwashed, uncombed, in rags and cold and misery—this could never come to be regarded as a trade or calling by which to make one's livelihood. Of the Ankret's sincerity we can scarcely entertain a doubt.

The following extracts from an unpublished chronicle by a nameless Brother may illustrate the Service of Consecration of an Ankret. The date appears to have been about the beginning of the reign of Henry IV. It will be observed that the practice of whispering or singing news, gossip and scandal instead of the appointed Psalms was practised at Westminster.

'After the singing of Mattins, on the morning of St. Thomas' or Mumping Day, when the Brethren began the Lauds for the Dead, it was whispered abroad that the Abbey Ankret was dead at last. Brother Innocent, my neighbour on the right, sang the news in my ear when we turned to the Altar for the *Gloria* : " Dead is our holy Ankret ; he is dead ; he died at midnight ; the Abbot confessed him ; he is dead." I for my part in like manner transmitted the news to Brother Franciscus. In this manner, though by our Rule it is a sin, do we lighten the labour of chanting and keep off the sleep which is sometimes ready to fall upon us.

'We knew that his time had come: he had reached the
extremity of age allowed to man—even, it was said, his
hundredth year. For sixty years he had been immured.
Those who conversed with him—but of late his discourse was

MONK OF THE ORDER OF ST. BENEDICT

wild—saw through an iron grating a long, bent figure, with
white hair and white beard reaching to his waist. His face
was like the face of some corpse which had escaped corruption
—so thin, so white, so sunken it was ; but for the gleaming
of his eyes one would have thought him the figure of Death

as he is painted in the cloister of Paul's. He was reckoned a very holy person ; the Brothers were justly proud of having an Ankret of such reputation for saintliness. Formerly, it was said, he would recount engagements with Devils, such as those which happened to St. Dunstan, our Founder, when he was a Recluse at Glastonbury, or those which happened to St. Anthony ; but of late, the Devils being routed, he was left to his meditations, and his discourse consisted of pious ejaculations, some of which have been written down by the Cancellarius ; and for the last year or two, his soul being rapt, his voice spoke only words uncertain. King Richard himself, that noble benefactor of the House, thought it not beneath his dignity to take counsel with the Ankret before he went forth to stay the rebellion. I know not what the holy man told the young king, but all men know how the leader was killed and the rebels were scattered. Like the renowned Mother Julian of Norwich, our Ankret brought honour and offerings to the House.

'Now he was dead. After daybreak, when we met in the Common Room, the air in the Cloisters being eager and cold, we whispered each other, "How shall we bury him ? With what honours ? Will he work a miracle ? Shall the House obtain at length a saint for itself ? If so, those of St. Albans and those of the Holy Trinity of London will not hold up their heads beside us. And who—if any—who will succeed him ? " And at this question we hung our heads and dropped our eyes, and murmured, "Nay, if one were worthy ; but these vows are too much for me." Yet there must be found some one, because an Abbey without an Ankret is like a ship without a rudder. We Monks pray for the world ; the Ankret prays for the Monks. Unless we know that all night long the Ankret in his cell is praying for the House and ourselves, who can sleep upon his bed ?

'The anxiety was speedily set at rest ; for it became known that one of the Brotherhood—a most unusual circum-

stance—the Sub-Prior—Heavens! nothing less than the
Sub-Prior, who might reasonably expect to be Prior, and even
Abbot!—had humbly offered himself to the Abbot for this
living sacrifice. Yet, when we considered the matter, it

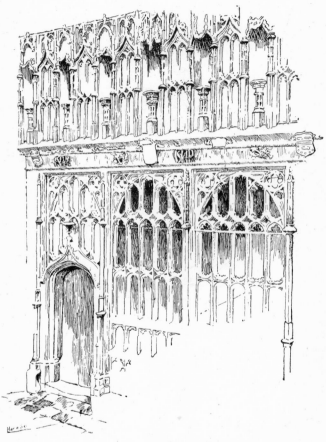

ABBOT ISLIP'S CHAPEL

seemed neither wonderful nor unexpected. The Sub-Prior—
Humphrey of Lambhythe—was always a silent man and
zealous in his duties. As one of the monitors he had been
thought too zealous, and many a Brother could show upon

his back the marks of the zeal which had placed him on the culprit's bench in Chapter. The Sub-Prior! Perhaps he would be more free to carry on his austerities in the Ankret's cell : he cared nothing for the Refectory, and his drink was only water. Heaven would doubtless reward him, and perhaps would grant to the Brothers of lower saintliness a milder Sub-Prior. In this life compassion and indulgence are more desirable than the strict investigation of every little sin.

'That night the Sub-Prior spent alone in the Abbey Church, after confessing to the Abbot and receiving absolution from him. In the morning we set him apart and consecrated him according to the Order prescribed. And the manner of his consecration was as follows :

'The Sub-Prior, being a priest, was taken into the choir, where he prostrated himself with bare feet. The Abbot and three of the Brethren who were priests having taken their places, the Cantor began the service with the Responsory, "*Beati in melius,*" after which the Abbot and assistants before the altar sang with the choir certain Psalms fourteen in number. After the Psalms followed a Litany, the choir singing after each clause, "*Ora pro eo.*" The Litany finished, the Abbot advanced towards the prostrate brother bearing a crucifix, a thurible, and holy water, and, standing over him, he thrice sprinkled him with water, censed him, and prayed over him. The Abbot then raised the candidate with his own hands, and gave him two lighted tapers, at the same time admonishing him to remain steadfast in the love of God. Then the candidate, standing, listened to the Deacon, who read first from the Prophet Isaiah, next the Gospel according to Saint Luke, as on the Festival of the Assumption of the Virgin Mary. After this the new garments which he was to put on were blessed. The candidate then took the vows, which were three only, and those the same as the vows at profession—viz., of chastity, of obedience, and of steadfastness.

'The candidate next kneeled at the altar, and, kissing it

three times, repeated each time the words *"Suscipe me, Domine,"* etc., the choir responding. This done, he offered the two tapers at the Altar, and again kneeled while the Abbot removed his monastic frock and clothed him with the garments newly blessed. Then followed a service of prayer.

THE WESTMINSTER SCHOOLROOM, FORMERLY THE ABBOT'S DORMITORY

It was the *Veni Creator*, with the *Pater noster* and " *Et ne nos.*" The Abbot then, standing on the north side of the Altar, preached to the Brethren and to the congregation assembled, commending the new Recluse to their prayers. The candidate then himself sang the Mass of the Holy Ghost.

'We had now completed that part of the consecration which takes place in the church. The Abbot then took the new Recluse by the hand, and led him down the nave of the church, followed by the choir and all the Brethren unto the little door leading into the West Cloister. The church was filled with people to see the sight. A new Recluse is not seen every day. There were the *domicellæ*, the maidens of the Queen, come from the Palace ; there were knights and pages, and even men-at-arms ; there were Sanctuary men, women and children ; men with hawks upon their wrists ; men with dogs ; merchants from the wool staple ; girls of wanton looks from the streets and taverns beyond the walls. The hawks jangled their bells, the dogs barked, the women chattered, the men talked loudly, the girls looked at the Brothers as they passed, and whispered and laughed ; and I heard one Brother say to another that this was a thing which would make the Sub-Prior return to the Monastery an he saw it. And all alike craned their necks to see the man who was going to be shut up in a narrow cell for the rest of his days.

'The Ankret's cell is on the south side of the Infirmary Cloister. It is built of stone, being twelve feet long, eight feet broad, and with an arched roof about ten feet high. On the side of the church there is a narrow opening by which the occupant can hear mass and can see the Elevation in the Chapel of St. Catherine. On the other side is a grating by which he can receive his food and converse with the world. But it is too high up for him to see out of it ; therefore he has nothing to look upon but the walls of his cell. This morning the west side had been broken down in order to remove the body of the dead man and to cleanse the cell for the new comer. So, while we gathered round in a circle and the people stood behind us, the Abbot entered the cell, and censed it, and sprinkled it with holy water, singing more Psalms and more prayers. When he came forth the Recluse himself entered, saying aloud : " *Hæc Requies mea in seculum seculi.*" The choir sang another Psalm. Then the Abbot sprinkled dust upon the head of the Recluse with the words beginning " *De terra plasmasti.*"

'This done, the *Operarius cum suis operariis* replaced the stones and built up the wall anew. And then, singing

TOMBS OF VITALIS, GERASMUS DE BLOIS, AND CRISPINUS, ABBOTS OF WESTMINSTER

another Psalm, we all went back to the cloister, leaving the Sub-Prior to begin his lifelong imprisonment. A stone bench for bed ; his frock for blanket ; a crucifix, and no other furniture. In the cold nights that followed, lying in my bed in dormitory, I often bethought myself of the former Sub-Prior alone in his dark cell, with Devils whispering temptation through the grating—Devils always assail every new Recluse—well-nigh frozen, praying with trembling lips and chattering teeth. No, I am not worthy. Such things are too high for me.

'But the new Sub-Prior proved to possess a heart full of compassion, and the House had rest for many years to come.'

NOTE (*'in another hand'*). This Recluse, formerly Humphrey of Lambhythe, surpassed in sanctity even his predecessor. It was to him that Henry V. repaired after the death of his father, as is thus recorded by Thomas of Elm-

TALLY FOR 6*s*. 8*d*. ISSUED BY TREASURER TO KING EDWARD I. TO THE SHERIFF OF LINCOLNSHIRE ABOUT 1290.

ham : 'The day of the funeral having been spent in weeping and lamentation, when the shades of night had fallen upon the face of the earth, the tearful Prince, taking advantage of the darkness, secretly repaired to the Recluse of Westminster, a man of perfect life, and unfolding to him the secret of his whole life, being washed in the bath of true penitence, received against the poison of his sins the antidote of absolution. Thus, having put off the cloak of iniquity, he returned decently garbed in the mantle of virtue.'

CHAPTER IV

THE ABBEY—II

THE Abbey must not, however, be dismissed without some reference to its history. There is a history of its buildings and there is a history of its people. The architectural history of the Abbey has been written in many volumes. Briefly, there was a monastery with its church here as early as the eighth century : this was destroyed by the Danes : then a new House with its church was founded and the House was rebuilt on a scale of great magnificence by Edward the Confessor. Next, Henry III. resolved to honour Edward the Confessor by pulling down his church and rebuilding it entirely. This he accomplished as far as the crossing of the transepts and the nave. The great feature of the new church was now the Shrine of the Confessor, raised high above the floor of the church by an artificial mound of earth brought from the Holy Land. St. Peter, to whom Edward had dedicated the church, was now supplanted by St. Edward. The nave was continued by Edward I. who built five bays, according to Gilbert Scott. The chantry of Henry V., Henry VII.'s Chapel, and the completion of the western towers by Wren or by his pupil Hawksmoor, have been added since the work of King Edward.

As for the domestic buildings of the Abbey there are still fragments remaining of the Confessor's work. But the buildings were in great part rebuilt by Abbot Litlington towards the end of the fourteenth century. The Cloisters, the Jerusalem Chamber, the Chapter House, the Abbot's dining hall, still remain : while the Cloisters, the Refectory, the Infirmary cloisters and fragments of the Chapel of St. Catherine also show in ruin, more or less complete, the beauty of his work. The history of a monastery apart from its architecture must be meagre. The more meagre it is, the more likely, one feels, is it that the House has sustained its pristine zeal. To the Benedictine of the ancient rule, behind his walls, cut off from the outer world, there were no events : he was buried : the world did not exist for him : the small events of the Abbey, the death of one Abbot and the election of another : an unexpected legacy : the building of another chapel : the addition of new carved stalls to the Abbey church : what else was there to chronicle ?

At Westminster the monks were noted for their scriptorium. The work of copying and illuminating was one which flourished in religious Houses first because it was work which required the attention and care of men who were not bound by any consideration of time—whether a missal was completed in a year or in ten years mattered nothing : the only point worthy of consideration was the excellence of the work : next, it was just the kind of delicate artistic work, conventional in its drawing and in its colouring, which a monk of artistic tastes would like. What else did the Westminster monks do ? They taught their novices : they received the sons of noblemen as scholars and wards : they administered their very large estates : they governed the rabble of Sanctuary : they carried on a tradition of learning but they produced no scholars : and they took part in every national and Royal Function held in the Abbey church. I think it may be conceded that, except in one deplorable case, there were few scandals attached to the Abbey of St. Peter's, Westminster. The stories connected with the poet Skelton point to a certain laxity as regards going outside the House and drinking in the Westminster taverns. Indeed it is plain that the monks were frequently seen in the streets and in public places. But we hear little of the monks, and this fact must be placed to their credit.

Twice is the silence broken. On one occasion some prophet announced that a high tide was coming up the Thames, which would overflow the Abbey buildings and drown the monks. Then the Abbot with all the brethren betook himself to a small House at Kilburn, the Priory of St. John the Baptist, where they took shelter until the tide was past and the prophet was covered with confusion.

The second case is that of Richard Podelicote, which deserves a longer notice.

This case occurred in the year 1303. It is certainly one of the most astonishing and daring attempts in history—only equalled by Col. Blood's attempt nearly four hundred years later. It was the Robbery of the Royal Treasury. The King's Treasure consisted of the Saxon Regalia ; the jewelled crowns, swords, cups of state, and precious vessels acquired by the Norman and Plantagenet kings : and of such moneys as the King had accumulated or set apart for special purposes, or acquired by ordinary means from year to year. The Treasury was the ancient Norman Chapel of the Pyx., i.e. Chapel of the Box which contained the things required for the assay and examination of new coins. In 1303 the chapel contained a far larger amount of specie than was usual. This money was lying there, ready for the use of the King in his Scottish campaign. It amounted to one hundred thousand pounds, an enormous sum, equivalent to something like a million or more of our own money.

The robbery apparently began with a raid upon the Refectory, and was not at first intended to go any farther. The robber was one Richard de Podelicote, described as a merchant of some kind formerly trading in the Low Countries. We must, of course, be careful not to suppose that a so-called ' merchant ' was necessarily a person with the dignity

I

and authority of a Whittington. Richard de Podelicote was probably an unsuccessful trader in foreign wares : not a craftsman or a retailer, else he would have been so described. Richard, who said in his confession that he had lost the sum of 14*l.* 17*s.* in a law-suit, was a broken man, desperate and cunning : he observed that the small gate in the wall which led from the Palace to the Abbey (at the door now by Poet's Corner) was unwatched and neglected. At this time the King himself with a great army was on his way to Scotland : the Palace was therefore deserted. All the grooms, armourers, blacksmiths, pages and men-at-arms were with the King. A crowd of servants followed with such gear as was wanted for the cooking, carrying provisions, wine and all kinds of things. There were left in the Palace only the Queen and her people, the canons, vicars, singing men, and boys of St. Stephen's ; the women and the children ; and some of the servants. The courts of the palace were therefore quiet and deserted : the strictness of the rules about closing and opening gates : and about watching those who entered or went out, was relaxed. This private way from the Palace to the Abbey was hardly ever used : perhaps it was well-nigh forgotten. The thief, therefore, would have no difficulty whatever, pretending to be a workman, sent perhaps to repair the roof, in introducing by this postern a ladder into the Abbey precinct. Or indeed he might have entered boldly by any of the remaining four gates into the Abbey.

At night all the gates, except this, being locked and made fast, and all the monks, even the two guardians of the church, being asleep, the thief was perfectly safe. No one could see him. He set his ladder against one of the Chapter House windows and so, opening a window and tying a rope round the stonework, he easily let himself down into the Chapter House and so into the Cloisters. There is mention of some kind of night-watch : there was such a watch in the

church : the Sacristan is said to have been responsible for a
night-watch in the Abbey : there was perhaps an irregular
patrol : perhaps the Sacristan, whose guilt in what afterwards
occurred is but too apparent, was already an accomplice.
However that might be, there were no watchmen out on the
night when Richard de Podelicote stood in the silent Cloisters
and glanced hurriedly around before he forced open the lock
of the Refectory door and proceeded to the job in hand.
This was to fill his bag with silver cups from the aumbries
or cupboards in the Refectory. Nobody disturbed him : he
retreated as he had entered : he climbed up his rope : he
replaced his ladder along the wall as if it had been left there
by a workman and he passed through the postern into the
Palace itself. To find a place for rest and concealment in
that deserted nest of houses, chambers, and offices was not
difficult : to carry out his bag in the morning —his bag full of
silver cups—was also easy. Perhaps, as happened later, the
custodian of the gate was an accomplice in this job as well.

The next chapter in the story is more difficult to understand. To rob the King's treasury was a far more serious job
than to rob the Refectory. For the Treasury was a chamber
with stone walls of great thickness, cemented firmly, only to
be dislodged by being taken away piecemeal with infinite
labour : and to carry out whole sacks and hampers full of
treasure was impossible for one man unaided. There must
be confederates. There must certainly have been confederates
within and without the Abbey : monks who would assist
in averting suspicion : people who would buy up the
plunder.

The story has been related by two writers from such
documents as remain—one of these is Mr. Joseph Burtt, late
Assistant Keeper of the Public Records, who contributed a
paper on the subject to Gilbert Scott's 'Gleanings from
Westminster Abbey,' and the other is Mr. Henry Harrod,
F.S.A., in a paper printed in the forty-fourth volume of

' Archæologia.' The differences between the two accounts are
very slight.

Mr. Harrod, however, endeavours to prove that the King's
Treasury was not the Chapel of the Pyx but the Crypt of
the Chapter House. I cannot think that he has made out
his case. It is true that the Crypt is a strong and massive
structure perfectly well adapted for such a purpose : but the
tradition which attaches to the chapel ; the strong iron
door: the provision about the keys : the nature of the things
actually stored there after the regalia was removed : seem to
me quite clearly to prove that this place and not the Crypt
was the Royal Treasury.

In considering the method of the robbery it makes a
very great difference whether the Treasury was in one or the
other place. Consider the plan (p. 79) of the Abbey. If the
Treasury was in the Chapter House the robber might if the
postern were closed work all day at the back of this house.
No one ever came into the cemetery which is now Henry
VII.'s Chapel. If the Treasury was in the Chapel of the Pyx,
he would have to work by night only in the passage frequented every day by the monks and leading from the
Chapter House to the Cloisters.

In any case the whole world knew the position of the
King's Treasury. In the reign of Edward I., just as now,
there was the massive and ponderous iron door, closely
locked, which could not be broken open in a single night by
a dozen men. The Abbot and the Prior were the official
guardians of the Treasury : they kept the keys. A key was
also kept by the Master of the King's Wardrobe.

Matthew of Westminster is deeply indignant at the
suspicion that any of the monks were concerned in the
robbery. But he is careful not to tell the story, which is
suspicious to the highest degree. Meantime it is perfectly
certain that no one unaided could effect this work without its
being discovered while incomplete. Dean Stanley (p. 369)

says that Richard 'concerted with friends, partly within, partly without the Precincts.' He refers to Matthew of Westminster under the year 1303. Unfortunately Matthew makes no reference whatever to any accomplices : he merely says 'Edward had his Treasury plundered by a single robber.' And this bald statement he repeats immediately afterwards.

The undeniable facts in the case are these—

1. At the end of April 1303, the King's Treasury at Westminster Abbey was broken open and a great quantity of treasure was stolen.

2. On June 6th, the King being then at Linlithgow, heard of the robbery and very naturally fell into a wrath more than royal. He despatched writ after writ, ordering the most searching investigation.

3. An investigation was made. In consequence of this all the monks of Westminster and forty other persons were taken to the Tower and kept there.

4. On the day of Annunciation 1306 the monks were released.

The evidence, so far as it has been preserved, shows how the robbery was planned and carried out.

First there is the confession of Podelicote himself—

' He was a travelling merchant for wool, cheese, and butter, and was arrested in Flanders for the King's debts in Bruges, and there were taken from him 14*l.* 17*s.*, for which he sued in the King's Court at Westminster at the beginning of August in the thirty-first year, and then he saw the condition of the Refectory of the Abbey, and saw the servants bringing in and out silver cups and spoons, and mazers. So he thought how he might obtain some of those goods, as he was so poor on account of his loss in Flanders, and so he spied about all the parts of the Abbey. And on the day when the King left the place for Barnes, on the following night, as he had spied out, he found a ladder at a house which was near the gate of the Palace towards the Abbey, and put that ladder to a window

of the Chapter House, which he opened and closed by a cord ;
and he entered by this cord, and thence he went to the door
of the Refectory, and found it closed with a lock, and he
opened it with his knife and entered, and there he found six
silver hanaps in an aumbry behind the door, and more
than thirty silver spoons in another aumbry, and the mazer
hanaps under a bench near together : and he carried them all
away, and closed the door after him without shutting the
lock.   And having spent the proceeds by Christmas he
thought how he could rob the King's Treasury.   And as he
knew the ways of the Abbey, and where the Treasury was, and
how he could get there, he began to set about the robbery
eight days before Christmas with the tools which he provided
for it, viz., two " tarrers," great and small knives and other
small " engines " of iron, and so was about the breaking open
during the night hours of eight days before Christmas to the
quinzain of Easter, when he first had entry on the night of a
Wednesday, the eve of St. Mark (April 24) ; and all the day
of St. Mark he stayed in there and arranged what he would
carry away, which he did the night after, and the night after
that, and the remainder he carried away with him out of the
gate behind the church of St. Margaret, and put it at the foot
of the wall beyond the gate, covering it with earth, and there
were there pitchers, cups with feet and covers.   And also he
put a great pitcher with stones and a cup in a certain tomb.
Besides he put three pouches full of jewels and vessels, of
which one was "hanaps" entire and in pieces.   In another a
great crucifix and jewels, a case of silver with gold spoons.
In the third " hanaps," nine dishes and saucers, and an image
of our Lady in silver-gilt, and two little pitchers of silver.
Besides he took to the ditch by the mews a pot and a cup of
silver.   Also he took with him spoons, saucers, spice dishes
of silver, a cup, rings, brooches, stones, crowns, girdles, and
other jewels which were afterwards found with him.   And he
says that what he took out of the Treasury he took at once out

of the gate near St. Margaret's Church, and left nothing behind within it.'

It will be observed that he takes the whole blame to himself and names no confederates. Was this loyalty to his friends? If so, it was loyalty of a very unusual kind. Another man, John de Rippingall, however, who also confessed, states that there were present two monks, two foresters, two knights, and about eight others.

The evidence of conspiracy was very strong. First, as regards the monks. Podelicote himself says that the work took him four months. Was there no help from within to keep this work secret? Consider: the robber was cutting through a massive stone wall: he would have to remove the stones one by one at night and replace them when he ceased at daybreak. But this kind of work cannot be done without making a considerable amount of mess. Now, the Sacrist and his officers had charge of the church and the close, and they were charged to watch ' in the cemetery.' By the cemetery is meant, I suppose, the ground lying between the East end of the Abbey and the wall, now covered by Henry VII.'s Chapel.

Stanley, without any discoverable authority, calls the cloister-garth the cemetery. During that time of four months the Sacrist's watch never once discovered this workman. I do not suppose a nightly patrol, but any kind of watch means some kind of irregular visit here and there.

The work would involve the removal of those stones which were underground. In order to effect this the flags must be taken up every night if the passage was paved: if it was not, the difficulty of opening and closing the cavity for working in was very greatly increased. It seems to me, in fact, impossible that the thing could have been managed at all without confederates in the Abbey itself.

There were other reasons for suspecting the Sacrist. He brought one day, before the discovery, a silver-gilt cup to the Abbot: he found it, he said, outside St. Margaret's Church.

It was debated whether the Abbot could rightly keep the cup thus found within the precincts. Where did the Sacrist get that cup? Did he give it up in fear of having it discovered in his possession? William the Palmer, Keeper of the Palace, deposed that he had seen a very unusual coming and going of the Sacrist, the Sub-Prior, and other monks, carrying things—What things? Some of the things were taken away in two great hampers by a boat from King's Bridge, the river stairs of the Palace. Another monk, John de Lynton, was proved to have sown the ground in the cloister with hempseed in the winter, so that when the hemp grew up there might be a convenient and unsuspected place to hide their plunder. One John Albas deposed that he was employed to make certain tools for the use of the robbers : and that Alexander de Pershore the monk threatened to kill him if he revealed the design : it was he who had seen the said Alexander and other monks taking two large panniers into a boat at the King's Bridge. John de Ramage, another confederate, went in and out of the Abbey a good deal at this time : he suddenly bought horses and arms and splendid attire. Where did the money come from? The robbers were also assisted by William de Paleys, who had charge of the Palace gate. He it was who passed the burglars in and let them out. Under his bed were found the richly jewelled case of the holy Cross of Neath, with other valuable things belonging to the Treasury.

They stole the King's money, a great quantity of gold and silver cups (some of these they broke up), and many rings, jewels and other precious things. They had the sense to understand that the King's crown and the greater jewels would be of no use at all to them : therefore they left these things behind : but they took the money and they took the things they could melt down and sell for silver or for gold. A good deal was sold in London, the purchasers not caring to inquire how this valuable stuff was obtained. Some of the jewels were sold by Podelicote in Northampton and Colchester. This worthy was actually found to be in possession of 2,000*l*. worth of property stolen from the Treasury.

Such is the story. It does not state in what manner the fact of the robbery was discovered. It took place at the end of April or the beginning of May. The King heard of it in June. It is stated, however, by Burtt that it was not till the 20th of June that the Master of the Wardrobe, John de Drokenesford, came with the Keeper of the Tower, the Justices, the Lord Mayor, and the Prior of Westminster, and opened the doors of the Treasury when he found 'the chests and coffers broken open and many goods carried away.' But the robbery was known before that date.—How? We cannot learn.

Many of the criminals were caught in actual possession of the spoil. Among these were Podelicote, William de Paleys, and John de Ramage. The history of this wonderful case is unfortunately incomplete. The fate of the ringleaders is unknown and the particulars of their trial have not been preserved. It is, however, quite certain that they were all hanged, most likely with the pleasing additions to hanging which prolonged the ceremony and gave it greater importance. In Rishanger there is a brief note on the subject. He is speaking of the robbery. 'Propter quod multi fuerunt—et quidam insontes forte—suspensi.' All the monks, forty of them, were sent to the Tower : another company of forty persons, not monks, were sent there as well. The monks were liberated after two years' imprisonment : what became of the rest I know not.

The following letter from the King, enjoining the Justices to make speed with the trial, is interesting, if only because it gives the names of the monks—

Rex dilectis et fidelibus suis Rogero Brabazan, Willielmo Bereford, Rogero de Higham, Radulpho de Sandwico et Waltero de Gloucestriâ, salutem.

Cum Walterus Abbas Westmonastriensis,

Frater Alexander de Pershore
,,   Rogerus de Bures
,,   Radulfus de Merton
,,   Thomas de Dene
,,   Adam de Warefield
,,   Johannes de Butterle
,,   Johannes de Nottele
,,   Robertus de Cherring
,,   Johannes de Salop
,,   Thomas de Lichfield
,,   Simon de Henle
,,   Walterus de Arthesden
,,   William de Charve
,,   Robertus de Bures
,,   Ricardus de Sudbury
,,   Henricus atte Ry
,,   Adam de Lilham
,,   Johannes de London
,,   Johannes de Wyttinge
,,   Robertus de Middleton
,,   Ricardus de Cullworth

Frater Rogerus de Aldenham
,,   Johannes de Wanetyng
,,   Willielmus de Breybroke
,,   Robertus de Roding
,,   Petrus de la Croyz
,,   Henricus Payn
,,   Henricus de Bircherton
,,   Philippus de Sutton
,,   Guido de Ashewell
,,   Willielmus de Kerchenton
,,   Thomas de Woberne
,,   Willielmus de Glaston
,,   Johannes de Wigorniâ
,,   Robertus Vil
,,   Raymundus de Wenlock
,,   Ricardus de Waltham
,,   Ricardus de Fanelon
,,   Henricus Temple
,,   Henricus de Wanetyng
,,   Johannes de Wenlok

Commonachi ejusdem domus ;

Gervase de St. Egidio
Rogerus de Presthope
Walterus de Ethelford
Rogerus de Wenlok
Hano de Wenlock
Adam le Skynnere
Johannes Sharpe
Ricardus Smart
Johannes de St. Albano
Johannes de Linton
Johannes de Lalham
Henricus le Ken
Ricardus de Weston
Rogerus de Bruger
Thomas de Dinglebrigge
Galfridus del Coler

Radulphus de Dutton
Radulphus de Humenden
Johannes de Sudbury
Ricardus Burle
Joceus de Cornubiâ
Galfridus de Kantia
Johannes de Oxoniâ
Ricardus del Ewe
Johannes de Bralyn
Johannes de Bramfleg
Robertus le Porter
Rogerus le Orfeuvre
Robertus le Bolthad
Maritius Morel
Godinus de Lernhote

—de fractione Thesaurariæ nostræ apud Westmonasterium

nuper furtive factâ et Thesauro ibidem ad valorem C. M. librarum capto et asportato indictati et eâ occasione in prisonâ nostrâ Turris nostræ London detenti, asseruerunt se inde falso et malitiose indictatos fuisse et nobis attente supplicaverunt quod veritatem inde inquiri et eis justitiam exhiberi faciamus. Assignavimus vos justiciarios ad inquirendum per sacramentum tum militum quum aliorum &c. . . . de comitatibus Middlesex et Surrey per quos &c. super negotio prædicto plenam veritatem et ad negotium illud audiendum et terminandum &c., &c.

The names suggest a few observations. First the monks with one or two exceptions all come from country villages or from small country towns—one is from Lichfield ; one from London. How are we to interpret this fact ? Surely by the very simple explanation that to be made a member of this rich and dignified foundation was a provision for a younger son. The wars carried off some of the sons— elder as well as younger : in the service of the King or of some great Lord some found employment and preferment : some were apprenticed in the great companies of London and perhaps of Bristol, York, and Norwich : some were put into the monasteries as children, and remained there all their lives. With three exceptions all the surnames are territorial. The three—Payn, Vil, and Temple—may have belonged to gentlehood, but I know not. A boy received as a novice was assured at least of a tranquil life, free from care. We are not to suppose that these rich endowments were given to boys taken from the plough. I say that the names in this list go to prove the fact that the monasteries were filled with the children of gentlefolk. For, granting that a rustic would also be called by the name of his village, how was a plain country lad from Pershore, Merton, Warefield, Henley, Sudbury, Rye, to get himself recommended and accepted by the Abbot of Westminster ?

The other names—those of the persons indicted who were

not monks—also illustrate the change and growth in the surname. There are thirty-one names—twenty-one are places of birth : four signify trade : six are names which I do not understand.

One more episode in the life of the Abbey—an episode which startled the Brotherhood in a way long remembered. There was a Spanish prisoner in the hands of his captors, two English knights named Shackle and Hawke. The prisoner was allowed to go home in order to collect his ransom leaving his son behind in his place. But the ransom was not sent. Then John of Gaunt, who pretended to the crown of Castile, demanded the release of the young Spaniard. This the two knights refused : they intended to secure their ransom : and according to the existing rules of the game as it was then played, they were quite right. John of Gaunt, without troubling himself about the legality of the thing, imprisoned them both in the Tower : but he could not find the young Spaniard. The knights escaped and took sanctuary at Westminster. Hither they were pursued by Alan Bloxhall, Constable of the Tower, and Sir Ralph Ferrers, with fifty armed men. It was on the 4th of August, in the forenoon, during the celebration of High Mass, that the two fugitives ran headlong into the church followed by their pursuers. Even in the rudest times such a thing as was then done would have been regarded as monstrous and horrible. For the knights and their servants ran round and round the choir, followed by the men of the Tower, and the words of the Gospel—they were at the Gospel of the day— were drowned by the clash of mailed heels and of weapons, by the shouts and yells of the murderers and the groans of the victims. Hawke fell dead in front of the Prior's stall : one of the monks was killed, no doubt trying to stop the men : and one of Hawke's servants. Then the Constable recalled his men and they all went back to the Tower, feeling, we may imagine, rather apprehensive of the consequences. And the Spanish prisoner was not caught after all. Now this young

Spaniard seems to have been the soul of honour : for he was with the knights all the time, disguised as one of the servants : it seems as if he might have given himself up at any moment.

Naturally, the Abbot and the monks set up an outcry that was heard over all Christendom. Was the like wickedness ever heard ? Not only to break sanctuary but to commit murder—a triple murder—in the Church itself and at the celebration of High Mass ! The Abbey Church was closed for four months : Parliament—which then met in the Chapter House—was suspended : the case was brought before the King : the two chief assailants were excommunicated : and they had to pay 200*l.* to the Abbey—a fine of about 3,000*l.* of our money. Meantime Shackle compromised the matter of the Spanish prisoner : he gave him up but received a sum of 500 marks down and an annuity of 100 marks.

Another breaking of sanctuary took place at the time of Wat Tyler's rebellion, when the unfortunate Marshal of the Marshalsea was dragged from the Confessor's shrine and murdered. But the rebels being dispersed and their leaders hanged there was nothing more said.

Such events as these from time to time broke the monotony of the monastic life. A coronation : a Royal wedding : a great funeral : the flight of a Queen—Elizabeth Woodville—or a Duchess—as the Duchess of Gloucester—to sanctuary : the death of a King—Henry IV. in the Abbey : these things gave the Brethren something to think about, something to quicken the slow march of Time.

There were, and are, however, other residents of the Abbey besides the monks : there are all the dead Kings and Queens and Princes : all the dead nobles and the dead ignobles : the dead men of letters and the arts who lie buried in this Campo Santo, the most sacred spot in all the Empire.

> ' Mortality, behold and fear !
> What a change of flesh is here !
> Think how many royal bones
> Sleep within these heaps of stones.'

The verger will show us the Royal tombs and the Royal waxworks, with the shrine of the Confessor, the armour of Henry V. and all the treasures that lie behind those iron gates. We can see for ourselves the monuments of the great unknown and the great illustrious who are buried in this cemetery. We can read in the historians of the Abbey about the tombs and the statues, the sculptors and the architects, the occupants and their royal achievements.

Let us turn to the men of Letters and of Art. Here lies Chaucer : buried in the church in the year 1400, not because he was a great poet, but because he was one of the Royal household. The monument was erected in the reign of Edward VI. Next to him lies Spenser, who died in King Street close by. All the poets were present at his funeral : elegies written by them for this occasion were thrown into the grave with the pens that wrote them. The Countess of Dorset erected the monument. Then come Drayton, Ben Jonson, Sir William Davenant, Abraham Cowley, John Dryden—whose monument was raised by Sheffield, Duke of Buckingham

> This Sheffield raised : the sacred dust below
> Was Dryden's once :—the rest who does not know?

But the lines were altered and Pope's proposed epitaph did not appear. John Milton's bust was put up in 1737 : his ashes lie in St. Giles' Cripplegate. Here are that remarkable pair Aphra Behn and Tom Brown. Here is Mrs. Steele, Dick Steele's first wife, and here lies Addison, the writer who is perhaps more loved than any other in our whole literary history. They knew how to honour so great a scholar and an essayist in the year 1719. His body lay in state in the Jerusalem Chamber. They buried him in the dead of night—funerals in the eighteenth century were often held at midnight when the darkness and the gleaming torches added to the impressiveness of the ceremony. Bishop Atterbury met the corpse ; the choir sang a hymn, and the procession was conducted by

torchlight round the Royal Tombs into Henry VII.'s Chapel.
Tickell has written upon the scene.

> Can I forget the dismal night that gave
> My soul's best part for ever to the grave?
> How silent did his old companions tread
> By midnight lamps the mansions of the dead;
> Through breaking statues, these unheeded things,
> Through rows of warriors and through walks of kings!
> What awe did the slow solemn knell inspire,
> The pealing organ and the pausing choir:
> The duties by the lawn-robed prelate pay'd:
> And the last words that dust to dust conveyed!

Matthew Prior and Gay followed Addison. Pope was
buried at Twickenham : Gray at Stoke Pogis : Goldsmith in
the Temple. Samuel Johnson lies in the Abbey—Sheridan,
Cumberland and Macpherson are buried here. And here of
moderns are Macaulay, Lord Lytton, Dickens and Tennyson.
Of actors and actresses Anne Oldfield, Anna Bracegirdle,
Betterton, Garrick and John Henderson are buried here.
Of musicians Purcell, John Blow, William Croft, Charles
Burney, Sterndale Bennett, and Handel are buried here. Of
painters there are none. This is a very remarkable omission.
How did it happen? Presumably because the successive Deans
and Canons have had no taste for art.

The list includes a goodly company. Whenever a great
man dies, the Dean should remove a monument—one of the
unknown—to make room for the new-comer : in that way the
Abbey would become more and more the Holy Field of the
British Empire.

One thing more before we leave the Abbey. We read
of the mediæval churches, especially such churches as old
St. Paul's, the Grey Friars, and Austin Friars, how they were
filled from end to end with tombs of princes and noble ladies,
carved and precious, with alabaster and marble : how between
and among the greater tombs were the tombs of the lesser

folk—but all of them, nobles and ladies and knights—the common sort lay outside—insomuch that the church was filled with their monuments. If we go into Westminster Abbey, alone of existing churches we can understand this wealth of sepulchral monuments formerly so common.

What says Addison?

'When I am in a serious humour I very often walk by myself in Westminster Abbey. When the gloominess of the place, and the use to which it is applied, with the solemnity of the building and the conditions of the people who lie in it, are apt to fill the mind with a kind of melancholy or rather thoughtfulness that is not disagreeable. . . . When I look upon the tombs of the great, every emotion of envy dies in me : when I read the epitaphs of the beautiful, every inordinate desire goes out : when I meet with the grief of parents upon a tombstone, my heart melts with compassion : when I see the tombs of the parents themselves, I consider the vanity of grieving for those whom we must quickly follow : when I see kings lying by those who deposed them, when I consider rival wits placed side by side ; or the holy men who divided the world with their contests and disputes, I reflect with sorrow and astonishment on the little competitions, factions, and debates of mankind.'

CHAPTER V

THE ABBEY—III

THE history of the successive Coronations performed in Westminster Abbey from that of the Conqueror to the present day—especially those which were picturesque—may be found in the pages of Stanley. There may be read the dramatic Coronation of William the Conqueror ; the joy of the people at the Crowning of Queen Maude ; the murder of the Jews at the Coronation of Richard ; here will be found Walpole's account of the Coronation of George III. ; and the somewhat unworthy note on the perspiring of George IV.

There are other points connected with the Coronations which may interest us. Thus, the creation of knights at every Coronation was a custom both graceful and symbolic. The candidate, after a bath, watched his arms all night : in the morning he confessed and heard mass : he thus entered upon his knightly duties cleansed and pure—body and soul : after the mass the new king conferred knighthood and presented him with robes. At the Coronation of Henry VI. there were thirty-six knights thus created : at that of Edward IV., thirty-two : at that of Charles II., sixty-eight. The part of the ceremony of a Coronation which most pleased the people was the procession from the Tower to Westminster. That of Henry IV. is thus described by Froissart :—

'The duke of Lancaster left the Tower this Sunday after dinner, on his return to Westminster : he was bare-headed, and had round his neck the order of the king of France. The prince of Wales, six dukes, six earls, eighteen barons, accom-

K

panied him ; and there were, of knights and other nobility, from eight to nine hundred horse with the procession. The duke was dressed in a jacket of the German fashion, of cloth of gold, mounted on a white courser, with a blue garter on his left leg. He passed through the streets of London, which were all handsomely decorated with tapestries and other rich hangings : there were nine fountains in Cheapside, and other streets he passed through, which perpetually ran with white and red wines. He was escorted by prodigious numbers of gentlemen, with their servants in liveries and badges ; and the different companies of London were led by their wardens clothed in their proper livery, and with ensigns of their trade. The whole cavalcade amounted to six thousand horse, which escorted the duke from the Tower to Westminster.'

Or in the words of Shakespeare :—

> Mounted upon a hot and fiery steed,
> Which his aspiring rider seemed to know,
> With slow but stately pace, kept on his course :
> While all tongues cried, God save thee, Bolingbroke !
> You would have thought the very windows spake,
> So many greedy looks of young and old
> Through casements darted their desiring eyes
> Upon his visage ; and that all the walls
> With painted imagery had said at once
> Jesu preserve thee ! welcome Bolingbroke !
> Whilst he, from one side to the other turning,
> Bare-headed, lower than his proud steed's neck,
> Bespoke them thus ; I thank you, countrymen ;
> And thus still doing, thus he passed along.[1]

Another magnificent procession was that in which Elizabeth, Henry VII.'s Queen, and, in the minds of many, the lawful heiress of the Crown, received her Coronation, when the King perceived that there would be discontent until that honour was paid to her. But she was not crowned, as Mary II. was afterwards crowned, as Queen Regnant, but

[1] *King Richard II.*

as the Queen Consort. This nice distinction, however, was not comprehended by the people.

The Queen came first from Greenwich to the Tower by water : 'there was attending upon her there the mayor, sheriffs, and aldermen of the city, and divers and many worshipful commoners, chosen out of every craft, in their liveries, in barges freshly furnished with banners and streamers of silk, richly beaton with the " armes and bagges " of their crafts ; and in especial a barge called the bachelors' barge, garnished and apparelled passing all other ; wherein was ordeynid a great red dragon spouting flames of fire into the Thames, and many other gentlemanly pageants, well and curiously devised to do her highness sport and pleasure with. And her grace, thus royally apparelled and accompanied, and also furnished in every behalf with trumpets, claryons, and other mynstrelles as apperteynid and was fitting to her estate Royal, came from Greenwich aforesaid and landed at the Tower wharf and entered into the Tower.'

Next day the court, in procession from the Tower to Westminster, dressed in white cloth of gold of damask, with a mantle of the same furred with ermine. She reclined on a litter and wore her fair yellow hair hanging down behind her back, 'with a calle of pipes over it.' Four knights carried over her a canopy of cloth of gold ; four peeresses rode behind her on grey palfreys ; the streets were cleaned and swept ; the houses were hung with tapestry and red cloth ; the crafts of London in their liveries lined the way, and singing children came dressed as angels, singing welcomes as the Queen was borne along.

The same kind of procession was that of Henry VIII. and Queen Katharine. In addition, at the end of Old Change stood virgins in white holding branches of white wax, while priests in copes with crosses of silver censed the King and Queen. Another procession much the same called forth similar rejoicings when Anne Boleyn was carried from the

Tower to Westminster, and equal popular rejoicing was shown
when Queen Mary rode through the City to her Corona
tion.

At the Coronation of Elizabeth a variety of pageants
were exhibited : the principal one was the presentation of
a Bible.

'Between two hills, representing a flourishing and a decayed
commonwealth, was made artificiallie one hollow place or
cave, with doore and locke inclosed, out of the which, a little
before the queenes' highnesse commyng thither, issued one
personage, whose name was Time, apparalled as an old man
with a sieth in his hand, havinge winges artificiallie made,
leading a personage of lesser stature than himselfe, which was
finelie and well apparalled, all clad in white silke, and directly
over her head was set her name and title in Latin and English,
Temporis filia, the daughter of Time.   Which two, as ap
pointed, went forwards toward the south side of the pageants,
where was another, and on her breast was written her proper
name, which was Veritas, Truth, who held a book in her hand,
upon the which was written Verbum Veritatis, the Word of
Truth.   And out of the south side of the pageant was cast a
standing for a child, which should interpret the same pageant.
Against whom when the queen's maiestie came, he spake vnto
her grace these sweet words :—

> This old man with a sieth
>   Old father Time they call,
> And her his daughter Truth,
>   Which holdeth yonder booke :
> Whome he out of his nooke
>   Hath brought foorth to us all,
> From whence this manie yeares
>   She durst not once out looke.
>
> Now sith that Time againe
>   His daughter Truth hath brought,
> We trust, ô worthie queene,
>   Thou wilt this truth embrace,

And sith thou vnderstandst
    The good estate and naught,
We trust wealth thou wilt plant,
    And barrenesse displace.

But for to heale the sore
    And cure that is not seene ;
Which thing the booke of truth,
    Dooth teach in writing plaine :
Shee doth present to thee
    The same, ô worthie queene,
For that, that words doo flie,
    But written dooth remaine.

Thus the queene's highnesse passed through the citie, which, without anie foreigne person, of itself beautified itselfe, and received her grace at all places, as hath been before mentioned, with most tender obedience and love, due to so gratious a queene and sovereigne a ladie.'

The alleged presence of Prince Charles at the Coronation feast of George III. is interesting and somewhat pathetic. Of kings in exile the chronicler of the Nineteenth Century will have a good deal to say. Volumes will be written on the shadowy Courts of Exile of our time. But the historian will find no exiled Prince more romantic in his youth, and until a life of disappointment, and with no aims or hopes, ruined him, than Prince Charles. It was fifteen years after Culloden : he was at this time perilously near forty : had he been detected one fears that even George III. could not have saved him : he came over : he entered Westminster Hall with the crowd : and he saw his rival seated where he would have been but for his grandfather's obstinacy. One gentleman recognised him and whispered, 'Your Royal Highness is the last of all mortals whom I should expect to see here.'

That the glove thrown by the Champion was picked up : or that a glove was thrown to the Champion from an upper seat in the Hall : was also reported ; but the thing seems doubtful.

As for the Coronation of Her Majesty Queen Victoria, wh
has described it in more fitting language than Dean Stanley
afterwards her friend and most faithful servant?

'The last Coronation doubtless still lives in the recollection
of all who witnessed it. They will long remember the early
summer morning, when, at break of day, the streets were
thronged, and the whole capital awake—the first sight of the
Abbey, crowded with the mass of gorgeous spectators, them
selves a pageant—the electric shock through the whole mass
when the first gun announced that the Queen was on her
way—and the thrill of expectation with which the iron rails
seemed to tremble in the hands of the spectators, as the long
procession closed with the entrance of the small figure
marked out from all beside by the regal train and attendants
floating like a crimson and silvery cloud behind her. At the
moment when she first came within the full view of the
Abbey, and paused, as if for breath, with clasped hands—as
she moved on, to her place by the altar—as in the deep
silence of the vast multitude, the tremulous voice of Arch
bishop Howley could be faintly heard, even to the remotest
corners of the Choir, asking for the recognition—as she sate
immovable on the throne, when the crown touched her head
amidst shout and trumpet and the roar of cannon, there must
have been many who felt a hope that the loyalty which had
waxed cold in the preceding reigns would once more revive
in a more serious form than it had, perhaps, ever worn before
Other solemnities they may have seen more beautiful, or
more strange, or more touching, but none at once so gorgeous
and so impressive, in recollections, in actual sight, and in
promise of what was to be.'

When the Commons separated from the Lords, they
met within the walls of Westminster Abbey while the Lords
took the Painted Chamber of the Palace. For two hundred
years the Commons assembled in the Cloister Court or in
the Refectory or in the Chapter House. They changed th

Chapter House for the no less beautiful church of St. Stephen in 1547, not long after the Dissolution of the Religious Houses. But the History of the Houses of Parliament belongs to the History of the Country.

We have now gone through the Abbey without attempting any description of it. That has been done over and over again ; now well, now ill. It is a treasury of architectural interest : it is crammed full of historical associations : one may linger among its ruins, among its monuments, under its noble roof, book in hand for days and weeks and years. I have shown you the monastic life and what it meant : I have told over again some of the stories that happened in the Abbey : I have shown you of what kind were the pageants and processions *outside* witnessed by the people belonging to the Coronations. Those who want the story of the Royal Tombs and Monuments, the Functions and Ceremonies, the Funerals and Weddings that have been celebrated within these walls, may consult the courtly page of Stanley, the learned page of Loftie, and the laborious page of Dart.

CHAPTER VI

SANCTUARY

ON the north-west corner of the Abbey precinct—that is to say, on the right hand as one entered by the High Gate from King Street, where now stands the Westminster 'Guildhall' —the earth formerly groaned beneath the weight of a ponderous structure resembling a square keep, not unlike that of Colchester, but very much smaller. It was a building of stone ; each side was seventy-five feet in length, and it was sixty feet in height. On the east side was a door—the only door, a heavy oaken door covered with plates of iron—which gave entrance to a curiously gloomy and narrow chapel, shaped as a double cross, the equal arms of which were only ten feet in width. Three of the four corners of this lower square consisted of solid stone sixteen feet square ; the third corner contained a circular staircase winding up to another chapel above. This, somewhat lighter and loftier than that below, was a plain single cross in form ; three of the angles contained rooms, in the fourth the stairs continued to the roof. King Edward III. built—or rebuilt, perhaps—on this corner a belfry, containing three great bells, which were only rung at the coronation and the death of kings. The roof was paved with stone; there was a parapet, but not embattled. On the outside—its construction dating perhaps after King Edward built the belfry—there stood a small circular tower containing stairs to the upper story. The strong walls of this gloomy fortress contained only one door and one window on the lower floor ; but in the upper story the walls were

only three feet thick. This place was St. Peter's Sanctuary
—the Westminster City of Refuge. It was made so strong
that it would resist any sudden attack, and give time for the
attacking party to bethink them of the sin of sacrilege. In

THE KING STREET GATE, WESTMINSTER, DEMOLISHED 1723

these two chapels the refugees heard mass; within these
walls the nobler sort of those who came here were placed for
greater safety; round these walls gathered the common sort,
in tenements forming a little colony or village. The building, of which there is very little mention anywhere, was

suffered to remain long after its original purpose was abolished.
It was pulled down piecemeal, by any who chose to take the
trouble, as stone was wanted for other buildings ; it is quite
possible that some of it was used for the White Hall ; but
the remaining portions of it were not finally taken away
until the middle of the last century ; and perhaps the foundations still remain.   It is strange that neither Stow nor,
after him, Strype, makes any mention of this building, which
the former could not fail to see, frowning and gloomy, as yet
untouched, whenever he visited Westminster ; and it is still
more remarkable that neither of these writers seems to attach
much importance to the ancient Sanctuary at Westminster.
That of St. Martin's-le-Grand, the remains of which were also
visible to Stow, he describes at length.

Like every other ecclesiastical foundation, the right of
Sanctuary was originally a beneficent and wise institution,
designed by the Church for the protection of the weak, and
the prevention of revenge, wild justice, violence and oppression.   If a man, in those days of swift wrath and ready
hand, should kill another in the madness of a moment ; if
by accident he should wound or maim another ; if by the
breaking of any law he should incur the penalties of justice ;
if by any action he should incur the hostility of a stronger
man ; if by some of the many changes and chances of fortune
he should lose his worldly goods and fall into debt or bank-
ruptcy, and so become liable to imprisonment ; if he had
cause to dread the displeasure of king, baron, or bishop,—the
right of Sanctuary was open to him.   Once on the frith-stool,
once clinging to the horns of the altar, he was as safe as an
Israelite within the walls of a city of refuge : the mighty hand
of the Church was over him ; his enemies could not touch
him, on pain of excommunication.

In theory every church was a sanctuary ; but it was easy
to blockade a church so that the refugee could be starved
into submission.   The only real safety for a fugitive from

justice or revenge was in those abbeys and places which possessed special charters and immunities. Foremost among these were the Sanctuaries of Westminster and St. Martin's-le-Grand. Outside London, the principal Sanctuaries appear to have been Beverley, Hexham, Durham and Beaulieu.

SOUTH-WEST VIEW OF THE ENTRANCE TO THE LITTLE SANCTUARY
FROM KING STREET

But perhaps every great abbey possessed its sanctuary as a part of its reason for existence. That of Westminster was, if not founded, defined and regulated by Edward the Confessor ; that of St Martin's, the existence of which was always a scandal and an offence to the City of London, was regulated by half a dozen charters of as many kings. Its refugees were principally bankrupts, debtors and common thieves—offenders against property, therefore specially hated by a trading community.

The privilege of Sanctuary was beautiful in theory. ' Come to me,' said the Church : ' I will keep thee in safety from the hand of violence and the arm of the law ; I will give thee lodging and food ; my doors shall be always open to thee, day and night ; I will lead thee to repentance. Come : in safety sit down and meditate on the sins which have brought thee hither.'

The invitation was extended to all, but with certain reservations. Traitors, Jews, infidels, and those who committed sacrilege were forbidden the safety of Sanctuary. Nor was it a formal invitation : Sanctuary was sought by multitudes. In Durham Cathedral two men slept every night in the Galilee to admit any fugitive who might ring the Galilee bell or lift the Galilee knocker. Nay, Sanctuary was actually converted into a city of refuge by the setting apart of a measured space, the whole of which was to be considered Sanctuary. At Hexham, where four roads met in the middle of the town, a cross was set up on every one of the roads to show where Sanctuary began. At Ripon and at Beverley a circle, whose radius was a mile, was the limit of Sanctuary. At St. Martin's-le-Grand the precinct was accurately laid down and jealously defended. It included many streets— the area is now almost entirely covered by the Post Office and the Telegraph Office. At Westminster the whole precinct of the Abbey—church, monastery buildings, close and cloisters and gardens—was sacred ground.

The right of Sanctuary was maintained with the greatest tenacity by the Church. When, as happened sometimes— men's passions carrying them beyond the fear of the Church —Sanctuary was violated, the Bishop or the Abbot allowed no rest or cessation from clamour, gave no relief from excommunication to the offender, until reparation and submission

had been obtained.   Thus, as we have seen, in the year 1378,
the Constable of the Tower pursued a small company of men,

VIEW OF LITTLE SANCTUARY FROM THE WEST, AS IT
APPEARED ABOUT A.D. 1800

fugitives, into Sanctuary, and actually had the temerity to slay
two of them in the church itself, before the Prior's stall, and

during the celebration of high mass. This seems to be the most flagrant case of violation on record. The Abbot closed the church for four months ; the perpetrator of the murder was excommunicated ; the guilty persons were very heavily fined ; the Abbot protested against the deed at the next meeting of Parliament; and the ancient privileges of St. Peter's Sanctuary were confirmed. There were other violations, especially in the lawless times of civil war. For instance, in the reign of Richard II., Tressilian, Lord Chief Justice, was dragged out of Sanctuary ; the Duke of York took John Holland, Duke of Exeter, out of Sanctuary. On the other hand, Henry VII. was careful to respect Sanctuary when Perkin Warbeck fled to Beaulieu Abbey. This was perhaps politic, and intended to show that he had nothing whatever to fear from that poor little Pretender.

Among the refugees of Westminster the most interesting figure is that of Elizabeth Woodville, Queen of Edward IV., and the most pathetic scene in the history of St. Peter's Sanctuary is that in which the mother takes leave of her boy, knowing full that she will see his dear face no more.

Twice did the Queen seek Sanctuary. Once when her husband, at the lowest point of misfortune, fled the country. Then, with her three daughters, she fled to this gloomy fortress, and there gave birth to her elder boy—' forsaken of all her friends and in great penury.' Here she laid the child in his father's arms on his return. A second time she fled hither, when Richard had seized the crown, and that boy, king for a little day, was in the Tower. What would happen to him ? What happened to King Henry VI. ? What happened to that king's son, Prince Edward ? What happened to the Duke of York ? What happened to the Duke of Exeter ? What happened to the Duke of Clarence ? What but murder could happen ? Murder was everywhere. The crown was made secure by murder. Every king murdered his actual or possible rival. How could the usurper reign in peace while those two boys were living ? So, in trembling and in haste, she passed from the Palace to the Abbey, and sat on the rushes, disconsolate, with her daughters and her second boy, while her servants fetched some household gear.

Outside, the King's Council deliberated. Richard would have seized the boy and dragged him out by force. The two

THE SANCTUARY. PULLED DOWN IN 1775

Archbishops stood before him. The wrath of St. Peter himself must be braved by him who would violate Sanctuary. But, said the casuist, Sanctuary is a place of refuge for criminals and debtors, and such as have incurred the penalties of the law. This child is not a criminal : he is too young to have committed any offence—Sanctuary is not for children ;

therefore to take this child is not to violate Sanctuary, and since His Highness the King takes him only in kindness and in love, and for a companion to his brother, the wrath of St. Peter will not be awakened. On the other hand, the Holy Apostle cannot but commend the action.

The Archbishops yielded. Let us remember, with the bloodstained chronicles of the time in our mind, that, among all the nobles present at that Council, there was not one who could possibly fail to understand that the two boys were going to be murdered. How else could Richard keep the crown upon his head? Yet the two Archbishops yielded. They consented, therefore, knowing with the greatest certainty that murder would follow. I think they may have argued in some such way as this. ' The time is evil: the country has been distracted and torn to pieces by civil wars for five-and-twenty years; nearly all the noble families have been destroyed, above and before everything else we need rest and peace and a strong hand. A hundred years ago, after the troubles in France, we had a boy for king, with consequences that may be still remembered by old men. If this boy reigns, there will be new disasters: if his uncle reigns, there may be peace. Life for two children, with more civil wars, more bloody fields, more ruin and starvation and rapine and violence—or the death of two children, with peace and rest for this long-suffering land— which shall it be?' A terrible alternative! The Archbishops sadly bowed their heads and stepped aside, while Richard climbed the winding stair, and in the upper chapel of the Sanctuary dragged the boy from his mother's arms.

' Farewell!' she cried, her words charged with the anguish of her heart : ' farewell, mine own sweet one! God send thee good keeping! Let me kiss thee once, ere you go. God knoweth when we shall kiss one another again!'

The right of Sanctuary in a modified form lasted long after the Dissolution of the Religious Houses. But when a great Abbey, as that of Beaulieu, standing in a retired and

unfrequented place, lay desolate and in ruins, the right of
Sanctuary was useless.   No one was left to assert the right—
no one to defend it : there was neither roof nor hearth nor

'THE BOAR'S HEAD' INN, KING STREET

L

altar.   In great towns it was different : the Abbey might be
desecrated, but the Sanctuary house remained.   Therefore on
the site of St. Martin's-le-Grand, on the site of Blackfriars,
and in Westminster round that old fortress-Church, still the
debtors ran to escape the bailiffs, and murderers and thieves
hid themselves, knowing that the law was weak indeed in the
network of courts and streets which formed these retreats.
Other places pretended to immunity from the sheriffs ; among
these were the streets on the site of Whitefriars, Salisbury
Court, Ram Alley and Mitre Court ; Fulwood's Rents in
Holborn, the Liberty of the Savoy, and, on the other side of the
river, Deadman's Place, the Clink, the Mint, and Montagu Close.
The ' privileges' of these places were finally abolished in 1697.

It was in the year of our Lord 1520, on a pleasant morning
in May, that one who greatly loved to walk abroad in order
to watch the ways of men and to hear them discourse stood
at the entrance of King Street, where the gate called after the
Cockpit hard by stood upon the bridge which spanned the
little stream flowing eastwards to join the river.   It was a
narrow street—on either side gabled houses.   Courts still
narrower opened out to right and left.   Lady Alley, where
were almshouses for poor women ; Boar's Head Court—in
the years to come one Cromwell, Member of Parliament,
would live here ; St. Stephen's Alley ; the Rhenish Wine
yard ; Thieven' Lane—a lane by which rogues could be taken
to the Gate House Prison without passing through the
Precinct and so being able to claim Sanctuary.   There were
taverns in it—Westminster was always full of taverns—the
Bell, the Boar's Head, and the Rhenish Wine House.   At the
south end stood the High Gate, built by Richard II.   The
visitor strolled slowly down the street, looking curiously about
him, as if the place was strange.   This indeed it was ; for he
had stepped straight out of the nineteenth century into the
sixteenth—out of King Street, mean and narrow, into King

Street narrow indeed, but not mean. The roadway was rough and full of holes ; a filthy stream ran down the middle ; all kinds of refuse were lying about ; there was no footpath nor any protection by means of posts for foot passengers,— when a loaded waggon lumbered along the people took refuge in the open doorways ; when a string of pack-horses plodded down the middle of the street splashing the mud of the stream

'THE COCK,' TOTHILL STREET

about it, the people retreated farther within the door. The street was full of pack-horses, because this was one of the two highways to Westminster—Palace and Castle both. In spite of the narrowness, the mud, the dirt and the inconvenience, the King Street which this visitor saw before him was far more picturesque than that which he had left behind. The houses rose up three and four stories high ; gabled all, with projecting fronts, story above story, the timbers of the fronts painted and gilt, some of them with scutcheons hung in front, the richly blazoned arms brightening the narrow way; from a window here and there hung out a bit of coloured cloth; some of the houses bore on their fronts a wealth of carven beams—some had signs hanging out; the men who lolled about the doors of the taverns wore bright liveries—those of King, Cardinal, Abbot, or great lord; in the windows above women and girls leaned out, talking and laughing with the men below; the sun (for it was nearly noon) shone straight up the street upon the stately Gate above and the stately Gate below, and upon the gilding, carving and painting, and windows of the houses on either side. The street was full of colour and of life: from the taverns came the tinkling of the mandoline, and now and then a lusty voice uplifted in a snatch of song,—in Westminster the drinking, gambling, singing and revelry went on all day and sometimes all night as well. Court and Camp and Church, all collected together on the Isle of Bramble, demanded, for their following, taverns innumerable and drink in oceans.

The stranger, of whom no one took any notice, passing through the High Gate, found himself within the Abbey Precinct. 'Is this,' he asked, 'a separate city?' For before him and to the right and to the left there lay heaped together, as close as they could stand, groups and rows and streets of houses, mostly small tenements mean and dirty in appearance. Only a clear space was left for the Church of St. Margaret's and for the Porch to the Abbey Church, the north side of which was hidden by houses. On the right hand—that is, on the west side—the houses were grouped round a great stone structure, gloomy and terrible; farther on they opened out for the Gate House, which led into the fields and so across the meadows to the great high road; and in the middle, opposite the west end of St. Margaret's, there was a shapeless mass of erections comprising private houses and old stone buildings and chapels. On the left more houses, and

under one a postern leading into New Palace Yard beyond.
The place was full of people—men, women and children.   As
the visitor threaded his way among the narrow lanes he
became conscious of a curious change.   Outside, in King
Street, everybody was alert, the street was filled with the
happiness of life ; the men-at-arms swaggered as they rolled
along, hand on sword hilt ; the children ran about and

ROOM IN ' THE KING'S ARMS,' TOTHILL STREET

laughed and sang and shrieked for mere joy of living ;
through open windows, down narrow courts, one could see
men at work ; the girls laughed and talked as they went
about the house, or leaned out of windows, or sat over their
sewing ; life was at full flow, like the broad river beyond.
But here—it was a City of Silence.   The men stood at the
doors moody and silent ; the women in the house went about
their work in moody silence ; the very children rolling in the

dust of the foul lanes had forgotten how to laugh ; there were
no cheerful sounds of work ; there were no swash-bucklers,
there were no roysterers, there were no taverns ; the men
carried no arms, they wore no liveries, except the Sanctuary
gown with the keys of the Abbey worked in white on the
left shoulder ; they were apparently plain burgesses of the
humbler sort, craftsmen or keepers of shops and stalls.   A
strange place !   A city apart ; a city of melancholy ; a city
of restlessness and discontent.   For the most part the men
sat or walked apart ; but here and there were groups of twos
and threes who whispered with each other, and showed things
secretly under cover of their gowns.   Villainous faces they
wore, and when they walked it was after the manner of the
wild beast which slinks behind the rocks.

The visitor found himself before the great square Tower
of which we have already spoken.   Gloomy and threatening
it looked down upon the tenements below, with its belfry in
one corner, its single door, its two windows above, its stair
tower beside the door, and its blackened massive walls.

As he stood there, wondering and trying to understand this
strange world, the door was opened, and a man came forth.

He was dressed as an ecclesiastic, in a black gown ; on
his left shoulder he wore the keys in white ; he was old and
somewhat bent ; a man of the middle height ; the thin hair
that showed from under the cap was white ; his nose was
broad and somewhat flat ; his eyes were large, and when he
spoke they became luminous and smiling ; his voice was still
young, and his laugh was ready—a thing unusual in a man
when he is past fifty ; but this man was close upon seventy—
the allotted span.   He was so near his end, and yet he
laughed.   It is given to few among mortals to find aught
that makes for mirth after the days of boyhood.   Mostly
their days are full of misery : men of violence rob them ;
kings and barons drive them forth to war ; they are flogged
and set in pillory and are clapped in prison.   How should

they laugh, when all they desire is rest, when they rejoice exceedingly and are glad if they think the grave is near ?

This man, as he came forth from the Sanctuary, espied the visitor, and greeted him.

'Sir,' he said, 'be welcome. I am John Skelton.' He

THE
GATE
HOUSE

drew himself up proudly. 'Johannes Skelton, Artium Magister, Laurea Ornatus. Were I free to leave this place—but my Lord the Cardinal takes care of that, so tender is he lest ill hap come to me—I could show you the cloak of white and green—the King's colours—with the laurel wreath embroidered on the shoulder and the word " Calliope" in cunning device within the wreath—here, on this spot'—he touched his left shoulder—'where are now the keys that are my safety—the keys of this Abbey.'

'And wherefore, Sir John,' asked the visitor, 'art thou in Sanctuary?'

'Come with me, and we will talk.'

So John Skelton led the way to a house of better appearance than most. It stood beside the Gate House, which was also the Abbot's prison. Over against it was the group of buildings called the Almonry, and from the windows there was a pleasant view across the gardens and the orchards of the Abbey.

'Come in, sir,' said the poet. 'Let us sit down and talk. Truly I have much to say. A man cannot discourse with the rabble of the Sanctuary. My patron the Abbot is oppressed with cares of state ; the monks, the good monks, the holy men,'—he smiled, he chuckled, he broke into a laugh, —'they have little learning outside the Psalms which they intone so well, and for poetry they have no love, or they might sing mine.'

He began to troll out, with a voice that had once been lusty,—

> 'Ye holy caterpillars,
> Ye helpe your well willers
> With prayers and psalmes,
> To devour the almes
> That Christians should give,
> To meynteyne and releve
> The people poore and needy ;
> But youe be greedy,
> And so grete a number
> The world ye encumber.

By Saynt Luke and *secundum Skeltonida*,' he concluded, with another laugh. 'Sir, let us drink before we go on.

Whereupon he went out, and presently returned carrying a black jack which held three quarts or so, and singing,—

> ' I care right nowghte,
> I take no thowte
> For clothes to keep me warme.
> Have I good dryncke,
> I surely thyncke
> Nothing can do me harm.
> For truly than
> I fear no man,
> Be he never so bolde,
> When I am armed
> And throwly warmed
> With joly good ale and olde.'

So he lifted the black jack to his lips, took a long draught, and handed it to his companion. 'Twas right October, strong and mellow.

The room was small and the furniture was scanty, yet with no suggestion of poverty ; there was a strong table of oak, the legs well carven ; there was a chair also of good workmanship, high backed, with arms and a cushion ; in the fireplace were two andirons and a pile of wood against the cold weather ; books were on the table, both printed books from the press of Caxton hard by, and written books ; there were writing materials ; there was a candlestick of latone ; in the corner stood a wooden coffer ; there was a curtain, to be drawn across the door in cold weather ; a silver mazer stood on the table ; a robe of perset, furred, hung over the back of the chair, and another of cloth, also furred, but the fur much eaten of moths, hung upon the wall. It was the room of a scholar. There was a long and broad seat in the window, which was glazed above with diamond panes and provided with a shutter below to keep out rain and cold ; but the day was warm, and so the shutter was up, and they sat down in the noonday sunshine—John Skelton at one end of the seat and his guest at the other, and the black jack between. And one listened while the other talked.

' It is now,' said the poèt, ' five years since I fled hither to escape the revenge of my Lord Cardinal Wolsey—Son of the Wolf, I call him. Well, he may compass my destruction, but my verses can he not destroy, for they are imprinted, and now fly here and there about the land, so that no one knows who they are that read them ; and wherever the Cardinal goeth, there he may find that my verses have gotten there before him. Nay, he will die, and after death not only the Lord but man will sit in judgment upon him ; and my verses will be there for all to read. Ha ! what said I ?—

> He is set so hye
> In his ierarchy
> Of franticke frenesy
> And folishe fantasy
> That in the Chamber of Starres
> All matters there he marres :
> Clapping his rod on the borde,
> No man dare speke a worde,
> For he hath all the sayenge,
> Without any renayinge.
> He rolleth in his recordes ;
> He sayth, " How saye ye, my Lordes ? "
> Some say yes, and some
> Syt styll as they were dumbe,
> He ruleth all the roste
> With braggynge and with boste,
> Borne up on every syde
> With pompe and with pryde.

The Cardinal will not forget these lines so long as he lives ; nor will the world forget them, any more than the world forgets the words of Ovid. When men shall speak of Cardinal Wolsey, they shall say, " He it was of whom Skelton—*poeta laurea donatus*—spoke when he said,—

> Borne up on every syde
> With pompe and with pryde."

By cock's blood, proud Sir Tyrmagant, I had rather my prison than thy shame!'

He paused and sighed.

' I confess, good sir, that I thought not to end my days in such a place as this. I thought to become a bishop—nay,

THE HOLBEIN GATE

even an archbishop, if it might please the Lord. All to-ragged as I am '—he was indeed somewhat frayed in the matter of linen—' and poor, insomuch that, unlike these losels among whom I live, who pay to the Abbey rent and fees for protection, I depend upon the bounty of the good Abbot Islip, whom may Christ and St. Peter spede. Yet, look you, I am John Skelton. You know not all that John Skelton has done. In the "Garlande of Laurell" you may find set forth at length all that I have written. Since Dan Chaucer there has been no poet like unto me. My fame hath gone forth into strange lands.' *Alma parens* was Cambridge ; but at Oxford was I honoured with the laurel : yea, and the ancient and venerable University of Louvain did also grant me a like honour. Had I time, I would read, gentle sir, certain noble Latin verses written in my honour by a scholar. " All the world," he truly writes,—" the woods, the forests, the rivers and the sea, the Loves, the Satyrs, the Nymphs, the Naiades and Oceanides, —all together sing my praise. And my fame shall be as everlasting as the stars—*fama perennis erit.*" Thus it is that the scholars speak of poets ; thus are we honoured. Why, I look around me and without : I am a Sanctuary man ; no bishop am I, nor chancellor,—only a Sanctuary man ; yet— *fama perennis erit.* Or would you know what Erasmus, that great light of learning, said of me ? Then read in his immortal Ode " De Laudibus Britanniæ," the dedication to Prince Henry. " Thou hast," he said, " at home Skelton, the only light and glory of British letters, one who can not only inflame thee with ardour, but also fill thee with learning." Yes, I was indeed the tutor of that young Prince, of whom I may proudly say that, if he is—all men know that he is—learned beyond any prince of his ancestry, mine own handiwork it is.'

Again he paused and sighed. Then he went on. ' I have not now to tell a tale of George a Green and Jack a Vale. 'Tis of John Skelton—unlucky John—that I must speak. They made me Rector of Diss in my native county, and there——' He paused and rubbed his chin and smiled. ' Understand, sir, we poets pay for the favour of the Muse in many ways. Some of us are merry when we should be grave ; and we are prone to fall in love despite our vows ; and we love better the company of our brothers, even in taverns and alehouses—even when they are but clowns and rustics of the baser sort—than the loneliness of the priest's house ; we laugh in season and out of season ; if we make songs we desire to sing them ; the rattling of pint-pots, the tinkling of mazers, is music in our ears ; we linger over the Psalms no longer than we must ; we invent merry conceits and quips ; men laugh with us : none so popular as the poet who makes mirth for the company.' Here he sighed and buried his face in the black jack. ' 'Tis right good ale,' he said. ' 'Tis solacyous ale, and from the Monastery cellar. Not such is the small stuff doled out to the rest. Drink, good sir. Ay ! tis easy to make good cheer ; but one is not the clown on the stage nor the fool, and they make men laugh as well. If the jester be also a grave scholar and a reverend Divine, there are presently rumours of things unseemly, things unworthy, things *tacenda*. Add to which that the poet inclineth often unto satire, like Horace and Juvenal ; and that those against whom the satire is directed are apt to chafe and even to become revengeful. Quarrels, therefore, I had with Sir Christopher Garnyshe, and with Masters Barclay, Gaguin and Lily. What ? I thumped them and they thumped me. And the world laughed ; and no one the worse. But one must not open mouth against the monks ; and by freedom of speech I brought upon me the wrath of the Dominicans. So there was admonishing from the Bishop, and I left Diss, coming to London, where, I hoped, Christ cross me spede and by the favour of His Highness the King, once my scholar apt and quick, to receive some great office.'

' Did you bring your wife with you, Sir John ? '

' Ha ! Sayest thou wife ? How ? Doth the whole world know that I was married ? Yea, I brought her with me—and my lusty boys. Sir, many there are—parish priests—who are married secretly and are thought to entertain a leman. By the King was I recommended to the Cardinal. And now, indeed, I thought my fortune made ; and so paid court to that great man, and strove to please him. Yea, I wrote for

him that admirable poem, profitable to the soul, entitled, "The
Boke of Three Fooles." And the "Garden of Laurel" I
dedicated to my Lord Cardinal's right noble Grace ·

> Go lytell quayre, apace
>   In moost humble wyse,
> Before his noble grace,
>   That caused you to devise
> This lytell enterprise ;
>   And hym most lowly pray,
> In his mynde to comprise
>   These wordes his grace dyd saye
>   On an ammas gray.
>   Je foy enterment en sa bonne grace.'

' You fell from his good grace ? '

' I did. How it boots not to relate. Tongue ! tongue !
that must needs be making rhymes, whether on Cardinal or
on Priest, on Lord or Varlet. He gave me nothing ; yet he
made much of me : gave me what they call Bowge a court
at his own great table, where he entertained a hundred daily
He heard my verses, and he smiled ; yet he gave me nothing.
He heard my jests, and laughed ; yet he gave me nothing.
Wherefore, the Muse working powerfully within me, not to
be resisted, I wrote such verses as I have already told you,
and fled hither. And here must I remain, for the Cardinal
can never forgive me, seeing that I have set upon him a mark
that he can in no way rub off. My only hope is that, as
King's favourites do fall as well as rise, and that His Highness
the King hath a temper which is like the wind in March, the
great man may fall before I die—otherwise, a Sanctuary man
shall I remain unto the end. Drink, good sir.'

Then, as his visitor would take no more of the strong
brown ale, he rose.

' Let us sally forth,' he said, ' and I will show thee this
Sanctuary or Common Sink of all rogues. Here,' he said, as
he stood before the Double Chapel, ' is the place where,
morning and evening, we must hear matins and vespers. So

sayeth the Rule : but who is there to examine and find out
whether the Rule be kept or not ?   'Tis a dark and gloomy
place, built for the better admonition of sinners and the
exhorting to repentance.   But of repentance is there little or
none.   I repent me only that I made not my verses the
stronger, so that my Lord Cardinal should feel them, day and

BROKEN CROSS WITHIN THE ABBEY PRECINCTS

night, pricking him like a hair shirt.   But these rogues are
full of sin ; they think all day long of iniquity ; Sanctuary is
wasted upon them.   Look now at yonder company '—they
were some of the men noticed before as whispering to each
other ; they had now got a flask of wine, and were drinking
about, but with no merriment—' those are murderers, house-

breakers, cutters of purses, common thieves, who come in to save their necks, and all day long plot new crimes, which by night—stealing out privily—they commit, bringing hither their stolen goods. Then there are the unthrifts, who, when they have spent their all, buy things for which they cannot pay and bring them here to live merrily upon them while they last. The wife comes here laden with her husband's plate, saying that the good man beats her, so that to live with him is intolerable. Then she sells the plate, and God knows what manner of life she leads here. Honest work there is none ; but all alike lie idle and unprofitable. Those who have money quickly lose it, paying at a monstrous rate for all things,— monks are ever unreasonable askers those who have none pig it as best they can. Sir, believe me, there is no life worse for man than the idle life. St. Benedict wisely ordained that the hours of rest from prayer should be hours of work with the hands. Alas ! In Sanctuary that Rule is clean forgotten.'

PICKERING CUP, BELONGING TO THE BURGESSES OF WESTMINSTER

Thus discoursing, they drew near to the Gate House, which opens to Tothill Street and Tothill Fields beyond.

'Here is the Abbot's Prison,' said Skelton : 'the prison of those who break the laws of Westminster—and of debtors—and sometimes of traitors. The debtors lie there like sheep ; and the longer they live the leaner they grow, because, look you, if a man is shut up he cannot work nor earn his daily bread, much less can he pay his debts.' As he spoke a long pole was pushed out of window with a box hanging at the end. 'It is their alms-box,' said Skelton. 'Bestow something upon them, so that they may eat and drink.'

As we stood in the gateway, looking out upon the pleasant fields and green pastures beyond, there came forth from a tavern—at the sign of the *Eagle*—a girl, the like of

THE SOUTHERN EXTREMITY OF THIEVING LANE, A.D. 1800

whom I had never seen for size and comeliness. She was over six feet high, and had shoulders for breadth like those of a porter, and arms—her sleeves rolled up—which belonged rather to a waterman than a maid. And at sight of her John

M

Skelton began to laugh, and called out, 'Meg! Long Meg! come hither. Let me gaze upon thee.' So the tall maid obeyed, showing by her smiles that she was willing to talk with the old man. 'Look at her, I say,' said Skelton, laughing. 'Saw'st ever woman so tall and strong? This is Long Meg. She is as lusty as she is tall. Let her tell how she knocked over Sir James of Castile, and cudgelled the robber, and fought the Vicar from the Abbey, so that he lay in the Infirmary for three weeks, and how she dragged the Catchpole through the pond, and how she bobbed Huffling Dick on the noll. And she is as good as she is tall and lusty. My modest Meg! my merry Meg! my valiant Meg! my pigsny Meg! Tell the gentleman, Meg.' But the girl hung her head modestly, and only said, 'Nay, Sir John, it becomes me not to tell these things.' Then replied Skelton, 'I will tell him for thee. And, Meg, we will come presently, in the afternoon, for a flask of Malmsey. Go, sweet maid: I would I were forty years younger for thy sake. Stay—what were the verses I made upon thee when first thou didst come to Westminster?'

Meg laughed, and, folding her hands behind her like a girl that says a lesson, began:

'Domine, Domine, unde hoc?
What is she in the gray cassock?'

'Right, Meg—right. But go on.'

'Methinks she is of a large length,
Of a tall pitch and a good strength.
With strange armes and stiff bones;
This is a wench for the nones.
I tell thee, Hostesse, I do not mocke,
Take her in the gray cassocke.'

'But I have no gray cassock now,' Meg added, laughing. 'This afternoon, Sir John, Will Sommers comes. There will be merry tales and songs. Farewell, good sir.'

So, with a reverence, this comely giantess, this thumping, handsome wench, ran back to the tavern.

'Now,' said Sir John, 'we will take a walk. First, I will show thee where Will Caxton put up his first printing press, at the sign of the Red Pale. 'Tis nigh on thirty years since he is dead. Ha! he printed books of mine. The printed book remains; for there are hundreds of each book, and the trade of the scrivener is well nigh gone. So much the better for the poet I am in good company on the shelf with Caxton's books; in the company of Virgil and Ovid; of Boethius, Chaucer and Gower and Alain Chartier. I march with uplifted head in such a company. Laureate of Oxford and Louvain, friend of these immortals. My Lord the Cardinal turns green when he

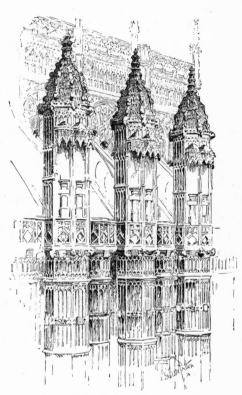

BUTTRESSES OF KING HENRY VII.'S CHAPEL

thinks upon it. Next,' he continued, 'we will walk about the Abbey. I cannot show thee the wealth of the monks, because that is spread out over the whole country—here a manor and there a manor; and no man, save the Abbot and the Prior, knoweth how great is their wealth; nor can I show thee the learning of the monks, because no man, not even the Abbot my benefactor, knoweth how small that is; nor can I show thee the piety of the Brothers, since that is known only to themselves; nor their fastings and macerations, because, the better to torment themselves, they sit down every day to a table covered with rich roasts and dainty confections; nor can I show thee the monks at work at the hours when they are not in their Church, because they work no more. But I will show thee the richest monastery in England, where the Brethren toil not, nor spin, and have no cares, but that they must grow old, and so daily draw nearer to the Fires of Purgatory. I will show thee gardens beautiful as the heart of man can desire; and, for their lodgings, the house of the Abbot is finer than the Palace of the King, and the chambers of the Prior and the Sub-Prior are delicate and dainty and desirable. What! think you that so great a Lord as the Abbot of Westminster . . . ? '

But here the original of this interview breaks off abruptly —*Explicit*—and I know not how the afternoon was spent, nor what jests and songs they had with Will Sommers and Long Meg.

CHAPTER VII

AT THE SIGN OF THE RED PALE

To write upon Westminster and not to speak of Caxton would be indeed impossible. As well write of America and forget Columbus. Even at the risk of doing over again what has already been done by the antiquary, as Blades, or by the historian, as Charles Knight—even though one may have

CAXTON'S DEVICE

found little to add to the investigations and discoveries of those who have gone before—we must still speak of Caxton, because through his agency was effected the change—that of printing for manuscript—which has proved the most momentous, the most far-reaching, the most fruitful of all the changes and inventions and discoveries of modern days. The

Reformation threw open the door for freedom of thought ; the Renascence restored to the world the literature and the philosophy of the past ; printing scattered broadcast the means of acquiring knowledge.

The humble beginnings of this revolution, the life and achievements of the man by whose hands it was effected in this country, are not so widely known that they may be assumed as common knowledge. Let us ask, for instance, who was Caxton ? How did he arrive at his printing press ? What did he print ? These are questions that the ordinary reader would perhaps find it difficult to answer.

To begin with, the setting up of his printing press was but an episode—albeit the last—in the long and busy life of this active man : an experiment, doubtful at first, which presently became the serious business of a man advanced in years, his occupation at an age when most men think of ease and retirement. The name and fame and praise of Caxton have gone forth into all lands ; but it is the fame of Caxton in old age — Caxton the printer, not Caxton in early life and in full manhood, Caxton of the Mercers' Company, Caxton the Merchant Adventurer, Caxton the Rector of the English House. If you ask any person of ordinary acquirements who invented printing, he will probably tell you that it was Caxton. Yet the person of a little more than ordinary acquirements very well knows that Caxton was not the inventor at all. What he did was to bring over the art of printing from the Netherlands to this country. Not such a very great thing, perhaps : had he not done so some one else would ; it was only a matter of time ; the invention was already beginning to leave its cradle ; other men already understood that here was a thing belonging to the whole world—a thing bound to travel over the whole world. Caxton, however, did actually give it to us ; he first brought it over here ; he introduced the new invention into this country. That is his great glory ; for that service he will never be forgotten : he has the honour that belongs to those

who understand, and advance, and associate with their own
lives and achievements, things invented by others who could
not, perhaps, see their importance.

SUPPOSED PORTRAIT OF CAXTON.   FROM BLADES' 'PENTATEUCH
OF PRINTING'

Perhaps everything that can be found out about Caxton has been already discovered. When we consider the antecedent improbability of learning anything at all about a merchant of the fifteenth century—not a merchant of the wealthier kind, neither a Whittington nor a Gresham—we may congratulate ourselves upon knowing a good deal about Caxton. To be sure, he gives us in his prefaces many valuable facts concerning himself. The learned Mr. William Blades has put together in his two books on Caxton all that he himself, or that others before him, had been able to discover. He has also added certain conjectures as to the most important step in Caxton's life: I will speak of these conjectures presently. The result is a tolerably complete biography. We cannot fill up the life year after year, but in general terms we know how it was spent and what things were done in the allotted span. That the personality is shadowy—yet not more shadowy than that of Shakespeare—cannot be denied.

No one, however, can say, in these times of research, when the documents of the past are overhauled and made to yield their secrets, that any point of archæological investigation is finally closed, so that nothing more will be discovered about it. Somewhere or other are lying hidden, documents, contracts, wills, conveyances, letters, reports, diaries—which may at any moment yield unexpected treasures to the finder. Let us remember how Peter Cunningham unearthed the accounts of the Revels and Masques among the papers of the Audit Office; how the debates of the House of Commons in the time of Cromwell were discovered; how Riley's researches in the archives of London have actually restored the mediæval city in every detail of its multi-coloured life; how the history of England has been already entirely rewritten during the last fifty years from newly discovered documents, and must in the next fifty years be again rewritten. Remembering these things, let us not conclude that concerning ny man, king, statesman, churchman, citizen, the last word as been spoken, the last discovery made.

For my own part, I have to contribute only those little iscoveries—some may call them theories—which always present themselves when another man from another point of iew approaches a certain array of facts. That is to say, I ave no new fact to announce, but I have one or two new onclusions to draw.

Let me endeavour, then, to present to you William Caxton s a reality, not a shadow : you shall see how and why he ecame, late in life, a printer ; what he was and what was is reputation before he became a printer. And you shall ee for yourselves what kind of book he produced, how he lustrated it, the kind of type he employed, and the binding f his books.

First, what manner of man was he, and of what origin ?

About four miles north-east of Tunbridge, in Kent, is the illage of Hadlow, part of which is covered by the manor f Causton. It is supposed, but it is by no means certain, hat from this manor sprang the family whose name Causton, Cauxton or Caxton, preserves the memory of their former olding. Long before the birth of William Caxton the nanor, if the family ever held it, had passed out of their ands. He says, himself, that he was born in the Weald of Kent. The Weald covers a large area ; but he does not tell us ny more, and it is not possible to get any closer information. n this part of the county he was born—somewhere. And n this part of the county there is a manor bearing his name. Can we safely conclude that a territorial name means that he family were once Lords of the Manor ? Certainly not. There is, however, reason to believe that he came of a City amily, and one long and honourably known in the City ; for he name of Caxton or Causton frequently occurs in the City ecords. In the year 1303 Aubin de Caustone, haberdasher, as appointed one of a committee to make scrutiny into the

manufacture of caps by methods and of materials forbidden
by law.   In 1307 William de Causton is one of those who
sign a letter addressed to the Bishop of Chester by the City
Fathers. In 1327 John de Causton, Alderman, is one of a Board
of Arbitrators between certain disputing trade companies
and he represented the City at the Council of Northampton
in 1337, for which service he received the sum of 60*l*.   In
1331 John de Caxton and Thomas de Caxton were butchers
— the latter, one regrets to find, obstructing the street with his
stall at the Poultry, for which his meat was forfeited.   In
1334 William de Causton, living in the parish of St. Vedast
was an Alderman.   In the year 1348 there were seven of the
name who paid their fees as liverymen of the Mercers
Company.   In 1364 Alice, wife of Robert de Causton, who
appears to have been a vintner, was sentenced to the 'thewe
for thickening the bottom of a quart pot with pitch, so that
he who ordered a quart of wine got short measure.   This
deplorable incident is the only one which tarnishes the honour
of the Caustons or Caxtons.   In 1401 William de Causton is
apprenticed to Thomas Gedeney.   In 1414 John Causton is
a butcher.   In 1424 Stevyn Causton is a liveryman of the
Mercers.   The family of Causton or Caxton, therefore, were
largely engaged in various branches of trade in London
during the whole of the fourteenth century.   Whether
William Caxton's father was himself a citizen and freeman
and if so, how the son came to be born in the Weald of Kent
is not known.   As the boy was apprenticed to the very
richest merchant in the City, and admitted a member of the
wealthiest company, it is quite certain that his people were of
some consideration in the City : to be received into the house
of a great merchant as an apprentice, to be admitted into the
Company of Mercers, proves beyond a doubt City connections of an honourable kind.   Either Caxton's father or his
grandfather must have been a man of weight and distinction
     ' I was born and learned my English in Kent in the

Weald, where I doubt not is spoken as broad and rude English as in any place of England.' These are his own words. In another place he writes, concerning his own style, ' whereof I humbly and with all my heart thank God, and also am bounden to pray for my father's and mother's souls, that in my youth set me to school, by which, by the sufferance of God, I got my living—I hope truly.' The Weald, in which he apparently spent his childhood, was at this time largely peopled by the descendants of the Flemish clothworkers brought over to England by Edward IV. He therefore heard as a child the Flemish language, or at least English with a large admixture of Flemish words—a fact which perhaps had something to do with his subsequent residence in Bruges. But where he went to school, what he learned there, and at what age he was taken from his lessons, he does not tell us.

He was born, I am sure, in the year 1424. It seems very clear that the usual age of apprenticeship was fourteen ; and Caxton was certainly apprenticed in the year 1438, and since the age of admission to the City freedom was twenty-four, ten years were passed in servitude : a long time, but not too long to learn the various branches of a merchant's work, and to acquire the habits of obedience which afterwards are trans-formed into the habit of authority.

It has been said that his master was the richest merchant of his time. He was Robert Large, Mercer, Warden of the Company in 1427, Sheriff in 1430, and Lord Mayor in 1440. When this great man received an apprentice he was receiving either the son of a personal friend or of some one whom he desired to oblige. It is significant that at the same time Large received another apprentice, the son of a brother mercer, named Harrowe, and that Harrowe received as apprentice another Caxton—Robert, perhaps brother of William—but concerning him nothing is discoverable.

Robert Large occupied a house already historic : it was

situated at the north-east corner of Old Jewry. In the thirteenth century the Jews who lived in that quarter buil for themselves a synagogue ; in the year 1262 there was a popular outbreak of hatred against the Jews, and a terrible massacre, in the course of which their synagogue was plun dered and taken from them. In the year 1271 Henry III gave the place as a House to a new order of Mendican Friars called *Fratres de Pœnitentiâ Jesu*, or *Fratres de Saccâ*.

This was a shortlived but extremely interesting Orde growing out of the Franciscans. It was founded in 1231 or as is also stated, in 1241. St. Francis, as we know, founde the Grey Friars, Fratres Minores : his disciple St. Clara founded the Clares or Sorores Minores, and the *Pœnitentiari* or *Fratres de Pœnitentiâ Jesu* or *Fratres de Saccâ* wer established shortly afterwards. The Order contained both men and women : the brothers and sisters might be married they might also hold property. They came over to England in the year 1257, and very soon possessed nine Houses, viz at Lynne, where Prior was the Head of the English Branch at London, Canterbury, Cambridge, Norwich, Worcester Newcastle, Lincoln and Leicester. The Council of Lyons in 1274 passed an edict permitting only four orders of Mendi cants. This edict seems to have been a deathblow to the *Fratres de Pœnitentiâ* : they languished and obtained little support—perhaps the people had no belief in friars who held property and were married. In 1305 Robert Fitzwalter obtained the permission of the King to assign their house to him : which was done, and the Penitential Friars disap peared from history. A hundred years later Robert Large obtained the house and held his Mayoralty in it : as did Lord Mayor Clipton in 1492. It was afterwards turned into a tavern called the Windmill.

In this house Caxton began his apprenticeship. He did not finish it here because unfortunately in the year 1441 Robert Large died.

As there is no document in which a man reveals himself so much as in a will, wherein may be found his religion, his superstition, his love, his hatred, his charity, the whole heart and soul of a man, I transfer to these pages a part of Robert Large's will, by which you may understand what manner of man was this rich merchant, Caxton's master, from whom he received his ideas of honourable trade.

He begins, after the usual preamble, by leaving money to the High Altar of his Parish Church ; to the structure of the church : to buy vestments for the church : the endowment of a chaplain to say mass daily. He then gives money to his widow and children : for the poor of the Mercers' Company : for a vestment in the Mercers' Chapel : to the four orders of Mendicants : to the Crutched Friars : for bedding in the Hospitals of St. Bartholomew and St. Mary Spital : to the parish church of Shallerton, where his father was buried : to the parish church of Alderton, where his ancestors were buried : to his servants and apprentices sums of money varying from one mark to twenty marks—there are five apprentices including William Caxton, who gets the larger sum—then there are more bequests to churches. To the poor of Coleman Street ward he gives twenty pounds. His soul thus cared for by so many gifts and bequests—a thing that no one in that age could possibly neglect : and his children and servants remembered : the testator applies himself to things practical and worldly. And here we observe what a practical citizen of the times most desired. He gave 400 marks towards the completion of an aqueduct lately begun in the City : he gave 100 marks towards the repairs of London Bridge : he gave 300 marks to the cleansing of Walbrook : also 100 marks to ten poor girls of good character on their marriage : also 100*l.* to be divided among poor servants in Lancashire and Warwickshire : also 20*l.* to be distributed by his executors where it might be most needed : also five marks for bedding at the Hospital of St. Mary of Bethlehem : also

forty shillings for bedding for St. Thomas's Hospital, and si.
pounds for bedding at the Lepers' Houses of Hackney, S
Giles, and St. George of Southwark. Also 100 shillings fo
the prisoners in Newgate and 100 shillings for the prisonei
in Ludgate.

He forgets nobody, this good citizen : he desires goo
water and plentiful : he wants the Bridge to be kept in repai
—where would trade be without the Bridge : he want
cleanliness in the City—why should Walbrook be allowe
to be converted into an open sewer ? Hospitals for the sick

THE ' DOMUS ANGLORUM,' BRUGES

marriage portions for girls : worn-out servants : prisoners
lepers : he remembers all. Surely to have been brought u
in the household of such a man, so kindly, so thoughtful, with
so great a heart, must have been an education for the boy.

At this time the principal market of Western Europe wa
Bruges, and the centre of the trade carried on by the Merchant
Adventurers—an association containing members of various
companies—was that city. There stood *Domus Anglorum*
the House of the English Merchants. It was not uncommor

or a young man to be sent to this House in order to learn ie foreign trade before he completed his time. Thither, ierefore, went Caxton, having seven years still to serve ; and iere he remained for thirty years.

Those who know the history of the Hanseatic Merchants nd the Steelyard will understand the position and meaning f the *Domus Anglorum*. The Englishmen in Bruges, just as ie Germans in London, lived separate and apart, a com- iunity by themselves, in their own house, which was irrounded by a wall, contained offices, warehouses, sleeping hambers, a common hall, and perhaps a chapel (I say erhaps, because a chapel belonged to every great house)· ˙he people of the London Steelyard, whether they had a hapel or no, worshipped in the Church of All Hallows the ِreat, just outside their walls ; and very likely the English ierchants observed the same practice. They lived separate ˙om the Flemings ; they were never allowed by the citizens f Bruges to consider themselves otherwise than as strangers nd foreigners ; they had certain privileges and rights ealously accorded, jealously watched, by the Duke of Bur- undy and by the worthy burghers of Bruges ; jealously uarded and resolutely claimed by the foreign merchants hemselves. In order to avoid, as much as possible, the ver present danger of a popular rising against strangers, ie Englishmen lived by strict rule : abroad they walked ˙ith circumspection ; they kept as much as possible within heir own walls. It is not likely that the prejudice against ˙reigners was so strong in any European country as it was i England ; certainly not at Bruges, Ghent, and Antwerp, ˙hither foreigners flocked from every part. At the same ime, to be a foreigner anywhere invited curiosity ; and iediæval curiosity was the mother of hostility ; and hostility ˙o often took a practical and an active line. The English actory, therefore, lived under rule, like the Germans of the Steel- ˙ard : they lived in a college ; they observed hours of closing

the gates ; they had a common table ; save for vows an
midnight prayers the life was monastic ; on no pretence wer
women to be admitted, and all the residents were unmarried

These factories or foreign stations of English merchant
were continued into quite modern times. In the seventeent
century, and perhaps later, there was an English factory a
Aleppo ; the Indian Empire sprang out of English factories
the establishment of a factory was the first step towards
footing in foreign trade.

The position of governor, or rector, of such a communit
was, it will be readily understood, one requiring special, rare
and valuable qualities. He must be, first of all, a man c
courteous and conciliatory manners ; he must know how t
be firm and how to assert his rights ; he must be watchfu
for the extension, and jealous for the observance, of privileges
he must be ready to seize every opportunity for advancin
the interests of the community ; he must not be afraid t
stand before kings ; he must be a linguist, and able to spea
the language of the court and the language of the marke
When we learn, therefore, that Caxton was presently raise
to the very important office of Governor of all the Englis
merchants, not only in Bruges, but in the other towns—Ghen
Antwerp, Damme, Sluys—we understand from this single fac
the manner of man he was supposed to be ; when we learn i
addition that he continued to hold this post till he was forty
five years of age, we understand what manner of man he mus
have been.

There is, as one who studies this time cannot fail t
remark, a special kind of dignity belonging to these centuries
it is the dignity which springs from the knowledge of one'
own rank or place, at a time when rank, place or statio
belonged to every possible occupation in life. A bricklaye
or a carpenter, as well as a mercer, or a monk or a pries
belonged to a trade association : he was 'prentice first, ful
member next, officer or even warden in due course. Th

most humble employment was dignified by the association of its members. Everybody, from the King to the lowest crafts-man, understood the dignity of associated labour ; everybody recognised office and authority, whether it was the episcopal office or the presidency of a Craft Company. You may see Caxton in every picture that presents a *bourgeois* of the time. He wears a long gown of red cloth, something like a cassock, the sleeves and neck trimmed with rich fur ; round his neck hangs a gold chain ; his belt is of leather gilt, and from it hangs his purse ; his hair is cut shorter than the nobles wear it, and it is seen under a round cap, the sides of which are turned up. It is a costume admitting of great splendour in the way of material ; the fur lining or trimming may be broad and costly ; the gold chain may be rich and heavy ; the belt may be embossed by an Italian artist,—all the advantages of mediæval costume are not with the knight and soldier. As for his face, it is grave ; his eyes are serious : it is not for him that the Court Fool plays his antics ; it is not for him that the minstrel strikes his mandoline : he is thinking what new concessions he can get from the Duke of Burgundy. Above all, at this moment he is troubled about the late quarrel in Antwerp between certain English sailors— young hotheads—and some Flemings, in a tavern, after which two of the latter were found dead. And the town, without considering who began the brawl, was of course in an uproar against the accursed English. The news has been brought home by a Flemish merchant just from Antwerp : the Englishmen have taken sanctuary ; there will be corre-spondence, excuses—fines, perhaps.

Or it is an Italian merchant—Caxton talks his language as well—who has things to propose, barter to effect. The Rector of the *Domus Anglorum* was, in fact, a kind of consul. He sent home regular reports on the state of trade, on prices and fluctuations, on supply and demand ; he received English merchants, made them pay an entrance fee,

N

instructed them in the laws and privileges of the factory, gav
them interpreters, and assisted them in their buying an
selling according to the customs of the town. He was als
agent to the Merchant Adventurers of London.

In the archives of the town two cases are recorded i
which Caxton was concerned, the first in which he ha
become surety to a merchant of the Staple at Calais, th
second in which he consented to arbitration. In the first h
is styled simply ' English Merchant.' In the second he i
' English Merchant and Governor of the English House.' A
a merchant, or as Rector of the English House, Caxton di
not become rich. This point seems to me abundantly prove
by the facts of the case. His biographers have sometime
represented him as returning to England enriched by hi
calling, and setting up his press as an occupation or recreatio
for his old age. Let us look again at the facts. Those whic
bear upon the point are the following :—

1. He remained in the *Domus* for thirty years, leaving i
at the age of forty-seven or thereabouts. Merchants who grov
rich do not continue in the service of their company so long

2. He married on leaving the *Domus*. Those who prospe
do not continue in celibacy till they are past their prime.

3. He then remained abroad for a time, and entered th
service of the Duchess of Burgundy. Wealthy merchants d
not remain in exile, nor did they at any time enter into th
service of a foreign prince.

4. During the whole thirty years of Caxton's residenc
abroad, his native country was torn to pieces by a long an
bitter civil war. It has been shown that the towns suffere
comparatively little from this conflict, but its effect upo
the Merchant Adventurers was most certainly disastrou
Where, when all the country was covered with armies an
every great noble had to take a side, was the market fo
imports ? Where were they to get the exports when th
land was ravaged throughout its length and breadth ? Th

Merchant Adventurers could neither sell their imports nor ship their exports. The condition of London was something like that when the Saxons overran the country on all sides ; and also, like that time, the flower of the London youth were called out to fight. Of money-making there was small thought : happy the merchant who could hold his own. ' I have known London,' Caxton writes, ' in my young age much more wealthy, prosperous, and richer than it is at this day.' While the Red and the White Roses were tearing at each other's throats one fears that the *Domus Angliæ* showed empty warehouses and a deserted hall.

Lastly, if there were any doubt on the subject of Caxton's comparative poverty, it should be removed by the grateful words in which he speaks of the money given him when he entered the service of the Duchess of Burgundy ; these are not the words of a prosperous man.

Caxton, therefore, one may be quite sure, left Bruges as slenderly provided as regards store and treasure as when he entered the city.

After this preamble, we now arrive at the invention of printing.

The fifteenth century—the beginning of the Renaissance —was also remarkable for the production of beautiful and costly books. The art of the illuminator had never been finer, the writing had never been more beautiful, the demand for books had never been so great, the numbers of those engaged outside the monasteries in the production of books rapidly increased. In every town they formed themselves into Guilds : thus, at Bruges, there was the Guild of St. John, in which were enrolled booksellers, painters, scriveners and copyists, illuminators, bookbinders, curriers, makers of parchment and vellum, and engravers. And they could not produce books fast enough to meet the increased demand. Now, it is perfectly certain that if the demand for anything that is made, grown or produced is increased from any cause, the methods of production of that thing will be reconsidered and men's ingenuity will devise means of making the production easier, cheaper, and more practicable.   What happened with the production of books was exactly what happened with everything else.   'Give us more books,' cried those who, a hundred years before, had wanted no books : ' Give us more books.'   Those who were interested in the production pondered continually over the enormous labour and cost of copying Could there be found any way to lessen that labour ?   The result was the invention of printing.

Who was the first printer ?

You may read all the books, pamphlets and articles ; you may consider all the arguments, and in the long run you will know no more than you knew at the beginning.   Perhaps it was Coster of Haarlem, or perhaps it was Gutenberg of Mainz.   No one knows, and really it matters little except for the antiquary and the historian.   At this period, as we have seen, some modification in the old method of copying was certain to be invented.   It was by the greatest good luck, I have always thought, that a sort of shorthand, a representation of words by little easy symbols, was not invented.   For instance, supposing a separate symbol for each of the prepositions, articles and auxiliary verbs, and other separate symbols for the commoner words, there might be some thousands of symbols in all to be learned by the scribe ; but his labour would be reduced to one-tenth.   They might have invented some such method.   Then, satisfied with the result we should have gone on for centuries, and the art of printing would still have to be invented.

But the time was come, and the invention, happily, came with it.   Had printing been invented two centuries before, it would have been neglected and speedily forgotten, because there was no demand for books.   Had it been invented two centuries later, it would have had to contend against some other contrivance for shortening labour and cheapening books

CAXTON'S HOUSE IN THE ALMONRY, WESTMINSTER

If an ingenious projector discovers some great truth or invents some useful contrivance before or after his time he is lost—he and his discovery. Thus, in the reign of James I. a man of great ingenuity contrived a submarine boat,—he was before his age. In the middle of the last century another ingenious person discovered a way of sending messages by electricity,—he was before his age. In a romance, now a hundred and fifty years old, the possibility of photography was imagined by another person before his age. Men whose ideas are much before their age receive, as their reward, contempt, certainly ; imprisonment, probably ; and perhaps death in one of its more unpleasant forms.

The generally received story, after all that has been said, is this. There was a certain Johann Gensfleisch von Sorgenloch, called Zum Gutenberg, a man of noble family, who was born in Mainz somewhere about the end of the fourteenth century. He removed from his native town to Strasbourg, where he began experimenting upon wood blocks. He then, with the idea of printing clearly defined in his mind, perhaps with type already cut in wood, went back to Mainz and entered into partnership with three others, named Riffe, Heitman and Dritzchen. Documents still exist which prove this partnership, and contemporary evidence is clear and strong upon the point that this Gutenberg, and none other, was the inventor of the art. The first partnership was speedily broken up. A second was formed with Fust or Faust, a goldsmith, and one Peter Schöffer, who seems to have been the working partner. Certainly he improved and carried the art to a high state of perfection.

That it should spread was certain : the work was simple ; the press was not a machine which could be kept secret. Before long printers were setting up their presses everywhere. At Bruges the first printer was one Colard Mansion, a native of the place. He was a member of that Fraternity or Guild of St. John already mentioned. He was himself a writer, or at least a translator, as well as a printer. Caxton followed him in this respect. He printed and published twenty-two works, of which one, called 'The Garden of Devotion,' was in Latin, the others were all in French except two, which were in English. These two were printed for Caxton. The use of French shows that the court and the nobles did not use Flemish. One of his books, the cost of which seems to have ruined the unfortunate printer, was a splendid edition in folio of Ovid's 'Metamorphoses,' translated into French and illustrated with numerous woodcuts. It is worthy of note that Colard's workshop was the chamber over the north porch of the Church of St. Donatus. The first 'chapel' of printers may have been begun in the modest room over a church porch. When troubles fell upon poor Colard he was fain to run away ; he left the city, and—he disappeared. History knows nothing more about Colard Mansion.

That he printed these two books for Caxton there seems no reason to doubt. Wynkyn de Worde, Caxton's successor, certainly says that they were printed at Cologne ; but contemporary evidence is not always to be trusted. The character of the type alone is held to prove that they are the work of Colard.

These are the earliest English-printed books. The first is a 'Recuyell of the Historyes of Troie'; the second is 'The Game and Playe of the Chesse.' The second is dedicated to the unfortunate Duke of Clarence : 'To the righte noble, righte excellent and vertuous Prince George, Duc of Clarence, Earle of Warwicke and of Salisburye, Grete Chamberlayne of Englonde and Lieutenant of Ireland, Oldest Brother of Kynge Edwarde, by the Grace of God Kynge of Englonde and of France, your most humble servant William Caxton amonge other of youre servantes sendes unto you Peas, Helthe, Joye and Victorye upon your Enemies.'

The 'Recuyell,' a translation, was completed in 1471. It was not printed until 1474. The conclusion is that Caxton found so great a demand for it that he could not get the book copied quickly enough to meet the demand ; that his attention was drawn to the newly invented art, and that he perceived something of the enormous possibilities which it presented. About this time he resigned the post he had held so long ; he left the claustral *Domus* over which he had presided ; he married a wife, and he entered into the service of the Duchess of Burgundy. It has been asked in what capacity he served. In no capacity at all : he was one of the 'following' ; he wore

Pirrus that was the sone of Achilles and o
adainie the doughter of kynge Lychame
hys moder syde. This kynge sieshomedes r
one of kynge Achastus that syued yet at that ty
2ndr this kynge Achastus that was moche olde
auncyent. hatedr stronglp pyrrus / But the historp
seth not wherfore ne for what cause this hate cam.
kynge Achastus hadr put the kynge Deleus oute o
royame of thesaplle / andr hadr sente hym m eryse.
sette esppes m manp places for to slee pyrrus m h
tourne fro tropes / Pirrus m his comyng fro trop
hdr manp parpllis m the see /

FACSIMILE OF THE 'RECUYELL OF THE HISTORYES OF TROIE'

the livery of the Duchess ; he was attached to the court ; he had rooms and rations and some allowance of money ; he was in the service and at the orders of the Duchess ; he was a secretary or an interpreter ; he swelled the pageant by his presence ; he conducted the Duchess' trade ventures ; he was Usher of the White Rod, Chamberlain, Gentleman-in-waiting —anything. Do not let us be deceived by the word 'service' and its modern meaning.

This 'service' lasted a very short time. He left the court

—one knows not why—and he returned, after this long absence, to his native land. Then began the third, the last, the most important chapter of his life. This was in the year

The fyfthe chappytre of the second book of the forme nd maners of the Rookes capitulo quinto

He rookes whiche ken vycayrs andy legates of the kynge ought to be maad a knyght vpon an hors & mantel and hood furrid with meneuia holdyng a staf in is hand/

FACSIMILE OF THE 'GAME AND PLAYE OF THE CHESSE'

1476. He brought over his presses and his workmen with him. And he settled in Westminster.

Why did he choose Westminster?

This point is elaborately discussed by Blades. He

suggests that Caxton went to Westminster on account of the Wool Staple, with which he may have had correspondence while at Bruges. He *may* have had : perhaps he did have—though it is not at all likely, because, as is most certain, he was in constant correspondence with the Merchant Adventurers of London, and with his own company of Mercers, whose representative he was ; and it is also certain that, as a citizen of London, he could not regard the Staple of Westminster with any favour. That reason, therefore, may be disregarded.

Or, Blades suggests, the Mercers rented of the Abbey a tavern called the 'Greyhound,' where they feasted once a year, and where they did business with the merchants of the Wool Staple. *Therefore* Caxton came here. This, again, is a reason that is no reason ; for, surely, the fact that there was this tavern in Westminster could not influence Caxton in the least. One might as well make him go to Gravesend because the Mercers had a farm not far from the town.

There are, however, two reasons which seem to me very plain and sufficient. The first shows why he did not set up his press in the City of London. The next shows why he did set it up in the town—not yet a city—of Westminster. The first reason is that he did not take a workshop in London because he could not. The thing was impossible ; he would not be allowed to work under the jurisdiction of the Lord Mayor. By this time every trade or craft carried on in the City had been formed into a company or attached to some company ; every craftsman belonged to a company ; every merchant and every retailer belonged to a company. There was, however, no trade of printing ; therefore no company : therefore, as yet, and until the point was raised and settled, no power of settling within the City.

Where, then, could he find a proper place ? Southwark was within the City jurisdiction. Without the walls there were hardly any suburbs. The Strand, which might be con-

sidered a suburb, was a long line of palaces built upon the
river bank, noble of aspect from the river ; on the other side
their gates opened upon a muddy road, on the north side of
which were fields.   Caxton wanted, however, not a suburb,
but a town ;. he wanted, also, patrons and customers for the
new trade.   Westminster was, in fact, the only place to which
he could go.   Doubtless he bore letters and recommendations.
from the Duchess of Burgundy to her brother Edward IV.
He wanted court favour, a thing which everybody wanted
at that time ; he wanted the patronage of great lords and
ladies ; and he wanted to attract the attention of colleges,
monasteries, and places where they wanted books and used
books.   In short, like every man in trade, Caxton wanted a
place which would be convenient for advertising, showing,
and proclaiming his business.   For all purposes Westminster
was admirably suited for the setting up of his press.

Where was his house ?

Long afterwards, until exactly fifty years ago, when it fell
down, there was shown a house traditionally assigned to
Caxton.   The representation certainly indicates a later origin,
but there may have been alterations.   There have been dis-
cussions and disputes over the site of the first printing
press : it has been placed on the site of Henry VII.'s
Chapel ; one is told that the monument in front of St.
Margaret's stands on the site.   For my own part I cannot
understand how there can be any doubt at all.   Stow, writing
a hundred years later, states with the greatest clearness
where the house stood.   He says, speaking of the ' Gate
House '—that is, the gate at the east end of Tothill Street
—' On the South side of this Gate King Henry VII. founded
an Almshouse for thirteen poor men . . . near unto this
house westward was an old chapel of St. Anne, over against
which the Lady Margaret, mother to King Henry VII.,
erected an almshouse for poor women, which is now turned
into lodgings for the singing men of the College.   The place

wherein this Chapel and Almshouse stand was called the
Eleemosynary or Almonry ; now, corruptly, the Ambry ; for
that the alms of the Abbey were here distributed to the
poor.

   ' And therein Islip, Abbot of Westminster, first practised
and erected the first press of Book printing that ever was
in England about the year of Christ 1471 ; W. Caxton,
Citizen of London, Mercer, brought it into England, and was
the first that practised it in the said Abbey.'

   Islip was not Abbot at that time, but Prior and afterwards
Abbot. As Prior, the details of the government of the
Abbey were in his hands.   If now we look at the map we
shall see that the place corresponds with what was called the
Great Almonry until a few years ago, when Victoria Street
was cut through the slums of Westminster, and the Westminster Palace Hotel was built, either covering the site or
effectually hiding it.   The thing does not seem to admit of
doubt or dispute.   Observe that Stow speaks of the ' Ambry '
as being ' in ' the Abbey, though it was outside the gate.   So
Caxton speaks of his presses as set up ' in ' the Abbey—an ex-
pression which has led many to think that he carried on his
work within the church.   The mistake was natural so long as
men had forgotten the meaning of the word ' Abbey,' and
thought that Westminster Abbey meant the Church of St.
Peter.   How many are there, even now, who have examined
the remains lying south of the church, and who understand
that these were buildings which, with the church, constituted
the Abbey ?

   The house was known by the sign of the Red Pale.   It
was a common sign among printers in Holland, some of
whom, however, had a Black Pale.

   It is not necessary to enumerate the books which Caxton
printed ; and the questions of type, process, binding and
illustrating must be left for the biographer.   But about
the trade of printer and publisher ?   On this point hear

Caxton himself. He speaks in a Prologue (hitherto undis-
covered).

'When,' he says, 'I resolved upon setting up a press in
Westminster, I knew full well that it was an enterprise full of
danger. For I had seen my friend Colard, printer of Bruges,
fain to fly from the city in poverty and debt; and I had seen
Melchior of Augsburg dying a bankrupt; and I had heard
how Sweynheim and Pannarts in Rome had petitioned the
Pope for help. Yet I hoped, by the favour and countenance

eth gyveth his herte and his Will, pytie & mercy ben
frendis, seking of Wysemen ben his fete, his lordship
justyce, his reigne is mesure, his Werke is grace, his
ʒy is peas, his awoie is saluacion, his knyghthode is the
seplle of Wysemen + his ornamentis ben strength, his
ure is Discipline, his loue is the companye of goode pe
his loue & al his desir is to fle sinne & to serue & loue god
And saide A grette trasur ys to haue frendys & is a
e affection, Wherfore it is conuenient to cherisshe & kepe
Wele, & to Winne one by another as ofte as byraes dra/
many into her company

FACSIMILE OF THE 'DICTES OR SAYINGS OF THE PHILOSOPHERS'

of His Highness the King, to succeed. This have I done:
yet not as I hoped to do. For I thought that the quick production and the cheapness of books would cause many to buy
them who hitherto had been content to live without the solace
of poetry and romance, and without the instruction of Cato
and Boethius. Again, I thought that there are schools and
colleges where books must be studied, and I hoped that they
would find it better to print than to copy. And there are
Religious Houses where they are for ever engaged in copying

Psalters and Service Books. Surely, I thought, it will be better for the good Monks to print than to copy. I forgot, moreover, that there was a great stock in hand of written books ; in every Monastery a store which must first be used up, and in every College there were written books for the student which must first be worn out before there would be question of replacing them with printed books. Also I forgot the great company of copyists, illuminators, limners, and those who make and sell vellum and fine parchment for the copyists. And I found, moreover, to my surprise, that there were many, great lords to wit, who cared nothing for cheapness, and who scoffed at my woodcuts compared with the illuminations in red and blue and gold which adorned their written books. He who would embark upon a new trade must reckon with those who make their livelihood in the old trade. Wherefore my Art of Printing had many enemies at the outset, and few friends. So that the demand for my books has not yet been found equal to the number which I have put forth, and I should have been ruined like Colard and bankrupt like Melchior were it not for the help of my Lord of Arundel and others, who protected me against the certain loss which threatened.'

There are many points connected with the first English printing press on which one would like to dwell : the mechanism of it, the forms of type, the paper used, the binding, the price. These things belong to a biography, and not to a chapter. It must suffice here to say that the form of the press was simple, being little more than such a screw press as is used now for copying letters.

As to the books themselves, Caxton, in the true spirit of trade, gave the world not what he himself may have wanted, but what the world wanted. Books of romance, chivalry and great achievements were demanded by the knights and nobles. Books of service were wanted by the Church. Caxton provided these. These things illustrate the character

Religion   Philosophy   Arts   Science

Fiat Lux

Dicts   Peregrinus
             Sept

Golden   ArtFlour
Legend   Salvatoris

Uen Bede   W. Caxton   Erasmus

CAXTON MEMORIAL WINDOW IN ST. MARGARET'S, WESTMINSTER

of the man—cautious, businesslike, anxious to run his press at a profit, so that he tried no experiments, and was content to be a servant rather than a teacher.

Those who will take the trouble to visit the British Museum and there examine for themselves the treasures which the nation possesses of early printing—the case full of Caxtons in the King's Library, the shelf filled with Caxtons in the vast Library which the general visitor is not allowed to see—will be astonished to observe the rapid advances already made in the Art of Printing when Caxton undertook its practice. Printing was first invented some time in the first half of the fifteenth century.[1] The type is clear and strong—clearer type we have never made since ; the ink is perfectly black to this day ; the lines are even and in perfect order ; the binding, when an ancient binding has been preserved, is like any binding of later times. But the shape of the book was not newly invented, nor the binding, nor the form of the type ; in these matters the printer followed the copyist. In the earlier examples the illuminator was called in to adorn the book, copy by copy, with his art-initials, coloured letters, pictures delicately and beautifully drawn, coloured and gilt in the printed page. The illuminator, however, very soon gave way to the engraver. The wood engravings of the late fifteenth century, rough though they are, and coarse in drawing and outline, are yet vigorous and direct ; they illustrate what they desire to illustrate. One can believe that those who could afford the illuminations continued to order and to buy the manuscripts, for the sake of their delicacy and beauty. But the printed book, with its rough engraving, was within the reach of student, priest, and squire, to whose slender means the illuminated work was forbidden.

The more one considers this figure of the fifteenth-century workman, the more clearly he stands out before us, grave,

---

[1] See Lacroix, *Les Arts au Moyen Age*, for a sensible *résumé* of the whole question.

anxious, resolute of face—the more he becomes admirable and wonderful. For thirty years engaged in protecting English interests in the Netherlands—patient, tenacious, conciliatory ; the friend and servant of the most powerful lady in Europe ; the friend of all those at home who regarded literature : himself a lover of poetry and of romance, and at the mature age of sixty-five engaged in translating the latter ; a good linguist ; a good scholar ; and, most certainly, one who could look into the future, and could foretell something of the influence which the press was destined to have upon the world. And all this in a simple liveryman of the Mercers' Company, without education other than that enjoyed by all lads of his position, without wealth and without family influence other than that derived from the long connection with the City in various trades of his kith and kin. Admirable and won-derful is the life of

FACSIMILE OF CAXTON'S HANDWRITING,
FROM THE PEPYSIAN LIBRARY

this great man ; admirable and wonderful are his achieve-ments.

He died in harness. Thus sayeth Wynkyn de Worden in the ' Vitæ Patrum ' : ' Thus endyth the most vertuouse hystorye of the devoute and righte renowned lyves of holy faders lyuynge in deserte, worthy of remembrance to all wel dysposed persons, which hath ben translated oute of French into Englishe by William Caxton of Westmynstre late deed and fynyshed at the laste daye of hys lyff.' He died in the year 1491, and was buried at St. Margaret's, where his wife, Maude, and perhaps his father, were also buried. He left one

O

child, a daughter. He left a will, which is lost ; but one clause was a bequest of fifteen copies of the ' Golden Legend ' to the parish church. These were afterwards sold at prices varying from 5*s*. 4*d*. to 6*s*. 8*d*. If money was then worth eight times its present value, we can understand that books, although they were greatly cheapened by being printed instead of written, had not yet become cheap.

Many of the books which he published were romances, as has been said, and tales of chivalry. He loved these tales himself, as much as the noble ladies and gallant knights for whom he published them. Let us end this notice with his own words on the excellence and the usefulness of romance. He is speaking of the ' History of King Blanchardine and Queen Eglantine his Wife,' translated by order of the Lady Margaret.

' I know full well that the story of it was honest and joyful to all virtuous young noble gentlemen and women for to read therein as for their pastime. For under correction, in my judgment, the stories of noble feats and valiant acts of arms and war . . . which have been actioned in old time by many noble princes, lords and knights, are as well for to see and know their valiantness, for to stand in the special grace and love of their ladies, and in like wise for gentle young ladies and demoiselles for to learn to be steadfast and constant in their part to them, that they once have promised and agreed to such as have put their lives oft in jeopardy for to please them to stand in grace, as it is to occupy the ken and study overmuch in books of contemplation.'

CHAPTER VIII

THE VANISHED PALACE

WESTMINSTER is the City of King's Houses. It contains, or has contained, five of them. Of these we have already considered one—the earliest and the most interesting. Of the four others, Buckingham Palace belongs to the present ; it is, in a way, part of ourselves, since it is the House of the Sovereign. Therefore we need not dwell upon it. There remain the Houses of Whitehall, of St. James's, and of Kensington. Of these three the two latter Palaces have apparently failed to impress the popular imagination with any sense of royal splendour or mystery. This sense belongs both to Westminster and to Whitehall ; but not to St. James's, or to Kensington. It is hard to say why this is so. As regards St. James's, the buildings are certainly not externally majestic ; nor does one who walks within its courts become immediately conscious of ancient associations and the atmosphere of Court Functions. Yet nearly all the Court Functions were held there for a hundred and fifty years. Again, there are personal associations, if one looks for them, clinging to St. James's, as there were at Whitehall ; but either we do not look for them, or they do not awaken any enthusiasm. Pilgrims do not journey to the Palace to visit its haunted chambers, as they do to Holyrood or to Windsor. Queen Mary, for instance, died in the Palace—Froude has told us in what mournful manner and in which room. Does any one ever ask or care for the room in which the most unhappy of all English Queens or Princesses breathed her last ?

King Charles spent his last night in this Palace. The Royal
martyr has still admirers, but they do not flock to St. James's
to weep over the unspeakable sadness of that night. The
elder Pretender was born here, but we have almost forgotten
his life, to say nothing of his birth, in spite of the romantic
warming-pan. There are stories of love and intrigue, of
jealousy, of ambition and disappointment, connected with
St. James's ; yet, with all this wealth of material, it is not
a palace of romance : at Whitehall, when we think of that
vanished House, the face, the eyes, the voice of Louise de
Querouaille light up the courts ; the Count de Grammont fills
the rooms for us with lovely ladies and gallant courtiers ; outside, from her windows looking into the Park, fair Nelly greets
the King with mirthful eyes and saucy tongue as he crosses
from Whitehall. Well, Miss Brett was perhaps quite as
beautiful as Nelly or Louise, but we do not in the least desire
to read about her. The book of the French courtier treats
entirely of the world, the flesh, and the devil,—we read it with
rapture ; the Chronicles of St. James's might be written so as
to treat of exactly the same subjects,—yet we turn from them.
Why ? Because it is impossible to throw over the Georges
the luminous halo of romance. George the First, the Second,
and the son of the Second, were perhaps as immoral as Charles
and James ; yet between them all they could not produce a
single romance. The first romantic episode in the history of
the house of Hanover is that simple little legend of Hannah
Lightfoot. Perhaps another reason why St. James's has never
become to the imagination a successor to Whitehall and
Westminster is that from the year 1714 to the year 1837
the old kind of loyalty to the sovereign no longer existed.
Compare the personal loyalty displayed to Henry V., to
Henry VIII., to Elizabeth, with that felt for William III., who
saved the country from Catholic rule, and for George I., who
carried on the Protestant succession. The country accepted
these kings, not because they had any personal love for them

Inigo Jones
1614.

but because they enabled the nation to have what it wanted.
The new kings did not try to become personally popular ; but
they were ready to lead the people in war for religious freedom, and they represented a principle.   But as for personal
loyalty of the ancient kind, that no longer existed.

For exactly a similar reason Kensington has never been
a palace in which the world is interested.   William III.
chose the house for his residence ; he died here.   An excellent king, a most useful king, but hardly possessed of the
nation's love.   George II. died here ; the Duke of Sussex died
here ; yet there is no curiosity or enthusiasm about the place.

With Whitehall the case is quite different.   It was the
Palace of Henry VIII., of Elizabeth, of the Tudors and the
Stuarts ; the Palace of sovereigns who ruled as well as
reigned, who were English and not Germans, who lived in
the open light and air for all to behold ; if they did not hide
their vices, they openly displayed their virtues : there is more
interest attaching to the Whitehall of Charles II. alone than
there is to the St. James's of all those who came after him.
Since, then, we can here consider one palace only out of the
remaining four, let us turn to the Palace of Whitehall.

We have seen that, of all the buildings which once
clustered round the Painted Chamber and formed the King's
House of Westminster, there now remain nothing more than
a single hall much changed, a crypt much restored, a cloister,
and a tower.   But this is autumnal opulence compared with
the Palace of Whitehall.   Of that broad, rambling place, as
taken over and enlarged by Henry VIII., there now remains
nothing at all—not a single chamber, not a tower, not a gateway, not a fragment ; everything is gone : even the disposition
of its courts and lanes, generally the last thing to be lost, can
no longer be traced.   And of the Stuart Whitehall which
succeeded there remains but one chamber, the Banqueting
Hall of Inigo Jones.   Perhaps no royal palace of recent
times, in any country, has been so lost and forgotten as that

HOLBEIN'S GATE AND THE BANQUETING HALL

From the original Picture by Samuel Scott, in possession of Mr. Andrew Chatto

of the Tudor Whitehall. Even the Ivory House of Ahab, or the Golden House of Nero, has not been more completely swept away. I wonder how many living men—even of the few who have seriously studied the Westminster of the past —could draw from memory a plan of Whitehall Palace, or describe in general terms its courts and buildings. Yet it was a very great house ; certainly not venerable or picturesque, such as that which stood beside the Abbey : there were no sculptured fronts, no tall gables, no tourelles, no gray walls, no narrow windows, no carved cloisters ; there was hardly any suggestion of a fortress ; it was a modern house from the first, the house of an ecclesiastic, built, like all the older houses, in a succession of courts. One who wishes to understand Whitehall must visit Hampton, and walk about the courts of St. James's.

The first mention of the House is in the year 1221, when it was bequeathed by Hubert de Burgh, Henry III.'s Justiciary, to the Dominicans of his foundation. The original home of the Black Friars in London was in Holborn, exactly north of Lincoln's Inn ; whence, fifty years later, they removed to the corner where the Fleet runs into the Thames, just outside the ancient City wall. Here their name still survives. The monks kept Hubert's house till 1276, when they sold it to the Archbishop of York. For two hundred and fifty years it was the town house of the Archbishop. Wolsey, the last Archbishop who held it, greatly enlarged and beautified the house. Concerning the magnificence with which he lived here—such magnificence as surpassed that of the King his master, such splendour as no king of England, not even Richard II., had ever shown at his court—we are informed by his biographer, Cavendish. Wolsey's following of eight hundred men, including ten peers of the realm and fifteen knights who were not too proud to enter the service of the Cardinal, was greater even than that of Warwick, the King-maker of the preceding century.

When one reads of the entertainments, the banquetings, the mumming, the music, the gold and silver plate, the cloth of gold, the blaze of colour everywhere—in the hangings, in the coats of arms, in the costumes, in the trappings of the horses—we must remember that this magnificence was not in those days regarded as ostentation. So to speak of it betrays nineteenth-century prejudice. It is only in this present century that the rich man has been expected to live, to travel, to dress, to entertain, very much like the men who are not so rich. Dives now drives in a carriage little better than that of the physician who attends him. He gives dinners little better than those of the lawyer who conducts his affairs. If he lives in a great house, it is in the country, unseen. To parade and flaunt and exhibit your wealth is, as we now understand things, bad form. In the time of Cardinal Wolsey it was not bad form : it was the right and proper use of wealth to entertain royally ; it was the part of a rich man to dress splendidly, to have a troop of gentlemen and valets in his service, to exhibit tables covered with gold and silver plate, to hang the walls with beautiful and costly arras. All this was right and proper. In this way the successful man showed his success to the world ; he invited the world to judge how successful he was—how rich, how powerful. A great deal of Wolsey's authority and power depended upon this outward and visible show. Perhaps he overdid the splendour and created jealousies. Yet kings delighted in seeing the splendour of their subjects. Had the Divorce business gone on smoothly, the King might have continued to rejoice in possessing a subject so great and powerful. We have ceased so long from open splendour that we find it difficult to understand it. Imagination refuses to restore the glory of York House, when its walls were hung with tapestry of many colours ; when, here and there, in place of tapestry, the walls were hung with cloth of gold, cloth of silver and cloth of tissue. Where, let me ask, can we find now a single

piece of this fine cloth of gold? There were long tables
spread with rich stuffs—satin, silk, velvet, damask : where
can we find a table now spread with these lovely things ?
There were sideboards set with the most splendid gold and
silver plate : where now can we see gold and silver plate—
save at a Lord Mayor's Dinner ? A following of eight hundred people rode with the Cardinal : what noble in the land
has such a following now ? Alas ! the richest and greatest
lord that we can produce has nothing but a couple of varlets
behind his carriage and two or three more in his hall, with
never a knight or squire or armiger among them. As for the
Cardinal himself, when he went abroad he was all scarlet and
red and gold and silver gilt. His saddle was of crimson
velvet, his shoes were set with gleaming diamonds, his stirrups
were silver gilt ; before him rode two monks carrying silver
crosses. Every day he entertained a multitude with a noble
feast and fine wines, with the singing of men and children
and with the music of all kinds of instruments. And afterwards there were masques and mummeries, and dances with
noble dames and gentle damsels.

What have we to show in comparison with this magnificence ? Nothing. The richest man, the most noble and the
most powerful, is no more splendid than a simple gentleman.
The King-maker, if he existed in the present day, would walk
to his club in Pall Mall ; and you would not distinguish him
from the briefless barrister taking his dinner—the same dinner,
mind—at the next table. The decay of magnificence accom-
panies the decay of rank, the decay of individual authority,
and the decay of territorial power.

Wolsey fell. Great and powerful must have been that
dread sovereign, that Occidental Star, that King who could
overthrow by a single word so mighty a Lord as the Cardinal.
And the King took over for his own use the town house of
the Archbishops of York.

At this time the old Palace of Westminster was in a

melancholy condition. A fire in 1512 destroyed a great part of it, including the principal offices and many of the chambers. The central part—the King's House—however, escaped, and here the King remained. Rooms for visitors were found at Baynard's Castle, Bridewell, and St. James's (which was built by Henry on the site of St. James's Hospital). Norden, who wrote in the year 1592, says that the old Palace at that time lay in ruins, but that the vaults, cellars, and walls still remaining, showed how extensive had been the buildings in former times.

In converting York House into a Palace Henry added a tennis court, a cockpit, a bowling alley and a tilt yard. He built a gateway after Holbein's designs across the main street; and besides these, according to the Act of Parliament which annexed Whitehall to the Palace of Westminster, he 'most sumptuously and curiously builded and edified many beautiful, costly, and pleasant lodgings.' He laid out the Park, and he began a collection of pictures, which Charles I. afterwards enlarged. James I. designed to erect a new and very costly Palace on the spot. He entrusted the work to Inigo Jones, but the design never got beyond the Banqueting Hall. Had the Palace been completed it would have shown a front of 1152 feet in length from north to south, and 874 feet from east to west.

The plan of the Palace, as it was in the reign of Charles II., exists. It is here reproduced from the Crace collection in the British Museum. It will be seen that the place was much less in area and contained fewer buildings than the Westminster Palace. The chief reason for these diminished proportions was the separation for the first time in English history of the High Courts of Justice from the King's Court, and the change from the army—King Cnut's huscarles—which the kings had always led about with them to a small body-guard. The place is rambling, as we should expect from the manner in which it grew.

THE WATERSIDE ELEVAT

On the south side the Palace began with the Bowling
Green ; next to this was the Privy Garden, a large piece of
ground laid out formally.   The front of the Palace consisted
of the Banqueting Hall, the present Whitehall, the Gate and
Gate Tower, neither stately nor in any way remarkable, and
a row of low gabled houses almost mean in appearance.   The
Gate opened upon a series of three courts or quadrangles.
The first and most important, called ' The Court,' had on its
west side the Banqueting House ; on the south there was a
row of offices or chambers ; on the north a low covered way
connected the Banqueting Hall with the other chambers ; on
the east side was the Great Hall or Presence Chamber, the
Chapel, and the private rooms of the King and Queen.   This
part of the Palace contained what was left of the old York
House.   The second court, that into which the principal gate
opened, was called the ' Courtyard.'   By this court was the

JONES' PALACE

vay to the Audience and Council Chambers, the Chapel, the
offices of the Palace, and the Water Gate. The Art Collections and Library were placed in the 'Stone Gallery,' which
ran along the east side of the Privy Garden. A third court
was called Scotland Yard; in this court was the Guard
House. The old custom of having everything made in the
Palace that could be made, and everything stored under
responsible officers, was continued at Whitehall as it had
been at Westminster. Thus we find cellars, pastry house,
pantry, cyder house, spicery, bakehouse, charcoal house,
scalding house, chandlery, poulterers' house, master glazier's,
confectionery—and the rest, each office with its responsible
officer, and each officer with his own quarters in the Palace.
One long building on the right hand of the picture was the
'Small Beer Buttery.' The length shows its importance; its
situation among the offices indicates for whom it was erected.

Remember that the common sort of Englishman has never at any time used water as a beverage unless there was nothing else to be had ; that as yet he had no tea ; that his habitual beverage was small beer ; and that in all great houses small beer was to be had for the asking in the intervals of work.

Beyond the Banqueting Hall and the Gate House there is a broad street, now Parliament Street, then a portion of the Palace. On the other side, where in King Henry's reign were the Tilt Yard and the Cockpit, are the old Horse Guards and Wallingford House, afterwards the Admiralty. Beyond these buildings is St. James's Park, with fine broad roads, which remain to the present day ; on the left is Rosamond's Pond in its setting of trees, to which reference is constantly made in the literature of the seventeenth century.

At the south end of the open space stood the beautiful gate erected by Holbein. It was removed in 1759.

The appearance of the Palace from the river has been preserved in several views, in none of which do the details all agree. The one produced here is taken from Wilkinson's 'Londina Illustrata,' and shows the Palace in the time of James II. The general aspect of the Palace is that of a great collection of chambers and offices built as they were required, for convenience and comfort, rather than for beauty or picturesqueness. There are no towers, cloisters, gables, or carved work. It is essentially—like St. James's, like Hampton—a palace of brick.

The greater part of Whitehall Palace was destroyed by fire in 1691 and 1697. After the deposition of James II. it ceased to be a royal residence. Then the site of the Palace was gradually built over by private persons. The Banqueting Hall was for a long time a Chapel Royal ; it has now become the house for the collections of the United Service Institute. One could wish that some of the Palace had been preserved : from the marriage of Anne Boleyn to the deposition of James II. is a period which contains a great many events of interest

nd importance, all of which are associated with this Palace.
The destruction of the ancient Faith, the dissolution of the
Religious Houses, the re-birth of Classical learning, the vast
developments of trade, the widening of the world, the begin-
ing of the Empire *outre mer*, the humbling of Spain, the

ST. JAMES'S PALACE

ccessful resistance of the nation against the king, the
rowth of a most glorious literature, the revival of the national
irit,—all these things belong to Whitehall Palace.   Other
emories it had, not so pleasing : the self-will of Henry, the
isery of his elder daughter, the execution of Charles I., the

licentious Court of Charles II.—one wishes that the place had
been spared.

We have copied the plan of the Palace. It is, however,
impossible to fill in the plan with the innumerable offices,
private rooms, galleries and chambers mentioned by one
writer and another. We must be content to know that it
was a vast nest of chambers and offices ; there were hundreds
of them ; the courts were crowded with people ; there was
a common thoroughfare through the middle of the Palace
from Charing Cross to Westminster : so many funerals, for
instance, were conducted along this road to St. Margaret's
that Henry VIII. constructed a new burial-ground at St.
Martin's. The Palace was accessible to all ; the Guard stood

KENSINGTON PALACE

at the gate, but everybody was admitted as to a town ; the
King moved freely about the Courts, in the Mall, in the
Park, sometimes unattended. The people drove their pack-
horses or their waggons up and down the road, and hardly
noticed the swarthy-faced man who stood under the shade
of a tree watching the players along the Mall. This easy
and fearless familiarity vanished with the Stuarts.

Between this Palace and that of Westminster there were
certain important points of difference. One, the absence of the
law courts, has already been noticed. At Whitehall there was
a Guard House ; it stood, as has been said, in Scotland Yard :
no doubt the Gate was guarded ; in 1641 the old ' Horse
Guards' was built for the Gentlemen Pensioners who formed

the Guard ; but there was no wall round the Palace, there was no suggestion of a fortress, there was no suggestion of a camp. Next, the Palace of Westminster was always, as had been intended by Edward the Confessor, connected with the Abbey. It had, to be sure, its own chapel—that of St. Stephen's ; but it was connected by historical associations of every kind with the Abbey. The ringing of the Abbey bells, the rolling of the organ, the chanting of the monks could be heard by day and by night above the music and the minstrelsy, the blare of trumpet and the clash of arms. At Whitehall there was a chapel, but the Abbey was out of hearing. When

BUCKINGHAM PALACE

Henry removed his Palace from Thorney Island to York House, it was a warning or a sign that he would shortly remove himself from the domination of the Church.

As for the Court in the reigns of Elizabeth and James we have full details. The Yeomen of the Guard, who were the body-guard, wore red cloth roses on back and breast. When the Court moved from Whitehall to Greenwich or to Theobalds, a vast quantity of baggage went with it. Three hundred carts were required to carry all that was wanted. What did these carts contain ? Not furniture, cer-

P

tainly. Table-linen, gold and silver plate, wine and stores
of all kinds, tapestry, dresses and bedding, kitchen vessels.
As for furniture, there were as yet no tables such as we now
use, but boards on trestles, which were put up for every meal ;
there were chairs and stools ; there was tapestry on the walls ;
there were beds ; there were cabinets and sideboards ; except
in the Presence Chamber or the Banqueting Hall there were
no carpets. All who write of England at this time speak
with admiration of the chambers strewn with sweet herbs,

THE HORSE GUARDS

the crushing of which by the feet brought out their fragrance ; the nosegays of flowers placed in the bedrooms ; and
the parlours trimmed with vine leaves, green boughs and
fresh herbs. It is a pleasant picture.

Of treasures such as exist at the present day in Buckingham Palace, Windsor and other royal residences, there were
few. Hentzner, a traveller in the year 1598, found a library
in Whitehall well stored with Greek, Latin, Italian and
French books ; he says nothing of English books. They

were all bound in red velvet, with clasps of gold and silver;
some had pearls and precious stones in the bindings. He also

OLD SCOTLAND YARD

found some pictures, including portraits of 'Henry, Richard
and Edward.' There were a few other curious things: a
cabinet of silver, daintily worked, in which the Queen kept

P 2

letter-paper ; a jewel box set with pearls ; toys and curiosities in clockwork. A few years later in 1613, the pictures in Whitehall are enumerated. There were then portraits of Henry VII., Henry VIII., Edward VI., Elizabeth, and Mary Queen of Scots. There were also portraits of French and Spanish kings and queens, and of the great ladies of Court. It is curious to remark that no portrait then existed in Whitehall either of Mary or of Philip. The list includes the portraits in the other palaces. There is not one of Mary.

Let us assist at a royal banquet It is an entertainment offered to Juan Fernandez de Velasco, Duke de Frias, Constable of Castile, on Sunday, August 10th, 1604, in which the King opened his mind without reserve as to peace with Spain. The Audience Chamber was furnished with a buffet of several stages, filled with gold and silver plate. People were freely admitted to look on, but a railing was put up on either side of the room to keep them from crowding or pressing. The table was fifteen feet long and three feet broad. The dishes were brought in by the King's gentlemen and servants, accompanied by the Lord Chamberlain. The Earls of Pembroke and Southampton were gentlemen-ushers The King and Queen, with Prince Henry, entered after the arrival of the Constable and his suite. After washing of hands,—the Lord Treasurer handing the bowl to the King and the Lord High Admiral to the Queen—grace was said, and they took their seats. The King and Queen occupied thrones at the head of the table under a canopy of state on chairs of brocade, with cushions. On the Queen's side sat the Constable on a tabouret of brocade, and on the King's side sat the Prince. The other guests were four gentlemen forming part of the Ambassador's suite. There was also at the table, says the historian, a large company of the principal noblemen in the realm. He enumerates twenty-one, and says there were others. How they were all placed at a table fifteen feet long and three feet broad he does not explain. Perhaps there was a second table. A band of instruments discoursed music during the banquet. The speeches and toasts went on during the course of the dinner. First the King rose, and, taking off his crown, he drank to the health of their Spanish Majesties. Next the Constable drank to the Health of the Queen 'out of the lid of a cup of agate of extraordinary beauty.' He then passed the cup to the King, asking him to drink out of

ROSAMOND'S POND, ST. JAMES'S PARK

it ; and then to the Prince. He then directed that the cup should remain on His Majesty's buffet. At this point the people present shouted out, ' Peace ! peace ! peace ! God save the King ! God save the King ! '

The banquet, thus cheered by compliments, toasts, and the shouts of the onlookers, lasted three hours. At its conclusion, which would be about three o'clock in the afternoon, a singular ceremony took place. ' The table was placed upon the ground, and their Majesties, standing upon it, proceeded to wash their hands.' The King and Queen then retired to their own apartments, while the Spanish guests were taken to the picture gallery. In an hour's time they returned to the Audience Chamber, where dancing had begun.

Fifty ladies-of-honour were present, 'richly dressed and extremely beautiful.' Prince Henry danced a *galliard* ; the Queen, with the Earl of Southampton, danced a *brando* ; the Prince danced another *galliard*—' con algunas cabriolas,' with certain capers ; then another *brando* was performed ; the Queen with the Earl of Southampton, and Prince Henry with another lady of the Court, danced a *correnta*. This ended the ball. They then all took their places at the windows, which looked out upon a court of the Palace. There they had the pleasure of seeing the King's bears fight with greyhounds, and there was very fine baiting of the bull. Then followed tumblers and rope-dancers. With these performances ended the entertainment and the day. The Lord Chamberlain accompanied the Constable to the farthest room ; the Earl of Devonshire and other gentlemen went with them to their coaches, and fifty halberdiers escorted them on their way home with torches. On the morrow, one is pained to read, the Constable had an attack of lumbago.

There are other notes on the Court which one finds in the descriptions of foreign travellers. Thus, the King was served on one knee ; while he drank his cupbearer remained on one knee ; he habitually drank Frontignac, a sweet, rich French wine ; when Queen Elizabeth passed through the street men fell on their knees (this practice seems to have been discontinued at her death) ; servants carried their masters' arms on the left sleeve ; the people, within or without the Court, were noisy and overbearing (all travellers agree on this point) ; they hated foreigners, and laughed at them ; they were magnificent in dress ; they allowed their wives the greatest liberty, and spent all they could afford upon their dresses ; the greatest pleasure the wives of the citizens had was to sit

in their doorways dressed in their best for the passers-by to
admire; they were accustomed to eat a great quantity of
meat; they loved sweet things, pouring honey over mutton
and mixing sugar with their wine; they ardently pursued
bull and bear baiting, hunting, fishing and sport of all kinds;

THE WATER GATE, NEW PALACE YARD

they ate saffron cakes to bring out the flavour of beer; they
spent great sums of money in tobacco, which was then 18*s.* a
pound, equal to more than 6*l.* of our money; their great
highway was the river, which was covered with boats of all
kinds plying up and down the stream, and was also covered
with thousands of swans. The river, indeed, maintained, as

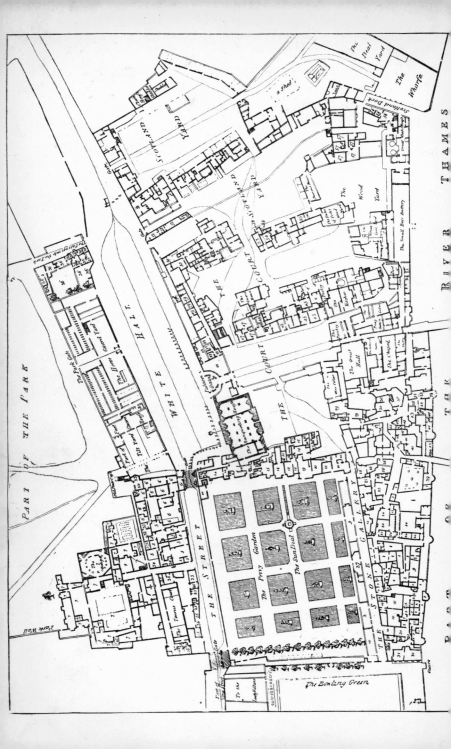

1. Lodgings belonging to his Majesty.
2. To his Royal Highness.
3. His Highness Prince Rupert.
4. The Duke of Richmond.
5. The Duke of Monmouth.
6. The Duke of Ormond.
7. The Duke of Albemarle.
8. The Earl of Bath.
9. The Earl of Lauderdale.
10. The Lord Peterborough.
11. The Lord Gerard.
12. The Lord Crofts.
13. The Lord Belassis.
14. The Lord Chamberlain.
15. The Lord Keeper.
16. The Council Office.
17. Sir Edward Walker.
18. The Treasury Chambers.
19. The King's Laboratory and Bath.
20. The Lord Arlington's Office.
21. Sir Robert Murrey.
22. The Wardrobe.
23. Her Majesty's Apartments.
24. The Maids of Honour.
25. The Countess of Suffolk.
26. The Queen's Wardrobe.
27. Madam Charlotte Killegrew.
28. The Lady Arlington.
29. The Lady Silvis.
30. The Countess of Falmouth.
31. Mrs Kirks.
32. Countess of Castlemaine's Kitchen.
33. Colonel Darcy's.
34. Sir Philip Killigrew.
35. Captain Cook.
36. Mrs. Kirke.
37. Mr. Hyde.
38. Mr. Povey.
39. Mr. Chiffinch.
40. Sir William Killegrew.
41. Sir Francis Clinton.
42. Dr. Frazier.
43. Father Patricks.
44. To Mr. Bryan.
45. Sir Henry Wood.
46. Sir George Carteret.
47. The Officers of ye Jewel Office.
48. The Quarter Waiters.
49. Sir John Trevors.
50. To Mr. Lightfoot.
51. To Mr. Vasse.
52. To Mr. Lis e.
53. Sir Paul Neale.
54. The King's Musick House.
55. To Mr. Early.
56. To Sir Stephen Fox.
57. To Mrs. Churchill.
58. To Mr. Dupper.

* On this spot King Charles I. was beheaded.

watermen, fishermen, lightermen, steve-dores, etc., as many as forty thousand men. When we read of James kissing his favourites—a practice nauseous to the modern Englishman—we must remember that it was then not an uncommon thing, but quite the contrary, for friends to kiss each other. In France and Germany men have always greeted each other with a kiss. On entering a room a visitor kissed all the ladies present. Thus it was reckoned unusual when the Duchess of Richmond (1625) admitted the Duke of Brunswick to Ely House on the proviso that he must not kiss her. He did not, but he kissed all her ladies twice over in a quarter of an hour. And the Constable of Castile, the day before the great banquet, kissed all the Queen's ladies-of-honour. Erasmus remarks that the English have a custom 'never to be sufficiently commended. Wherever you go, you are received with a kiss from all; when you take your leave, you are dismissed with kisses; you return — kisses are repeated; they come to visit you—kisses again.'

Those who read—and trust—the gossiping and scandalous memoirs of the day acquire a very imperfect idea of King James's Court. The physical defects and weaknesses of the King are exaggerated: we are told that his legs were weak, and that he rolled in his gait; the foreign ambassadors, however, speak of him as a man of great strength and strong constitution : we are told that he spoke thickly ; there is nothing said of this defect in the letters written by these visitors. That he lived privately, and went not abroad, as Queen Elizabeth had done, is acknowledged ; that his Court was in any way ridiculous does not appear, except in such a writer as Anthony Welldon. In this place, happily, we have not to consider his foreign or domestic policy, or his lofty ideas on Divine Right ; but only his Court. In the fierce light which beats upon a throne every weakness is made visible and appears out of proportion. We must remember, however, that the blemishes are not visible to him who only occasionally visits the Court, or witnesses a Court function. We, for instance, are only outsiders : we know nothing of the whispers which run round the inner circle. Those who are about the person of the sovereign must experience, one would think, something of degradation when they make the inevitable discovery that the King's most excellent Majesty, whom they have been wont to serve on bended knee, is afflicted, like the meanest of his servants, with human infirmities, and with weaknesses physical and mental. There are, however, two kings : the one as he appears to the outer world, which only sees him at Court functions ; the other as he appears to his servants and those about his person. If one of these servants reveals to the world that the sovereign in hours of privacy was wont to relax from the cares of state in the company of persons little better than buffoons, we may acknowledge that the dignity maintained by the King in public and before the eyes of the world was greater than James could always sustain. He relaxed, therefore, too much in the opposite direction. Why parade the fact ? When one of his servants describes a drunken orgy at the Palace, we remark that James was king for more than twenty years, that there is no mention of any other drunken orgy, and that this deplorable evening was in honour of the Queen's brother, King of Denmark, who probably thought that general excess of wine was part of the

honour paid to him.   When we are told that James was afraid
of a drawn sword, and turned his eyes away when he knighted
a certain person, we remark that this outward and visible sign
of fear is only recorded of him once and by one writer, that
no one else speaks of it, and that there is no proof whatever
that on this occasion he turned his head in sign of fear.   That
he loved hunting excessively is only saying that he joined in
the sports of his time, and that he was always pleased to escape
the cares and fatigues of his place.   That saint whom English
Catholics still revere, Edward the Confessor, was also excessively fond of hunting.   When all this is said we may add
that this King, who loved buffoonery so much, was a good
scholar and a diligent student, a lover of literature and of
scholars, a writer of considerable power, a disputant of no
mean order.   King James wrote the *Doron Basilikon* ; he
wrote a book on Dæmonology (who can expect a king to be
in advance of his age ?) ; he wrote against the use of tobacco ;
he translated many of the Psalms ; he was constantly saying
things witty, unexpected, shrewd and epigrammatic ; he was
as tolerant as could be expected in matters of religion.

Lastly, James made the Court of Whitehall magnificent
during the whole of his reign, by the splendour of the Masques.

When we think of this vanished Palace our thoughts turn
to the Masques, which belong especially to Whitehall,—there
were none at Westminster and none at St. James's.   The
Masque is of the sixteenth and seventeenth centuries.   It was
a play performed on one night only ; not by professional
actors, but by lords and ladies of the Court.   The jewels
worn were real jewels ; the dresses were of velvet and silk,
embroidered with gold and pearls ; the scenery was costly
and elaborate ; the music was new and composed for the
occasion ; the dances were newly invented for that night only ;
the scene-painter and stage manager was the greatest architect
of the day ; the words were written by the poet who, in his
lifetime, was esteemed by many the first of living poets.   The

Masque was a costly, splendid thing—a thing of courtly pomp
—a fit plaything for queen and princess ; a form of drama
perfected by Ben Jonson, not disdained by Milton, put upon
the stage by Inigo Jones.   As for the play itself, the *motif*
was always simple, sometimes allegorical, generally grave ;
the treatment was classical.   The Masques of Ben Jonson
would be wearisome for the length of the speeches and the
slowness of the movement, did we not keep before our eyes
the scenery and the grouping of the figures.   Their tedium in
the reading is also retrieved by the lovely verses and songs
scattered freely over the piece : the acting, the music, the
scenes, the singing, the dancing kept up the life and action
and interest of the piece.   There was an immense amount
of stage management, stage machinery and decorations.
Shakespeare and his actors at the Globe and the Fortune
could neither afford these splendours, nor did they attempt
even a distant imitation of them.   When the King commanded
a play, it was put on the stage with none of the accessories
which belonged to the Masque.   At Whitehall, as at Bankside,
the back of the stage represented a wall, a palace or a castle ;
the hangings—black or blue—showed whether it was night or
day.   But the Masque was not a show for the people : it is
certain that the ' groundlings ' of the Globe would not have
understood the classical allusions with which it was crammed.
At the present day a masque would be only endured as a
spectacle for the picturesque grouping, the beauty of the
actresses, the splendour of the dresses, the perfection of the
dancing, the lovely songs, and the admirable skill and discipline of the company.   When the principal actress was no
other than the Queen herself, who led off a dance, followed
by ladies representing mythological characters perfectly well
understood by a Court of scholars, when the scenery, new
and beautiful, was changed again and again, even though the
fable was no great thing the entertainment was delightful.

    The general care of these and other shows was entrusted

to the Master of Revels. This office is described in an official book compiled by Edmund Tylney, a Master of Revels 1579–1610. He says : ' The office of yᵉ Revels consisteth of a Wardropp and other several Roomes, for Artificers to worke in—viz., Taylors, Imbrotherers, Property-makers, Paynters, Wyer drawers and Carpenters, togeather with a convenient place for yᵉ rehearsals and setting forthe of Playes and other Showes for those Services.'

The first Master of Revels was Sir Thomas Cawerden, appointed in 1546. He was followed by Sir Thomas Benger, Edmund Tylney, Sir George Busk, Sir John Astley, and Sir Henry Herbert. With him the importance of the post ceased ; the office, however, was still continued. It survives —or lingers—in the Licenser of Plays.

So few read Ben Jonson's Masques that I ask no excuse for presenting one. We will take the masque called *The Hue and Cry after Cupid*. It was written as a wedding entertainment.

The scene represented a high, steep red cliff mounting to the sky—a red cliff because the occasion was the wedding of one of the Radcliffs. The cliff was also ' a note of height, greatness, and antiquity.' Before the cliff on the two sides were two pilasters charged with spoils and trophies of Venus and Cupid : hearts transfixed, hearts burning, young men and maidens buried with roses, garlands, arrows, and so forth—all of burnished gold. Over the pillars hovered the figures of Triumph and Victory, twice the size of life, completing the arch and holding a garland of myrtle for the key.

Beyond the cliff, cloud and obscurity.

Then music began ; the clouds vanished ; two doves followed by two swans drew forth a triumphant chariot, in which sat Venus crowned with her star, and beneath her the three Graces, ' all attired according to their antique figures '— which is obscure and doubtful.

Venus descends from the chariot, and is followed by the Graces :

" It is no common cause, you will conceive,
　My lovely Graces, makes your goddess leave
　Her state in Heaven to-night, to visit earth.
　Love late is fled away, my eldest birth,
　Cupid, whom I did joy to call my son ;
　And whom long absent, Venus is undone.
　Spy, if you can, his footsteps on the green ;
　For here, as I am told, he late hath been.

　　　　·　　　·　　　·　　　·　　　·

　Find ye no track of his stray'd feet ?
1st. G. Not I.
2nd G.　　　Not I.
3rd G.　　　　　　Not I.
Venus. Stay, nymphs ; we then will try
　A nearer way.　Look all these ladies' eyes,
　And see if there he not concealèd lies.
　Perchance he hath some simple heart to hide
　His subtle shape in. . .

　　　·　　　·　　　·　　　·

　Begin, soft Graces, and proclaim reward
　To her that brings him in.　Speak to be heard."

Then the Graces begin, and one after the other for nine
verses sing the ' Hue and Cry for Cupid ' :—

" 1st G. Beauties, have ye seen this toy
　　Callèd Love, a little boy,
　　Almost naked, wanton, blind ;
　　Cruel now, and then as kind ?
　　If he be amongst ye, say ?
　　He is Venus' runaway.

　　　·　　　·　　　·　　　·

2nd G. Trust him not ; his words, though sweet,
　　Seldom with his heart do meet.
　　All his practice is deceit ;
　　Any gift it is a bait ;
　　Not a kiss but poison bears,
　　And most treason in his tears.

　　　·　　　·　　　·　　　·

1st G. If by these ye please to know him,
　　Beauties, be not nice, but show him.

> *2nd G.* Though ye had a will to hide him,
>   Now, we hope, ye'll not abide him.
> *3rd G.* Since you hear his falser play,
>   And that he's Venus' runaway."

After this Cupid himself comes running out from behind
the trophies : he is armed ; he is followed by twelve boys
most antickly ' attired, representing the Sports and pretty
Lightnesses that accompany Love under the titles of *Joci*
and *Risus*.

> "*Cupid.* Come, my little jocund sports,
>   Come away ; the time now sorts
>   With your pastime ; this same night
>   Is Cupid's day. Advance your light,
>   With your revel fill the room,
>   That our triumphs be not dumb."

Then the boys ' fall into a subtle, capricious ' dance, bearing
torches with ridiculous gestures. Venus all the time stands
on one side, the Graces grouped around her. Can we realise
what a pretty picture this would make ? When the dance is
over, Venus and her maidens surround Cupid and apprehend
him. What has he been doing ?—

> " Have you shot Minerva or the Thespian dames ?
>   Heat agèd Ops again with youthful flames ?
>   Or have you made the colder Moon to visit,
>   Once more, a sheepcote ? Say what conquest is it
>   Can make you hope such a renown to win ?
>   Is there a second Hercules brought to spin ?
>   Or, for some new disguise, leaves Jove his thunder ? "

At this point Hymen entered, and the manner of his entry
was thus. He wore a saffron-coloured robe, his under-vesture
white, his socks yellow, a yellow veil of silk on his left arm,
his head crowned with roses and marjoram, in his right hand
a torch of pine tree. After him came a youth in white,
bearing another torch of white thorn ; behind him two others
in white, the one bearing a distaff and the other a spindle.
Then followed the Auspices, those who ' handfasted ' the pair

and wished them luck —*i.e.*, prayed for them. Tnen one whc
bore water and another who bore fire ; and lastly musicians.
Cupid at sight of Hymen breaks off—

> " Hymen's presence bids away ;
> 'Tis already at his night :
> He can give you further light.
> You, my Sports, may here abide,
> Till I call to light the bride."

Hymen addresses Venus, paying the most charming
compliments to King James under the name of Æneas. He
tells her that he is come to grace the marriage of a noble
virgin styled the Maid of the Redcliffe, and that Vulcan witl
the Cyclopes are at that moment forging something strange
and curious to grace the nuptials ; and indeed, at tha
moment Vulcan himself, dressed like the blacksmith that he
is, comes upon the stage.   He has completed the work :

> "Cleave, solid rock, and bring the wonder forth ! "

Then, with a burst of music, the cliff falls open and disclose
'an illustrious concave filled with an ample and glistering
light in which an artificial sphere was made of silver, eighteen
feet in diameter, that turned perpetually ; the *coluri* were
heightened with gold ; so were the arctic and the antarctic
circles, the tropics, the equinoctial, the meridian and horizon
only the zodiac was of pure gold, in which the masquer
under the characters of the twelve signs were placed
answering them in number.'

This is the description.   The system of the Zodiac seem
a strange thing to present as part of a wedding entertainment
but such a thing was not then part of school work, and when
Vulcan called out at the masquers, Aries the Ram, Tauru
the Bull, Gemini the Twins, and the rest, explaining how
they apply to the conjugal condition, no doubt there wa
much delight.   This done, Venus, Vulcan, Hymen and thei
trains sat or stood while the masquers, assisted by th

Cyclopes, alternately sang and danced. There are seven verses to the song, and there were four dances. The dances were invented by Master Thomas Giles and Master Hieronymus Herne; the tunes were composed by Master Alphonso Ferrabosco; the scenes by Master Inigo Jones; and the verse, with the invention of the whole, by Ben Jonson himself. 'The attire,' says the poet, 'of the masquers throughout was most graceful and noble; partaking of the best both ancient and later figure. The colours, carnation and silver, enriched with embroidery and lace. The dressing of their heads, feathers and jewels.' The names of the masquers were the Duke of Lenox, the Earls of Arundell, Pembroke, and Montgomery, Lords D'Aubigny, Walden, Hay and Sankre, Sir Robert Rothe, Sir Joseph Kennethir, and Master Erskine. Here are two of the verses :—

"What joy or honours can compare
  With holy nuptials when they are
      Made out of equal parts
  Of years, of states, of hands, of hearts !
      When in the happy choice
  The spouse and spousèd have the foremost vice !
      Such, glad of Hymen's war,
        Live what they are
      And long perfection see :
        And such ours be—
  Shine, Hesperus, shine forth, thou wishèd star !

"Love's common wealth consists of toys :
  His council are those antic boys.
      Games, laughter, sports, delights,
  That triumph with him on these nights,
      To whom we must give way,
  For now their reign begins and lasts till day.
      They sweeten Hymen's war,
        And, in that jar,
      Make all, that married be,
        Perfection see.
  Shine, Hesperus, shine forth, thou wishèd star !"

The Masque was short-lived. It was stately and dignified ; it was courtly ; it was classical ; it was serious : nobody
laughed much, except perhaps at the 'antic' dances which
were sometimes introduced. It required fine if not the finest
poetic work. It could not be adequately presented without
lavish expenditure. It demanded the performance of
amateurs. When the troubles of the next reign began there
was little desire for such entertainments, and no money to
spare for the production of a Masque on the old scale of
splendour. When Charles II. returned all the world wanted
to laugh and to sing ; the Masque, slow and stately, was out
of fashion. Charles made an attempt to revive it, but
without success. It was quite forgotten : the old properties
were stowed away and mouldered in the cellars till the Fire
came and burned them all. And the stage effects, the sudden
changes of scene, the clouds and the rocks and streams were
all forgotten, until they were revived in the present century.

There are many memories of Whitehall on which we
might enlarge : scenes in the later life of Henry VIII. ;
scenes in the Court of Queen Mary ; tilts, feasts and entertainments by Queen Elizabeth ; the death of Charles ; the occupation by Cromwell ; the mistresses of Charles the Deplorable—
with a great many more. These, however, belong to the things
already narrated. I have endeavoured to recall certain associations which have hitherto belonged to the book of the things
left out ; and among them there are none so pleasing and so
characteristic as the Masque in the reign of James I.

Now there is nothing left of Elizabeth's Palace at all ; of
Charles's Palace, only the latest and last construction, the
Banqueting Hall. When the fires of 1691 and 1697 swept
all away except this building, there perished a collection of
courts and houses for the most part dingy, without the
picturesque appearance of the old Palace, which, if it was
crowded and huddled together, was full of lovely mediæval
towers, gables, and carved work. Whitehall as a building

was without dignity and without nobility. Yet one wishes that it had remained to the present day. Hampton Court, as I have said above, remains to show the world what Whitehall Palace was like.

William III. talked of rebuilding the place ; but he died. Queen Anne took up her residence in St. James's. And Whitehall Palace vanished.

CHAPTER IX

THE CITY

THE Houses of Parliament,—their history, their buildings, their constitution—belong to the history of the Empire. They happen to stand in the City of Westminster ; but their history does not form part of the City history. The House of Commons has been called to Westminster almost without interruption for six hundred years. It sat for three hundred years in the Chapter House of the Abbey ; then for three hundred years more in the Chapel of St. Stephen ; when that was burned down the site was preserved and set apart for the New House which arose when the ashes of the old had been cleared away. That site must not be considered a part of Westminster ; it is part of the Island—part of the Empire.

In a certain special sense, however, the House of Commons did belong to the City of Westminster for a long time. A great many of the country members lodged in the narrow streets round the Abbey. The reason is plain : there were no streets or houses in the meadows lying north and west of the Houses of Parliament ; either the members must lodge in the City of London and take boat for St. Stephen's, or they must lodge in Westminster itself. It is stated by a writer of the last century that the principal means of support for the people of Westminster were the lodging and the entertainment of the members. The monks were gone ; Sanctuary was gone ; the Court was gone ; but the members remained, and so the taverns remained too, and the ancient reputation of Westminster as a thirsty city was happily uninjured.

In another way Westminster created for itself a new distinction. As a borough it became notorious for the turbulence and the violence of the elections. Its central position, the King's House always lying within its boundaries, the City of London its near neighbour, naturally caused an election at Westminster to attract more attention than an election at Oxford, say, or Winchester. Again, the electors of West-

THE HOUSE OF COMMONS AND WESTMINSTER HALL FROM THE RIVER IN 1798 (FROM A CONTEMPORARY DRAWING)

minster were not, probably, fiercer partisans than those of any other place, nor were their candidates always of greater importance ; yet it is certain that for downright bludgeon rowdiness and riot, the rabble at Westminster, when it turned out at election time, was equalled by few towns and surpassed by none.

Let us observe one point, which is instructive : the rabble had no votes ; the butchers, those patriotic thinkers, who paraded the streets with clubs to the music of marrow-bones and cleavers ; the chairmen, equal patriots of opposite convictions, who marched to the Way of War and the breaking of

heads with their poles—formidable as pike or spear ; the
jolly sailors, convinced as to the foundations of order, who
came along with bludgeons, thirsting for the display of their
political principles,—none of these brave fellows had any
vote. Yet the share they took, the part they played, the
influence they exercised in every election, cannot be disputed.
The vote, you see, about which nowadays we make such a
fuss, is by no means everything : in those days one stout
fellow with a cudgel at the bottom of the steps of the hustings
might be worth to his party fifty votes a day : he might represent as many voters sent home discouraged, or even persuaded
by a broken head, to a radical change of political principles.

   In the year 1710, Swift says that the rabble surrounded
his coach, and he was afraid of having dead cats thrown in at
the window, or getting his glass broken. The part played by
the dead cat in all eighteenth-century functions, elections,
pillories, and outdoor speeches, was quite remarkable. In
times of peace and quiet we hear of no dead cats. The streets
did not then, and do not now, provide a supply of dead cats
to meet all demands. It would seem as if all the cats of all
the slums were slaughtered for the occasion. Throughout
the last century the elections of Westminster became more
and more riotous ; there were riots and ructions in 1711 and
in 1721 ; in 1741 these were quite surpassed by the contested
election in which Lord Sundon and Sir Charles Wager were
candidates on the one side—the Court side—and Admiral
Vernon and Mr. Charles Edwin on the other. Lord Sundon,
a newly created Irish peer, took upon himself to close the
poll by the help of a detachment of Guards before it was
finished. One vote an hour was supposed to keep the poll
open. The returning officer, however, disregarding this con-
vention, and by Lord Sundon's order, declared the poll closed
and Lord Sundon with Sir Charles Wager duly elected.
There was indignation, there was a question, which led to a
debate in the House ; and finally the election was declared

illegal. The victory thus obtained by the populace against the Court party was celebrated long afterwards by an annual dinner of the 'Independent Electors.' It marks the change in our management of these things that there should have been a Court party, and that the Court should think it consistent with its dignity to take an active part in any election.

That the king should openly side with this or that candidate shows that the sovereign a hundred and fifty years ago stood on a much lower level than the sovereign of to-day.

OAK DOORWAY DISCOVERED IN THE SPEAKER'S DINING-ROOM AFTER THE FIRE

The longest and fiercest contest, the one with the most doubtful issues, the most violent of all the Westminster elections, was that of the year 1784. Of this election there was published a most careful record from day to day. I suppose there is no other election on record of which such a daily diary has been preserved. It appeared towards the end of the same year, and was published by Debrett, a Piccadilly bookseller. The anonymous authors, who modestly call themselves 'Lovers of Truth and Justice,' begin the work with a narrative of the events which led to the Dissolution of March 25th, 1784; they then proceed to set down the story of the Westminster election from day to day;

they have reproduced many of the caricatures, rough, coarse, and vigorous, with which Rowlandson illustrated the contest ; they have published all the speeches ; they have collected the whole of the Election literature, with the poems, squibs, epigrams, attacks, and eulogies, which appeared on either side.   Not only is there no other record, so far as I know, of any election so complete as this ; but there has never been any other election, so far as I know, where the fight was fiercer, more determined, more unscrupulous, and of longer duration.   The volume is, I believe, somewhat scarce and difficult to procure.   Its full title is 'The History of the Westminster Election, containing every Material Occurrence, from its Commencement, on the First of April, to the Final Close of the Poll, on 17th of May, to which is Prefixed a Summary Account of the Proceedings of the Late Parliament, so far as they appear Connected with the East India Business and the Dismission of the Portland Administration, with other Select and Interesting Occurrences at the Westminster Meetings, Previous to its Dissolution on the 25th Day of March 1784.'

This long title-page promises no more than the volume performs.   It is proposed, therefore, to reproduce in these pages, with the assistance of the 'Lovers of Truth and Justice,' the history of an election as it was conducted a hundred years ago.

The Dissolution of March 1784, and the causes which led to it, belong to the history of the country and to the life of Charles James Fox.   Let us accept the fact that a General Election was held in April ; that the candidates for Westminster were Admiral Lord Hood and Sir Cecil Wray on the Ministerial side, and Fox for the Opposition.   The former was also the Court side : the candidates on that side were called the King's friends ; the King himself took the keenest interest in the daily progress of the poll ; he peremptorily ordered all the Court servants, the Court tradesmen and the

Court dependents to vote for Hood and Wray ; and he actually sent a body of two hundred and eighty Guards to vote on that side. No king, in fact, ever interfered with an election more openly, more actively, or with less dignity. The

THE HOUSE OF LORDS AT THE BEGINNING
OF THE CENTURY

struggle, remember, of King *v.* Commons was not completed when William of Orange succeeded James. The lesson taught by the struggle of the seventeenth century was most imperfectly grasped by King George III. On the other hand, the Prince of Wales, with the filial loyalty which characterised him as well as his grandfather, used all his influence on the side of Fox.

The temper of the City of Westminster, and the certain prospect of a stormy time, was shown two months before the Dissolution, when a document purporting to be a humble address to the King from the Dean, the High Steward and the Burgesses assembled at the Guildhall, Westminster, was passed about for signature. It was accepted for what it pretended to be, and was signed by 2,800 people, among whom were a great many electors. Lastly, it was presented by Sir Cecil Wray, one of the members, as from the Dean and High Steward.

A few days later, a meeting of the electors was called at the Shakespeare Tavern, Covent Garden, at which this document was very severely handled. It was affirmed that the Dean and the High Steward actually knew nothing of the address, and that their names had been most improperly affixed without their sanction. This was the beginning of a great cataract of lies. Whether the names had been used with or without sanction, mattered little : the allegation presented an excuse for a resolution of confidence in Fox which was passed with acclamation.

On February 10th another meeting, with Sir Cecil Wray in the chair, adopted an address to his Majesty expressing confidence in the Ministry. This meeting was, of course, described by one side as 'very numerous and most respectable,' and by the other as exactly the reverse : ' Never was there, perhaps in the annals of all the meetings ever held in England, so motley a group, so noisy an assembly, or one less respectable for its company.'

Then followed handbills for distribution. The struggle, it must be remembered, was one which could hardly occur in these days : it was, in fact, nothing short of a declaration of confidence in the King or the opposite—for or against secret influence—for or against Court direction, and the extension of prerogative. Here is a specimen of what was written at the outset :—

' Of all the features which mark the political character of the English nation the most striking and remarkable is a perpetual jealousy of prerogative. . . . Ask an Englishman

THE HOUSE OF COMMONS AT THE BEGINNING OF THE CENTURY

what sort of Judge, Crown Lawyer, or Minister, he most dreads : his uniform answer is a *prerogative* Judge, a *prerogative* Lawyer, a *prerogative* Minister. Is then a *prerogative* King of so little danger to us that we are all at once to forget these jealousies, which seem to have been twisted with our existence, and to fall into a miraculous fondness for that prerogative which our ancestors have shed their dearest blood to check and limit ?   Let the people of England once confederate with the Crown and the Lords in *such* a conflict, and who is the man that will answer for one hour of legal liberty afterwards ?

'Can the people confide in His Majesty's secret advisers ? I say NO.   And I demand one instance, in the twenty-three years of this wretched reign, when a regard to the liberty of the people can be traced in any measure to the *secret system.*'

This document, which went on in a similar strain to a great length, was handed about from house to house : no doubt a copy was given to the King.

A general meeting of all the electors was called on March 14th, in Westminster Hall.   This assemblage proved everything that could be desired ; the hall was completely packed with an uproarious mob, chiefly on the King's side ; the hustings were made a battlefield for the possession of the chair, which was pulled to pieces in the struggle ; then the hustings broke down, and a good many on either side were trampled upon and injured. Nobody could be heard ; when it was understood that the meeting was asked to express an opinion on the Address to the King, nearly all the hands went up : Fox tried to speak ; a bag of assafœtida was thrown in his face ; his friends carried him out on their shoulders ; finally he addressed the crowd from the bow-window of the King's Head Tavern, in Palace Yard.   After the speech they took the horses from his carriage and dragged him all the way to Devonshire House, in Piccadilly, with shouts and cheers.

A so-called report of the meeting was then drawn up by Fox's friends, stating that the chair had been taken by Fox and that a new Address to the King had been unanimously adopted.   At the outset, therefore, neither side was in the least degree desirous to present the bald, bare, cold, unsatisfying truth.

On March 19th the Friends of Liberty held a great banquet

at Willis's Rooms.   They numbered five hundred ; the dinner
was fixed for half-past five, but such was the ardour of the

THE ENTRANCE TO SPEAKER'S YARD AS IT APPEARED BEFORE THE FIRE

company, so great their determination to do justice to the feast, that they began to assemble at half-past three.

It is pleasant to read of civic and electioneering banquets —to see pictures of the patriots enjoying some of the rewards of virtue. The dinner was spread on six tables ; and, in order to prevent confusion, everything was put on the table at once, so that when the covers—if there were any covers— were removed, the company ' saw their dinner.' Then friends and neighbours helped each other with loving zeal from the dishes before them ; the waiters looked to the bottles, while the guests handed the plates to each other. Only to think of this dinner makes one hear the clatter of knives and forks, the buzz of talk—serious talk, because the average elector of Westminster in 1784 was not a person who laughed much— indeed, one imagines that, after the humiliations and disgraces of the American war, there could be very little laughter left in the country at all, even among the young and the light- hearted. Music there was, however—music to uplift the hearts of the despondent—violins and a 'cello, with perhaps flutes and horns. Singing there was, also, after dinner. During the banquet there was not much drinking : it would be sinful, with the whole night before one, to destroy a generous thirst at the outset. Men of that age were very powerful performers at the table ; we neither eat nor drink with the noble, copious and indiscriminate voracity of our ancestors : without any scientific observance of order these Friends of Liberty tackled all that stood before them—beef and mutton, fish and apple pie, turkey, tongue, ham, chicken, soup and jelly—' plentifully dispersed and fashionably set out.' Faces grew shiny with long-continued exercise ; those who wore wigs pushed them back, those who wore powder found it slipping from their hair on their shoulders ; bones—the suc- culent bones of duck and chicken—were freely gnawed and sucked, as was still the custom even in circles much higher than that which these Friends of Liberty adorned.

At last the dishes were removed, and the business of the evening, with the drinking, began. It is not stated, unfortunately, whether the Friends of Liberty drank port or punch. Contemporary pictures incline one to favour the theory of punch.

We of too degenerate age are wont to complain of the after-dinner speech. Which of us could now sit out the speeches and the toasts at this banquet, and survive? Even the speaker would recoil in terror at the prospect of such a night.

They did not drink the health of the King. His name was purposely omitted —a thing astonishing to us, who cannot remember personal hostility to the sovereign. Fox, who was in the chair, began with the 'Independent Electors of the City of Westminster'; he followed with 'The Majesty of the People of England,' 'The Cause of Freedom all over the World,' 'The Glorious and Immortal Memory of King William the Third.' Twenty-seven toasts are enumerated at length, with the ominous words at the end, 'Several other toasts were given.' Songs were sung by Captain Morris of Anacreontic fame, Mr. Bannister, and others of the tuneful choir.

'THEMISTOCLES' (LORD HOOD), FROM 'THE RIVAL CANDIDATES.'

In the midst of this growing excitement it was learned that the Great Seal of England, which was in the custody of the Lord Chancellor, had been stolen. Men looked at each other in amazement and dismay. What did this thing portend? Who had caused it to be done? What did it mean? Was it ordered by the King, or by Pitt, or by Fox? What deep-laid plot did the

burglary conceal? Nobody could tell. The King, rising to
the occasion, ordered a new seal to be made without delay.
The robbery, which had no political significance, was forgotten,
and the mind of the public returned to the General Election.

On March 25th the House of Commons was dissolved,
and the candidates made haste to issue their addresses to the

'DEMOSTHENES' (CHARLES JAMES FOX), FROM 'THE RIVAL CANDIDATES'

'Worthy and Independent Electors of the City of Westminster.' The Committee of Hood and Wray met at Wood's
Hotel, and that of Fox at the Shakespeare Tavern, both in
Covent Garden. The Westminster hustings were at that
time put up in front of St. Paul's, Covent Garden. If I
remember aright, the hustings of the election of 1868 were
erected in Trafalgar Square; and I think they were the last.

Then, pending the opening of the poll, the merry game of
abuse and misrepresentation began, and was carried on with the
greatest vigour on both sides. Against Hood nothing at all
could be alleged by the most rancorous opponent : he was an
Irish peer, newly created, and a victorious admiral. Against
Sir Cecil Wray, however, there were two
or three unfortunate circumstances.

Thus, he had been put into his seat by
the recommendation and influence of Fox,
whom he now deserted. Of course, therefore, he was Judas, Judas Iscariot, Traitor,
Monster of Ingratitude. That was the
first charge : in default of anything else it
was a good solid charge, to which his enemies could always return. Plain ingratitude, however, has always failed to command popular indignation. What can one
expect ? What does everybody's experience teach ? ' Gratitude, sir,' says the dis-
appointed man of Virtue, ' no one expects ;
but . . .' I do not suppose that the charge
of ingratitude lost Sir Cecil Wray one
single vote, any more than unexpected
inconsistency or a sudden change of
front or a sudden change of principle in
these days affects the seat of a modern
politician. The electors, therefore, heard
with unmoved faces that Sir Cecil was
worse than Judas Iscariot as regards

'JUDAS ISCARIOT' (SIR
CECIL WRAY), FROM
'THE RIVAL CANDI-
DATES'

treachery and ingratitude : what had the Election to do with
private gratitude ? They therefore proceeded to vote for him.

There was, however, another weapon—and one far more
effective. He had once called the attention of the House to
the lavish expenditure of Chelsea Hospital, which maintained
the old soldiers of the country at an annual cost of 51*l.* apiece.

R

And on that occasion he declared that, rather than continue this prodigality, he would like to see the abolition of the Hospital! The abolition of Chelsea Hospital! And Chelsea Hospital was in Westminster Borough! And that a Westminster member should say this monstrous thing! And, after he had said it, should dare to become a candidate again!

'THE WESTMINSTER MENDICANT' (SIR CECIL WRAY)

Here, indeed, seemed a chance for the other side! Would the electors—the patriotic, enlightened electors of Westminster—return one who would actually abolish, because it cost a little money, the old soldiers' hospital?

And there was a third weapon. Sir Cecil Wray had even proposed a tax on housemaids! Horrible! Wicked! This Monster would actually drive out of their places all the housemaids in the country! What would become of these poor girls? What would they do? Must they be thrown, weeping and reluctant, into the arms of Vice? Eloquence was exhausted, tears were shed, wrath was aroused by the mere description of what would have happened to these poor girls had this tax been passed. In vain did Sir Cecil explain away his words. There they were! In vain did he say that it would be cheaper and better to give every man a pension of twenty pounds a year, with permission to live where he wished : he had wounded the popular sentiment—he said he would willingly abolish Chelsea Hospital. As regards the housemaids, it was quite useless to explain that the master would pay the tax, not the maid : the average elector did not want to pay any more taxes ; rather than pay this tax he would go without his maidservant—then what was the poor girl to do? With such excellent weapons as these, the caricaturist, the lampooner, the writer of squibs and the poet were amply provided.

First, by way of catechism : —

"Who, in his advertisement, professes to be the protector of the fair sex ?

Sir Cecil Wray.

Who proposed a tax on the poorest of the fair sex ?

Sir Cecil Wray.

Who calls himself a soldier and a man of humanity ?

Sir Cecil Wray.

Who proposed to pull down Chelsea Hospital?

Sir Cecil Wray.

Who has forfeited the good opinion of every man of honour, humanity, and consistency?

Sir Cecil Wray."

Next, which is always a sure method of creating a laugh, and is moreover very easy to manage, a leaflet in the Biblical style :—

"And it came to pass that there were dissensions amongst the rulers of the nation.

And the Counsellors of the Back Stairs said, ' Let us take advantage, and yoke the people, even as oxen and rule them with a rod of iron.

' And let us break up the Assembly of Privileges, and get a new one of Prerogatives, and let us hire false prophets to deceive the people.' And they did so.

Then Judas Iscariot went among the citizens, saying, ' Choose me one of your elders, and I will tax your innocent damsels, and I will take their bread from the helpless, lame and blind,' " etc., etc., etc.

Or by way of posters, as the following :—

To be sold by Auction

By

JUDAS ISCARIOT,

At the Prerogative Arms, Westminster,

CHELSEA HOSPITAL,

With all the live and dead Stock,

In which is included the Cloaks, Crutches, Fire Arms, etc., of the poor worn-out Veterans, who have bled in their Country's Cause, their existence being declared a Public Nuisance.

Likewise the Virtue, Innocence, and Modesty of the harmless, inoffensive Servant Maids.

The Sale of this last lot was intended by Judas for the purpose of raising the supplies for the Tax on Maid Servants.

JUDAS ISCARIOT

is extremely sorry he cannot put up for Sale

PUBLIC INGRATITUDE,

Having Reserved that Article for Himself.

N.B.—To be disposed of, A large Quantity of Patent Dark Lanterns, and the best Price will be given for a set of Fellows who will go through thick and thin for a rotten back staircase.

Huzza for Prerogative ! A Fig for the Constitution !

It was then discovered — or alleged, which came to the same thing—that Sir Cecil had married his own housemaid.

The following not very brilliant epigram is written 'on Sir Cecil proposing a tax on Maid Servants after having married his own':—

> When Cecil first the plan laid down,
>   Poor servant girls to curse,
> He looked at home, and took his own
>   For better and for worse.

The Chelsea business provoked a more worthy effusion :—

> And will you turn us out of doors,
>   In age, to want a prey—
> When cold winds blow and tempest roars?
>   Oh ! Hard Sir Cecil Wray !
>
> This house our haven is, and port
>   After a stormy sea :
> Then shall it be cast down in sport,
>   By hard Sir Cecil Wray ?
>
> 'Twill break our heart these scenes to leave,
>   But soldiers must obey ;
> Yet in my conscience I believe
>   You're mad, Sir Cecil Wray.
>
> For who will see us poor and lame,
>   Exposed on the highway,
> And not with curses load the name
>   Of thee, Sir Cecil Wray ?
>
> These walls can talk of Minden's plain,
>   Of England's proudest day :
> I think I hear these walls complain
>   Of thee, Sir Cecil Wray.
>
> If thou art bent the poor to harm,
>   Attack the young and gay :
> Girls both in health and beauty warm,—
>   But we are old, Sir Wray.

But Sir Cecil Wray had once published a volume of poems. Perhaps the cruelest stroke of all—if the poor man had the sensitive nature of most poets—must have been certain parodies of these verses. Here are some. The notes are, of course, part of the parody.

On Celia killing a Flea

Thou great epitome of little death, all hail !
How blest thy fate beneath my Celia's lovely nail !
No more thou'lt skip from sheet to sheet alive and well,
The furious nail and finger toll'd thy passing bell.

N.B.—The allusion to the noise made by the animal's sudden death is beautifully descriptive of a passing bell.

On a Black Sow with a Litter of Thirteen Pigs

To the head of that sow, what a back, chine,[1] and tail ![2]
Here, John, bring to Porkey[3] some milk and some meal.
Desire your mistress and Patty[4] my cousin
Come look at the mother and her baker's dozen.[5]

How sweet is the smell of the straw in her stye ![6]
It's a mixture of oaten, and wheaten, and rye.
What an eye has this fat little creature, indeed !
But no wonder at that, 'tis the true Chinese Breed.[7]

.   .   .   .

The thirteenth my dear wife has told me she means
To dress here at home, with sage[8] chopped in the brains :
And the belly,[9] she says, shall be stuffed with sweet things
With prunes and with currants—a Dish fit for Kings :
And egg sauce[10] we will have, and potatoes,[11] and butter,
And will eat till neither one word more can we utter.

[1] The chine is always considered the nicest part of the pork, either roasted or boiled, and is monstrous fine eating when the Norfolk Turkies are in season.

[2] The tail of a little roasted pig is a nice morsel.

[3] Porkey was the Sow's name.

[4] Patty is an abbreviation of the Christian name Martha. Patty contains five letters—Martha has six.   [5] A baker's dozen is thirteen.

[6] Stye is the name of a place where hogs, pigs, and sows are usually kept.

[7] China is a great place in the Eastern world, where I have never been in. But I have cups and saucers, and tea, and a mandarin, and two fire screens that were actually made there.

[8] Sage chopped in the brains is very common, and if the little tongue is put among them, it makes the dish better.

[9] The place which contains the entrails, and when stuffed with sweet things is delicious.   [10] Egg sauce is common in Ireland with pigs.

[11] Potatoes—a vegetable something like a turnip, but more like an apple. They are sold in Covent Garden, and the Irish are fond of them.

The Election took place during the time of dismal
depression following the humiliation of the American War.
There was one branch of the service, and only one, which the
country could regard with pride or even satisfaction. This
was the Navy ; and of all the brave men who, in that
disastrous war, endeavoured to uphold the honour of the
British flag, Lord Hood was the popular favourite. He was
at this time in his fiftieth year, and in the middle of his

'PROCESSION TO THE HUSTINGS AFTER A SUCCESSFUL CANVASS'
(AFTER A PRINT, A.D. 1784)

career. It is evident, from the silence with which the writers
on the other side treated him, that it was not considered safe
to attack him. Even the malignity of electioneering warfare
was compelled to spare the name of Hood. He was returned,
of course, and he continued to represent Westminster until
the long war begun in 1793.

As regards Sir Cecil Wray, the attacks made upon him,
of which we have seen some, were villainous enough to meet

the case of the greatest monster or the most brazen turn-coat :
they were also powerless, for the simple reason that the real
foundation for attack was so extremely weak.   One can
already perceive, behind this onslaught of combined bludgeon
and rapier, a harmless man of blameless private character ;
cultivated ; probably rather weak ; who was ill-advised when
he opposed his old friend Fox, and when he brought forward
Hood, a man enormously superior to himself.   That he
obtained so many votes and nearly defeated his opponent
was due to the influence of the Court.

As for Fox, he was at this time forty-five years of age,
and in the midst of his unbounded activity.   At the age of
nineteen he was returned for Midhurst.   Before the age of
twenty-five he had become a power in the House of Commons ;
he had run racehorses ;   he was a notorious gambler ;   and
had incurred debts to the total of 240,000*l.* ;   he was regarded
as an enemy of the King and a friend of the people.   We
shall see what the other side could rake up against him.

First there were questions suggested—' Did you not ' say,
or do this or that ?—abuse Lord North and then join him—
promise great things and perform nothing—buy up all the
usual scribblers in the City—cringe to the electors ?   Then
there were sarcastic reasons why Fox should be supported :
the admirable economy with which he conducted his own
affairs—his general consistency—his great landed estates—
his hatred of gambling.

Another set of questions insinuated that he was a private
friend of one Tyrle, executed for high treason in sending
information to France.   Virtuous indignation, of course, and
not political expediency, compelled the plain and honest
' Father ' to ask whether the electors would vote for the ' high
priest of drunkenness, gaming, and every species of de-
bauchery that can contaminate the principles we should wish
to inculcate in our offspring.'

They called him Carlo Khan, and Cogdie Shufflecard

Reynardine, and they made the most infamous attacks on the Duchess of Devonshire and the other ladies who canvassed for him. Most of them are not to be quoted : the following extracts are the most decent :—

> Hail, Duchess, first of womankind !
> Far, far you leave your sex behind ;
>   With you none can compare :
> For who but you, from street to street,
> Would run about, a vote to get,
>   Thrice, thrice bewitching fair !
>
> Each day you visit every shop,
> Into the house your head you pop,
>   Nor do you act the prude :
> For every man salutes your Grace ;
> Some kiss your hand and some your face,
>   And some are rather rude.
>
> The girl condemned to walk the streets
> And pick each blackguard up she meets,
>   And get him in her clutches,
> Has lost her trade ; for they despise
> Her wanton airs, her leering eyes,
>   Now they can kiss a Duchess !

The following lyrics are the commencement of a short satiric poem, compelled, like the remonstrance of the ' Father,' by the indignant heart of the poet :—

> See modest Duchesses, no longer nice,
> In Virtue's honour haunt the sinks of Vice :
> In Freedom's cause the guilty bribe convey,
> And perjured wretches piously betray.

In a lighter strain the following :—

> Her mien like Cytherea's dove,
>   Her lips like Hybla's honey :
> Who would not give a vote for love,
>   Unless he wanted money ?
>
> Alas ! To reputation blind !
>   I wonder some folks bore it :
> You've lost your fame, and those that find
>   Can ne'er again restore it.

On the other side there was one capable of putting the Duchess in a more amiable light :—

> Arrayed in matchless beauty, Devon's fair,
> In Fox's favour takes a zealous part :
> But, oh ! where'er the pilferer comes, beware—
> She supplicates a vote and steals a heart.

All the ladies were not on the side of Fox : Lady Buckinghamshire came into the field for Hood and Wray. Unfortunately she was inferior to the Duchess in personal charms, and the friends of Fox, one regrets to say, had the bad taste to call her Madame Blubber. They made at least one song about her, of which one can quote the first two stanzas :—

> A certain lady I won't name
>   Must take an active part, sir,
> To show that Devon's beauteous dame
>   Should not engage each heart, sir.
> She canvassed all—both great and small,
>   And thundered at each door, sir ;
> She rummaged every shop and stall,
>   The Duchess was still before, sir.
>
> Sam Marrowbones had shut his shop,
>   And just had lit his pipe, sir,
> When in the lady needs must pop,
>   Exceeding plump and ripe, sir.
> 'Gad zounds !' said he, 'how late you be !
>   For votes you come to bore me,—
> But let us feel, are you beef or veal?
>   The Duchess has been before ye.'

On Thursday, April 1st, the polling began. The hustings were put up in Covent Garden, and at eleven a.m. the candidates appeared before an enormous mob. Fox's address was drowned in clamours and shouts and curses, and by the delectable music of marrowbones and cleavers. The show of hands was declared in favour of Hood and Wray : a poll was demanded, and was opened immediately.

The polling went on, day after day, for more than six
weeks. It was not until Monday, May 17th, that it was finally
closed. During the whole of that time Westminster was the
scene of continual fighting, feasting and drinking. Lord
Hood, about whose return there seems to have been no doubt

THE SPEAKER'S COURT AS IT APPEARED BEFORE THE FIRE

from the beginning, thought it necessary to protect his voters
by a body of sailors brought from Wapping. These gallant
fellows were stationed in front of the hustings, displaying the
King's colours, and actually commanded by naval officers.
It seems incredible that such a thing should have been

tolerated. But it was a hundred years ago. The sailors assaulted and knocked down the voters on the other side. When complaints were made, Hood's Committee refused to send them away.

On Saturday, April 3rd, a body of Guards, nearly three hundred strong, were marched to Covent Garden under orders to vote for Hood and Wray.

On April 5th the sailors met their match, for the chairmen, all stout and sturdy Irishmen, came down to Covent Garden in a body, and after a battle with cudgels and chair-poles in the fine old eighteenth-century fashion—a form of fight which gave every possible advantage to the valiant, and every opportunity for personal distinction—they drove the sailors from the field and remained in possession. The routed sailors made for St. James's Street, proposing to destroy the chairs ; but they were followed by the chairmen, resolute to preserve their property. Again the sailors were driven from the field. The rioting continued, more or less, during the whole of the Election. For the most part it was carried on in Covent Garden, outside Wood's Hotel, which was the headquarters of Hood and Wray ; and outside the Shakespeare Tavern, where sat Fox's Committee. For instance, one day a certain party of amiable and honest butchers marched into Covent Garden wearing Fox's colours. Of course it was quite accidental that this procession, with its band of marrowbones and cleavers, should strike up an inspiriting strain, accompanied by derisive cheers, in front of Wood's Hotel, and of course they did not expect what followed—the appearance on the scene of the sailors armed with bludgeons and cutlasses. A fight followed, in which the sailors were driven back ; some one from the hotel windows fired into the mob, upon which the windows were broken. The arrival of the Guards prevented fresh hostilities. A good many were wounded in this affair ; happily, no one was killed.

A more serious riot took place on May 11th. It was

supposed that the polling would conclude on that day ; the Westminster magistrates, apprehending a riot, called together a large number of special constables, and sent them to Covent Garden to keep the peace. The polling went on quietly until three o'clock, when it closed for the day. Then the fighting began between the butchers and the constables. Who provoked it ? The constables were sent, it was said, in order to get up a riot. The butchers, it was said, began. Fox himself was knocked down. The constables were defeated, one man being killed ; and the soldiers were called in.

Mr. John Hunter, surgeon, gave evidence in the inquest that followed. The man was killed by injuries inflicted by some blunt weapon, presumably a bludgeon. The jury returned a verdict of wilful murder against some person or persons unknown. The funeral of the unfortunate man was carefully conducted so as to throw the odium of his death on Fox's side. He was buried, though a Whitechapel man, in the churchyard of St. Paul's, Covent Garden. The other people declared that he was really buried at Whitechapel, and that the coffin placed in St. Paul's was empty. The funeral was conducted, of course, very slowly past the Shakespeare Tavern and before the hustings. The widow followed in a mourning coach, crying out of the window ' Blood for Blood ! ' The procession was admirably arranged in order to provoke another riot, which would certainly have happened, had not Fox's Committee caused the polling to be stopped at two instead of three o'clock, so that when the funeral arrived Covent Garden was comparatively quiet. The last day of the struggle was on May 17th, after forty-seven days of polling. The result was :—

Lord Hood 6694
Charles James Fox 6234
Sir Cecil Wray 5998

Sir Cecil Wray demanded a scrutiny, to which Fox objected. The reason of his objection appeared later on, when the subject was discussed in the House, and it appeared that a scrutiny would probably last five years and would cost 30,000*l.*, which would have to be paid by the candidates. It was therefore abandoned.

But the fun was not yet finished.   A Triumphal Procession was formed, and the successful candidate was escorted on his way to Devonshire House.   The following was the order of the Procession :—

Heralds on Horseback.
Twenty-four marrow-bones and cleavers.
The Arms of Westminster.
Thirty Firemen of Westminster.
Martial Music.
Committees of the seven Parishes, with white Wands, following their respective banners and attended by numberless gentlemen of the several Districts.
Squadron of Gentlemen on Horseback in Buff and Blue.
Trumpets.
Flag—The Rights of the Commons.
Grand Band of Music.
Flag—The Men of the People.
Marshals on Foot.
Triumphal Chair
Decorated with Laurels, in which was seated
The Right Hon. Charles James Fox.
Trumpets.
Flag—The Whig Cause.
Second Squadron of Horse.
Liberty Boys of Newport Market.
Mr. Fox's Carriage crowned with Laurels.
Banner Sacred to Female Patriotism.
Blue Standard.   Inscribed
Independence !
State carriages of the Duchess of Portland and the Duchess of Devonshire, drawn by six horses superbly caparisoned, with six running footmen attending on each.
Gentlemen's Servants closing the Procession—two and two.

The Procession over, they all adjourned—Marrow-bones,

Cleavers, Liberty Boys and all, to Willis'ʄ Rooms, where they made a glorious night of it.

The Prince of Wales gave a *déjeuner* in honour of the occasion to six hundred 'of the first persons of fashion.' They danced all night and till six in the morning, and they all met again in the evening at Mrs. Crewe's Ball. Captain Morris took the chair after supper, and sang the 'Baby and Nurse.' He then proposed a toast, 'Buff and Blue and Mrs. Crewe!' to which the fair hostess responded, wittily and gracefully, with 'Buff and Blue and all for you!' Then Captain Morris gave them a succession of songs 'with a spirit that made every fair eye in the room dance with delight.' At four o'clock they went back to the dancing and kept it up till six or seven.

So ended the fiercest contest and the longest of which any history remains. It is also, to repeat what has been already advanced, the only election of which there has been preserved so complete a record. Page after page, in the volume from which I have quoted, is filled with paragraphs cut from the papers of the day, in which the most astonishing ingenuity is devoted to the invention of new libels, the distortion of old speeches, and the perversion of facts. We have seen that against Sir Cecil Wray absolutely nothing of the least import-ance could be alleged, because it was absurd to suppose that he was to be Fox's henchman for life. Fox had certainly introduced Wray to the Westminster electors, and that was the only service he had rendered him. Against Fox himself very little of importance could be alleged, because, even if he was a prodigal, a gambler and of doubtful virtue, the average Briton has always loved a sportsman, and has never—at least, not until quite recently—thought that a man's gifts and powers as a statesman depend upon his private morals. All the abuse, all the libels, all the monstrous lies hurled about on either side, were absolutely useless: I do not believe that they influenced a single elector. Were the gentlemen who played so beautifully with the marrow-bones and cleavers influenced ? Were the Liberty Boys of Newport Market influenced ? Were the residents of Peter Street, Orchard Street, the Almonry influenced ? They were not voters. The voting qualification of 1784 was the burgage holding, the tenant who paid scot and lot, and the potwaller. Did the presence of the sailors assist the Court party ? Did the valiant chairman prove of any real help to Fox ? I think not. All these things amused the mob : none of these things moved the elector. The one thing that damaged Fox was his late coalition with Lord North, the man most heartily and thoroughly detested in all the length and breadth of the country—the man universally regarded as the chief cause of the national disasters and humiliations. And I think that what hurt Sir Cecil Wray most was the marching of the three hundred Guards in a body to vote as they were ordered, and the interference of the Court in commanding every person connected with the Household to vote against Fox. And for my own part, had I been able to vote at that election, Fox should have had a plumper from me if only to win one of the Duchess's smiles ; and if any other reason were wanting, I should have voted for Fox because, of all the men of that most disagreeable period, Fox, to my mind, with all his faults, stands out as the bravest, the most genial, and the most patriotic.

CHAPTER X

THE STREETS AND THE PEOPLE

AFTER the Palace and the Monastery, the City of Refuge, the Sign of the Red Pale, and the Borough at Election-time, we turn to the City streets and the people.

Now, if we include that part of the City lying west and north of Charing Cross and Pall Mall, the part which has been built and occupied since the seventeenth century, we are face to face with nothing less than the history of the British aristocracy during the last two centuries. This history has never been written ; it is a work which cannot even be touched upon in these pages : to consider any part of it in a single chapter would be absurd. It belongs, like the history of the House of Commons, to the City of Westminster because most of its events took place, and most of the people concerned lived, within the limits of that City. Also, like the House of Commons, the quarter where the aristo-cracy have had their town houses for two hundred years belongs to the national history, and must be treated inde-pendently of the City.

The British aristocracy was never so much a Caste apart as during the hundred and fifty years ending about the middle of this century. Their younger sons had quite abandoned the ancient practice of entering the City and going into trade : every kind of money-making, except the collection of rents from land, had become unworthy of a gentleman. No one could buy or sell and continue to call himself a gentleman. There was a noble Caste and a trading

Caste, quite separate and apart.   The noble Caste possessed
everything worth having : the whole of the land was theirs ;
all the great offices of state, all the lesser offices worth
having, were theirs ; the commands in the army and the
navy were theirs—not only the command of armies and
fleets, but also of regiments and men-o'-war ;   the rich
preferments of the Church,—the deaneries, canonries and
bishoprics,—were theirs ; the House of Commons belonged
to them (even the popular or radical members belonged to
the Caste : in the election which was treated in the last
chapter, Fox, the Friend of Liberty, the Chosen of the Independent Electors, belonged to the Caste as much as his
opponents, Lord Hood and Sir Cecil Wray).   Everything
was theirs, except the right to trade : they must not trade.
To be a banker was to be in trade ; the richest merchant
was a tradesman as much as the grocer who sold sugar and
treacle.

The materials for this history are abundant : there are
memoirs, letters, biographies, autobiographies, recollections,
in profusion. ⸍ The life of the Caste during this period of a
hundred and fifty years can be fully written.   The historian,
if we were able to exercise the art of selection, would present
a series of highly dramatic chapters : there would be found
in them love, jealousy and intrigue ; there would be ambition and cabal; there would be back-stairs interest ; there
would be Court gossip and scandal and whisperings ; there
would be gaming, racing, coursing, prizefighting, drinking ;
there would be young Mohocks and old profligates ; there
would be ruined rakes and splendid adventurers,— in a word,
there would be the whole life of pleasure and the whole
life of ambition.   It would be, worthily treated, a noble
work.

This Caste, which enjoyed all the fruits of the earth, for
which the rest of the nation toiled with the pious contentment
enjoined by the Church, created for its own separate use a

GRIFFINS FROM THE ROOF OF HENRY VII.'S CHAPEL

society which was at the same time free and unrestrained, yet courtly and stately. No one not born and bred in the Caste could attain its manners ; if an outsider by any accident found himself in this circle he thought he had got into the wrong paradise, and asked leave to exchange. Again, among the Caste, which, with a few brilliant exceptions, was without learning and without taste, were found all the patrons of art, poetry and *Belles Lettres.* Still more remarkable, while the Caste had no religion, it owned the patronage of all the best livings in the Church. And, while it enjoyed an immunity never before claimed by any class of men from morality, principle, and self-restraint, the Caste was the encouraging and fostering patron of every useful and admirable virtue, such as thrift, fidelity, temperance, industry, perseverance, frugality and contentment. A wonderful history indeed —and all of it connected with Westminster !

Of course another side presents

itself : the Caste was brave—its courage was undoubted ; it was never without ability of the very highest kind, though a great deal of its ability was allowed to lie waste for want of stimulus : it was proud ; if the occasion had arrived—it was very near arriving—the Caste would have faced the mob as dauntlessly as its cousin in France, whom the mob might kill, but could neither terrify nor degrade.

Again, there is the literary side. With the exception of a few names belonging to Fleet Street and a few belonging to Grub Street, most of our literary history belongs to the quarter lying west of Temple Bar—in other words, to Westminster. One might go from street to street pointing out the residence of Byron here and of Moore there, of Swift, of Pope, of Addison. And in this way one could compile a chapter as interesting as a catalogue.

In the same way, the connection of street and noble residents might be carefully noted down, with the same result. This, indeed, has been already done by Jesse. If you read one or two of his chapters, taken almost at random, you will presently feel that your wits are wandering. For instance, here is a passage concerning one of the least distinguished streets in Westminster :—

'In Cannon Row stood the magnificent residence of Anne Stanhope, the scorned and turbulent wife of the great Protector, Duke of Somerset. Here, in the reign of Queen Elizabeth, was the inn or palace of the Stanleys, Earls of Derby. Close by was the mansion of Henry, second Earl of Lincoln, who sat in judgment on Mary Queen of Scots, and who was one of the peers deputed by Queen Elizabeth to arrest the Earl of Essex in his house. Here, in the reign of James I., the Sackvilles, Earls of Dorset, had their town residence ; and here, in the time of Queen Elizabeth, was the mansion of the great family of the Cliffords, Earls of Cumberland.'

How much, gentle reader, are you likely to remember of

such information as this after reading twenty pages of it ? How much, indeed, is it desirable to remember ?. Why cumber the brain with names and titles which are meaningless to your mind, and can restore for you no more of the past life and the bygone actors than a handful of Helen's dust could restore her beauty ?

There is, however, another part of Westminster—a part which concerns us more than Caste Land. It is the part which lies around the ancient precincts of the Abbey. Here we touch Westminster ; here we are not on land that belongs to the country, nor among people who belong to the country : we are in Westminster proper—in the streets which cannot even now, when all the former spaces of separation are covered up and built over, be called a part of London or a suburb of London. They are Westminster.

These streets possessed, until quite recently, the picturesqueness

GRIFFINS FROM THE ROOF OF HENRY VII.'S CHAPEL

that belongs to the aged vagrom man. He hardly exists in these days ; but one remembers him. He was old—age had lent no touch of reverence or dignity ; he was clad in many-coloured rags and fluttering duds ; he leaned upon a stick ; his white locks were the only part of him that presented any appearance of cleanliness ; his face was lined and puckered, his features were weatherbeaten and prominent, his eyes were wolfish. He was admirable—in a picture. Such were the streets, such the houses, of Westminster—that part of the City lying round about the Abbey. Those on the west and south of the Abbey are comparatively new streets. In the excellent map by Richard Newcourt showing London and Westminster in the year 1658 we find Tothill Street completely built ; Rochester Row

GRIFFIN FROM THE ROOF OF HENRY VII.'S CHAPEL.

ROOM IN 'THE KING'S ARMS,' TOTHILL STREET, WESTMINSTER

does not exist; Great St. Peter Street has a few houses, Great College Street none; St. Anne's Street has houses with gardens. The crowded part of Westminster in the seventeenth century was that narrow area north of New Palace Yard of which King Street was the most important thoroughfare. When we consider that this place was a great centre of trade long before and long after the building of London Bridge; that for six hundred years it was close to the King's House, with all his followers,—huscarles, archers, or body-guard,—we are not surprised that there has always been about these streets the flavour of the tavern— always the smell of casks and pint pots, of stale beer and yesterday's wine. Where there are soldiers there are taverns; there also are the minstrels and the music and the girls. It may also be concluded beyond a doubt that the Sanctuary was a thirsty place. Long after Court and Camp and Sanctuary had left the place the name and fame of Westminster for its taverns and its dens remained. These streets were a byword and a reproach well into the present century. One or two streets there were that claimed for a generation or so a kind of respectability. They were the streets lying between New Palace Yard and Whitehall, such as King Street and Cannon Street, with one or two of later growth—of seventeenth and eighteenth century respectability—such as Petty France, Cowley Street and College Street.

King Street, especially, if one may brave the reproach of cataloguing, is full of history. Here lived Oliver Cromwell: his house is said to have stood on the north side of the Blue Boar's Head, of which the court still remains. Sir Henry Wootton lived here; one of Caxton's successors set up his press in this street. It was formerly, as we have already seen, a picturesque and beautiful street, with its gate at either end, its overhanging gables, and its signs. Half a dozen taverns stood in this street—the Swan, the Dog, the Bell, the Blue Boar's Head, etc. This little street, now so insignifi-

cant, was formerly, we are always, by every writer, called
upon to observe, the 'highway' between London and Westminster. But then nobody went by
road who could go by river. The
Thames was the highway—not King
Street—between London and Westminster : by the Thames the Port of
London sent its goods to the Court
of Westminster or Whitehall ; by the
river came down country produce for
Court and Abbey. There was doubtless some traffic which found its way
along King Street ; but for communication between Westminster and all
other parts of the country except
the City and the Strand, we must
remember that there
was not only the
river, but the old, old
road, that which
formerly ran down
from the North to the
marsh at St. James'
Park, and began again
on the other side of
the river ; the marsh
was now drained, and
the road, no longer
a ford, ran across it
and formed the most
direct entrance to the
Court or the Abbey

GRIFFINS FROM THE ROOF OF HENRY VII.'S
CHAPEL

from the North. We
must remember, again, that nobody walked who could ride ;
and that nobody rode who could take boat : walking along

streets unpaved, foul with every kind of refuse, muddy after rain, stinking in dry weather, was never pleasant ; therefore no one went afoot who could go any other way. The streets which contained shops, such as Cheapside, were kept clean and protected by posts ; but King Street was not one of these. Men who rode into Westminster entered either by King Street or by Tothill Street ; but no one came afoot if they could come by boat.

In King Street died Spenser ' for lack of bread,' said Ben Jonson. But he goes on to add that the dying poet refused money sent him by the Earl of Essex. The story has been accepted without question by almost every one who writes upon Spenser. Yet it is incredible on the face of it, when one begins to consider, for the simple reason that starving men never do refuse help, even at the last gasp. There is no doubt that in the Irish Rebellion Spenser lost one child, who perished in the flames of the burning house. He escaped, it is said, with his wife. That he was desperately poor at this juncture we need not doubt ; that he was wretched is also without doubt ; that he died in misery we need not doubt ; but if the Earl of Essex sent him money he would certainly have taken it if he was starving ; if his wife was with him he would have taken it for her sake if he was dying.

As a matter of fact he was not suffering from want of money : and since the death of an infant does not often kill the child's father, we need not suppose that he died of heart-break. Nor is it probable that he died of a broken heart over the loss of MSS. He was Sheriff of Cork : he had his estate, which was not lost, although the rebels burned his house —they burned his house because he was Sheriff : he had, beside the estate, a small pension : he had still his wife and his children, and his friends : he was only forty-six years of age, a time when the world is still lying fair and far stretched out before the pilgrim. None the less he died—of what ? Of fever caused by the excitement and the trouble of the ebellion : by exposure : by this or by that—he died. He was buried in the Abbey near the resting-place of Chaucer : all he poets wrote elegies and threw them, together with the pens that wrote them, into the grave of 'the little man who wore short hair.' And his widow married again and quarrelled with her eldest son about the estate : and there were descendants of Edmund Spenser in Ireland until a hundred years ago, when the last one died.

Queen Square, which is now Queen Anne's Gate, and Petty France, now York Street, represent the respectable side of Old Westminster. Peg Woffington lived in Queen Square ; so did Bentham. In Petty France Milton lived when he gave up his chambers in Whitehall Palace. His house was taken down a year or two ago. Hazlitt occupied Milton's house for some years.

Another respectable quarter was the group of streets at the back of Dean's Yard, known as Great College Street, Barton Street, and Cowley Street. There is not anywhere in and about the cities of London and Westminster a more secluded, peaceful retreat than can be found in these three streets. The first, whose upper windows look out upon the broad lawns and noble trees, formerly the garden of the Infirmary, now the garden of the Canons, might be a street in Amsterdam if its ground-floor windows were only higher ; under this street still flows the stream which once helped to separate the Isle of Bramble from the marshes and the meadows ; half-way down, hidden by stables, stands the old Jewel House of the King's House of Westminster ; at the west end is the modern gateway, still preserving some semblance of its former appearance, the last that is left of the four gateways of the Abbey. It leads into Dean's Yard, the quietest of squares, and, under ancient gates, into ancient cloisters and covered ways, and the relics and fragments of the Benedictine Abbey. Behind Great College Street stand Barton Street and Cowley Street. And for quiet and solitude these should belong to a city of the dead ; or, better still, they should be what they pretend to be. For the houses among themselves pretend to be the Cathedral Close ; they whisper to the stray traveller : 'Seek no farther. This, and none other, is the Close of the Cathedral or Collegiate Church of St. Peter. In this quiet retreat live, we assure you, the canons and the minor canons. Step lightly, lest you disturb their meditations.' There are many such spots about London which thus pretend, and so carry themselves with pride : one such, for instance, is in Bermondsey, affected by the memory of the Abbey and the presence of the Parish Church ; and another there is at Hampstead ; and in most country towns there is such a quiet, dignified street ; one such street, so quiet, so dignified, stands in Albany, New York State ; and one in Boston, Massachusetts.

Once there was a tavern in Barton Street, known to all men by its sign, as The Salutation. The excellence of the painting is proved by the fact that in the Commonwealth the same sign without alteration served for a new name—viz., The Soldier and Citizen. After the Restoration the Soldier once more became an Angel and the Citizen returned to the Virgin Mary. But I think that the tavern languished. Cowley Street was not named after the poet, as one would like to believe, but after the village of Cowley, in Middlesex, by Mr. Booth Barton, who built the two streets. There are other associations about these streets : the name of Keats is mentioned. But they belong to the catalogue. It is enough for us to recall the babbling brook which once ran along the roadway here—on this side of the grey stone wall which still stands, the wall of the Monastery. It ran then through the bending reeds and the tall grasses of the marsh, and so out into the silver Thames ; the swans came sailing up the brook, and made nests in the low bank of the eyot. The Abbot's barge was moored close by the gateway, of which a modern successor still stands ; and there were drawn up on the bank

the boats in which the Abbot's fishermen went out to catch
salmon and sturgeon in the river.   Later on they built these
quiet houses along one side, something after the Dutch style ;
and they hung up before their fronts a curtain of green
Virginia creeper, but not to hide from the windows the view

WOOD CARVING AND ORIGINAL SIGN OF 'THE COCK' INN,
TOTHILL STREET, WESTMINSTER

of the broad lawns, the flower-beds and the walnut trees of
the garden behind the wall.

This part of Westminster has always been full of taverns ;
first for the solace of the men-at-arms, afterwards for that of
the Members of Parliament. The tavern has always been
the national place of recreation and rest : for a time, it is true,

the coffee-house displaced it, but only for a time,—the tavern
came back again to favour.   The signs of these inns show
the date of their erection.   There was the White Hart o
Richard II. ; the Brown Bear of Warwick ; the White Swan
of Henry V. ; the Old Rose of Henry VII.   And there wer
the more common signs : the Blue Boar, the Salutation
the George, the Green Dragon, the Barley Mow, the Heave
tavern, the Fleece.   One of the oldest of these taverns, th
Cock, remained with its open court and its galleries till twent
years ago, when it was pulled down to make room for th

Aquarium.   The rafters and tim
bers of this tavern were of cedar
and the interior was also adorne
with many curious carvings.

More remarkable than th
taverns, which we have with u
everywhere, were the Almshouse
of Westminster.   Until they wer
destroyed they were remarkabl
for their number, for their endow
ments, and for the quaint pleasant
ness and beauty of their appear
ance.   You may now look in vain
for the old buildings : they are

ORIGINAL SIGN, 'COCK' INN

gone ; in their place we have the consolidated almshouse
and the consolidated schools.

There were almshouses—eight of them—in the Wool
staple, which is now Cannon Street : they looked out upon
the river, and the bedesmen turned an honest penny by
letting them in lodgings for Parliament men.   There were
other almshouses founded by Henry VII. outside the Gate-
house in Tothill Street.   There was an almshouse for women
founded by Lady Margaret in the Almonry.   But these were
ancient things.   Perhaps they disappeared with the Dissolution ; perhaps they were 'consolidated' the other day.   Of

the modern almshouses with schools attached, the most important was Emanuel College, a lovely House of Refuge, which stood until yesterday in James Street, on the way from Buckingham Gate to Victoria. After leaving the great

MILTON'S HOUSE IN PETTY FRANCE

mansions near the Park one came suddenly upon the low red brick quadrangle open on one side, with its chapel in the middle and its broad smooth lawn and flower-beds in front— as peaceful a spot as could be found anywhere. It made one glad to think that Dives had really remembered Lazarus; it made one reflect that perhaps money can be put to no better use than to consecrate it to the maintenance of age. And now that College is taken down: soon the site will be covered with residential flats, and Lazarus will retire to his

EMANUEL HOSPITAL, LATELY DEMOLISHED
By permission of ' The Architect '

place upon the doorstep. Lazarus is old and worn out in the service of Dives: he ought to be in an almshouse; he has got rheumatism in all his joints; he wants a warm place and a quiet place to lie down and rest in. While this venerable Hospital stood, the world—the world of fashion, the world of pleasure—was reminded of Lazarus. It has disappeared: this means that Lazarus is shoved aside, put out of sight, forgotten; he spends his strength and his skill in the service of the rich man, who knows and thinks nothing about him, and when his strength and his skill fail there is nothing to remind his master that thus and thus should he deal with his old and faithful servant.

THE GRILLE, EMANUEL HOSPITAL
By permission of 'The Architect'

All the romance of Westminster City lay in its almshouses and schools. The City of London was fighting the battle of

T

civic freedom ; the City of London was finding money to fill the King's Treasury ; the City of London was sending its sails out to the uttermost parts of the earth. This other City, which was not really a city, but only a collection of houses, under the rule of Abbot and of Dean—which had no trade, which had no municipality, which was a gathering of riffraff and Sanctuary rabble—presented a continual spectacle of poverty, misery, and crime, lying at the very gate of Abbey and of King's House. Lazarus, actual or prospective, lived in every house. The Dean and Chapter had the poor always with them, as their tenants. They had not only the impotent and the worn-out, but also the vicious and the mischievous—the people who would not work. They had but to step outside their gates in order to obtain illustrations for their sermons on the extreme misery which, even in this world, follows such a life. The general wretchedness moved the hearts of many. London itself once had admirable almshouses ; but those of Westminster, considering the difference in population, are much more important. The City contained an unparalleled collection of almshouses and free schools. But I do not find any that were founded by the landlords of the City, the Dean and Chapter of the Cathedral.

If you walk down Rochester Row, you will find on the west side a large modern building, with a hall and offices on one side of a quadrangle and red-brick houses of pleasing appearance on the other side. These are the consolidated or United Westminster Charities. They pulled down the old almshouses, which were so picturesque and so lovely of aspect : they destroyed the individual character belonging to every one, they rolled them all together, and with the lump sum, subtracting the leakage that went to conveyancers and architects, they built this pile.

Yes, it is very well : the pile is perhaps handsome ; but I doubt if there are so many bedesmen in the United Charity

as there were in the separate charities. And it is no longer
the same thing. Each House formerly had its own garden, in
which the almsmen took the air ; and its own chapel, in
which those on the foundation could remember the founder—

GREY COAT HOSPITAL : THE ENTRANCE

Lady Dacre, to wit ; or Cornelius Van Dun, Yeoman of the
Guard to Henry VIII., Queen Mary, and Queen Elizabeth
(his house stood near the present Town Hall) ; or Emery
Hill, or George Whicher, or Judith Kifford, or Nicholas
Butler Palmer. Busts and tablets outside the new buildings

T 2

commemorate these worthies, but where are their buildings
gone ? The Almshouses of Westminster are all destroyed,
and with them have perished the sentiment and the romance
of the streets.

Something still remains ; for, with the most laudable
desire to destroy whatever can teach or suggest or soften
manners or point to heaven, the Charity Commissioners have
not been able to destroy one or two of the schools. There
were formerly the Grey Coat Schools, the Green Coat School,
the Blue Coat School, and the Black Coat School. The Grey
Coat School has become a school for nearly four hundred girls :
their old house still remains for them—a most beautiful monument, built in the seventeenth century for a poorhouse. The
great hall in which the paupers formerly lived is now the school
hall ; above it ran the old low dormitory, now thrown open to
the roof ; there are panelled old rooms for board rooms ; there
are broad passages and corridors ; there are schoolrooms of
later date ; and at the back, still uninjured, lie the broad
gardens that belong to the time when every house in Westminster had its garden.

In any map of London except those of the actual present
—say, in Crutchley's of 1838—there is laid down in its place,
just north of Rochester Row (which is now Artillery Place),
St. Margaret's Hospital, otherwise called the Green Coat
School. This part of Westminster was once called Palmer's
Village ; the Hospital was founded by the parish for the
benefit of orphans. Charles II. endowed it ; the Duchess of
Somerset gave the school a thousand pounds ; other benefac-
tions flowed in. Forty years ago the place was thus described
by a writer who is not often eloquent in praise (Walcott's
‘ Westminster ’) :—

‘ The Hospital of St. Margaret consists of a large quadrangle. Upon the east side are the schoolroom, lavatory
and dormitories. The Master's house fronts the entrance—
a detached building ornamented with a bust of the kingly

founder, and the Royal arms painted in colours widely carved and gilded, which were, according to tradition, only preserved from the destructive hands of the Puritans by a thick coating of plaster laid over the obnoxious remembrancers of the rightful dynasty. The south side is formed by the refectory and board room, wainscoted—once, it is said, with old portions of the woodwork which stood in St. Margaret's

GREY COAT BOY   GREY COAT GIRL
FROM THE STATUE IN FRONT OF THE HOSPITAL

chancel—to a considerable height, in large panels, upon which are hung full-length paintings of King Charles II. by Sir Peter Lely, and Emery Hill, an ancient benefactor to the institution, in the manner of the same master. Over the mantelpiece is a beautiful portrait of King Charles I. by Vandyke. The windows command a view of the Hospital Garden, with its fragrant flower-beds and grassy plots—a pleasant relief to the eye wearied with the interminable brick buildings of the outer street, and well attesting the constant care bestowed upon it.

' Upon this foundation are maintained twenty-nine boys, who wear a long green skirt, bound round with a red girdle, similar in form to that worn by the boys of Christ's Hospital.'

Where is this lovely place now ? It is gone. On its site are some branches of the Army and Navy Stores. Think what a city loses by the destruction of such a place ! The daily object-lesson in our duty to the friendless and the helpless ; the memory of bygone worthies ; the sentiment of brotherhood. That is one way of considering the loss. Another way is to think of it as a place of singular beauty, of such beauty as we cannot possibly reproduce. And we have wilfully and needlessly destroyed it ! It is a national disaster of the gravest, the most irreparable kind, that such monuments as old almshouses, old City churches, old schools, old gates, old foundations of any kind, should be given over to any body of men, with permission to tear down and destroy at their will, and under pretence of benefiting the parish. Can one benefit a man by destroying his memory ? Can one improve a parish by cutting off its connection with the past ?

There is one other endowed school not yet destroyed. It is the Blue Coat School, first opened in 1688 for boys. In the year 1709 the present school buildings were erected. They consist of a charming red-brick hall with the figure of a scholar over the porch ; a little garden full of greenery is at the back ; at one side is the master's residence, a two-storied house covered all over with a curtain of Virginia creeper ; another little garden, full of such flowers as will grow in the London air, is behind this house. But master and boys, when they look around them, begin to tremble, for their place is old, it is beautiful, it adorns the street, it is sacred to the memory of two hundred years of Boy—thirty generations of Boy : it is still most useful—therefore one feels certain that it is doomed ; it must soon go, to make room for residential flats and mansions fifteen stories high ; it must, we have no doubt, follow the other monuments of the Past, and be absorbed into Consolidated Schools. If there were any other reason wanted for the destruction of the School, it is the tradition that Wren built it.

To my mind Wesminster possesses, apart from the Abbey, but one Church—that of St. Margaret's. Other modern churches there are, but one does not heed them : they are things of to-day—even St. John's and St. Martin's are but of

GREY COAT HOSPITAL FROM THE GARDEN

yesterday : St. Margaret's is eight hundred years old ; if not built by the Confessor, it was built—that is to say, the first church on this site was built—soon after his death. The history of St. Margaret's Church must be told by an ecclesi-astic ; we need only remember that Caxton lies buried here ; there is a tablet to his memory put up in 1820 by the Rox-burgh Club. Raleigh is buried here—within the chancel. James Harrington, author of 'Oceana,' is buried here. John Skelton, with whom we have conversed in Sanctuary, is buried here. Here Milton was married to Katharine Woodcock, who died in child-birth a year later :

Methought I saw my late espousèd saint
Brought to me, like Alcestis, from the grave.
Mine, such as yet once more I trust to have
Full sight of her in heaven, without restraint,
Came vested all in white, pure as her mind.
Her face was veiled ; yet to my fancied sight
Love, sweetness, goodness in her person shined.

In the churchyard of St. Margaret's were interred the remains of those persons who were turned out of the Abbey at the Restoration : the mother of Cromwell ; his daughter ;

CARVING FROM THE DOORWAY OF EMANUEL HOSPITAL

Admiral Blake, whose remains ought to have been taken back again long ago ; and in this church, or this churchyard, have been buried a crowd of persons illustrious and of high degree in their generation, whose deeds have not survived them and whose memory is only kept alive by the monuments on the walls and nothing else. It is a church filled with monuments : it reminds one of such a church as the Grey Friars' in the City, which was crowded with tombs of the illustrious Forgotten.

Not far from the church is the old-new Burial Ground, in the Horseferry Road. It is now a public garden, and a pleasant garden, with seats and asphalted paths and beds of

grass and flowers. Against the wall are ranged the tomb-
stones of the obscure Forgotten. I suppose it makes very
little difference to a man whether he has a headstone provided
for him against the wall of a public garden, or a tablet—nay,
a monument—against the wall of St. Margaret's Church, as
soon as he is properly and completely forgotten.

St. Margaret's, then, is the only church of which one

MEDAL WORN BY THE CAPTAIN OF THE GREY COAT BOYS

thinks in connection with Westminster. There is one scene,
one little drama, enacted or partly enacted in this church,
which perhaps may belong to the pen of the layman. It is
the famous case brought before a Court of Chivalry in the
year 1387 to decide the dispute between Sir Richard le
Scrope and Sir Robert Grosvenor respecting the right of
either party to a certain coat-of-arms. This was no common
case: it was the alleged violation of a family possession, a

family distinction. The case was considered so important that more than three hundred witnesses were called. They are nearly all shadows and empty names now; but one there is who stands out prominent : his name is Geoffrey Chaucer.

BLUE COAT SCHOOL, CAXTON STREET

The following is the evidence given by the poet in this great heraldic case :—

'Geoffrey Chaucer, Esquire, forty years of age and more, having borne arms for twenty-eight years, produced for the side of Sir Richard le Scrope, sworn and examined. Asked if the arms Azure with a bend Or belonged or ought to belong to the said Richard of right and inheritance, said, " Yes "; for he had seen him thus armed in France before the city of Retters, and Sir Henry le Scrope with the same arms with a white label and a banner, and the said Sir Richard with the complete arms—Azure and a bend Or ; and thus had he seen them armed during the whole time that the said Geoffrey was

BLUE COAT SCHOOL, FROM THE GARDEN

present. Asked why he knew that the said arms belonged to the said Sir Richard, said that he had heard speech of old knights and squires, and that they had always continued their possession of the said arms, and for all his time reputed for these arms in common fame and public ways. And also he said that he had seen the same arms on banners, on windows, on paintings, on robes, commonly called the arms of Le Scrope.　Asked if he had ever heard who was the first ancestor of the said Sir Richard, who first bore the said arms, said " No " ; but that he had never heard of any, but that they had come of an old stock and of old gentlefolk, and had held the same arms.　Asked if he had ever heard of any interruption or challenge made by Sir Robert Grosvenor, or by his ancestors, or by any one in his name, to the said Sir Richard or to any of his ancestors, said " No " ; but that he was once in Friday Street in London, and as he went along the street he saw hanging out a new sign made of the said arms, and he asked what house was this that had hung out the arms of Scrope ; and one other replied, and said, " Not so : and they are not hung out for the arms of Scrope, nor painted for those arms, but they are painted and put up there for a knight of the County of Chester, a man named Robert Grosvenor ' ; and that this was the first time that ever he heard tell of Sir Robert Grosvenor or his ancestors or anybody bearing the name of Grosvenor.'

The case, at which between three and four hundred witnesses were heard, was finally decided by ' Thomas Fitz au Roy, Duc de Gloucestre, Counte de Bukyngham et Dessex, Constable Dengleterre,' who, after due care and deliberation, and the weighing of all the evidence, and consultation with wise and discreet persons, finally adjudged ' les dites armes d'azure ove une bend dor avoir esté et estre les armes du dit Richard Lescrop.'　And so ended this great case, which somehow puts the poet before us more clearly than even his ' Canterbury Pilgrims.'

And so we come back to the streets proper of Westminster —i.e. the slums on the west and south of the Monastery.

There have always been slums here, even before the Sanctuary rabble and after.　The streets lying about Tothill Lane, however, which were slums from the beginning, only began in the sixteenth century.　The map of Anthony Van

den Wyngeerde (A.D. 1543) shows only a few houses standing
round about the Sanctuary in the north-west corner of the
enclosure ; there is a crowd of houses between King Street
and the river, and on the west there is nothing but open
country : that part of the City which contained the most

LOVING CUP PRESENTED TO THE GUARDIANS OF ST. MARGARET'S,
WESTMINSTER, BY SAMUEL PIERSON IN 1764

infamous dens and the vilest ruffians, which was called the
' Desert ' of Westminster, lying to the south of Tothill Fields,
grew up and ran to waste and seed in the course of the seventeenth century. In the eighteenth we reaped the harvest of
that seed ; at the end of the nineteenth we are still pulling
up the weeds and planting new flowers and sowing better seed.

The ' Desert ' was bounded on the north by Tothill Street, Broadway, and Petty France, all with their courts—their sweet and desirable courts ; its southern boundary was the Horseferry Road ; the Abbey lay along the east ; and the western marsh was the fringe of Tothill Fields, now marked by Rochester Row, or perhaps Francis Street. A little remains—here a court, there a bit of street—to mark what the place was like.

Hear what was written about Westminster so late as the year 1839 (Bardsley on ' Westminster Improvements ') : ' Thorney Island consisted chiefly of narrow, dirty streets lined with wretched dwellings, and of numerous miserable courts and alleys, situate in the environs of the Palace and Abbey, where in the olden time the many lawless characters claiming sanctuary found shelter ; and so great had been the force of long custom that the houses continued to be rebuilt, century after century, in a miserable manner for the reception of similar degraded outcasts. The inhabitants of these courts and alleys are stated in the reign of Queen Elizabeth " to be the most part of no trade or mystery, to be poor, and many of them wholly given to vice and idleness." And in James I.'s time " almost every fourth house is an alehouse, harbouring all sorts of lewde and badde people." And again : " In these narrow streets, and in their close and insalubrious lanes, courts and alleys, where squalid misery and poverty struggle with filth and wretchedness, where vice reigns unchecked, and in the atmosphere of which the worst diseases are generated and diffused." '

In the little space of a thousand feet by twelve hundred the courts were sometimes so narrow that the people could shake hands across ; the tenements were sometimes built of boards nailed together ; there were no sanitary arrangements at all ; there was no drainage ; typhus always held possession ; and actually under the very shadow of the Cathedral were gathered together the most dangerous and most villainous wretches in

the whole country. Old Pye Street, Orchard Street, Duck
Lane, the Almonry and St. Anne's Street were the homes of
the professional street beggar and the professional thief. No
respectable person could venture with safety into these streets.

They are now quite safe ; the people are rough to look at,
but they are no longer thieves and cut-throats by calling.
Let us take a short, a very short walk about the Desert.
Alas ! its glories are gone ; the place is not even picturesque :
Vice, we know, is sometimes picturesque, even in its most

OLD PYE STREET AND THE RAGGED SCHOOL

hideous mien. Orchard Street has one side pulled down, and
the other side presents a squalid, dilapidated appearance in
grey brick ; it was once a fit entrance for the most wicked
part of London. The streets into which it leads—Great St.
Anne's Street, Pye Street, Peter Street, Duck Lane (now St.
Matthew Street) are all transformed. Huge barracks of
lodging-houses stand over the dark and malodorous courts ;
the place is now no doubt tolerably virtuous, but the artist
turns from it with a shudder. There was a time when these

streets were country lanes, having few houses and no courts ; at this time many pleasant, ingenious and interesting persons lived in this quarter. For example, Herrick the poet and Purcell the musician lived in St. Anne's Street. But we have already condemned the catalogue of connections. He who seriously studies the streets learns the associations as he goes along.

Outside these streets stretched Tothill Fields and Five Fields. These fields were to Westminster much as Smithfield and Moorfields were to the City of London. Anything out of the common could be done in Tothill Fields. To begin with, they were a pleasant place for walking ; in the spring they were full of flowers—the cuckoo flower, the marsh mallow, the spurge, the willow herb, the wild parsley, are enumerated ; they contained ponds and streams ; in the streams grew watercress, always a favourite ' sallet ' to the people ; in the ponds there were ducks—the Westminster boys used to hire dogs to worry the ducks—it is not stated who paid for those ducks. On the north side of the Fields was St. James's Park, with its decoy and Rosamond's Pond, a rectangular pool lying across what is now Birdcage Walk, opposite the Wellington Barracks. Later on, market gardens were laid out in these low-lying meadows.

Tournaments were held in the Fields—not the ordinary exercises or displays of the tilt yard, but the grander occasions, as in 1226 at the coronation of Queen Eleanor. Here, in the same reign, but later, the Prior of Beverley entertained the Kings and Queens of England and Scotland, the King's son, and many great lords, in tents erected on the field.

Executions were carried out in the Fields, as when was taken Margaret Gourdemains, ' a witch of Eye beside Westminster'—was it Battersea (' Peter's Ey ') ? or was it Chelsea (' Shingle Ey ') ?—' whose sorcerie and witchcraft Dame Eleanour Cobham had long time used, and by her medicines and drinks enforced the Duke of Gloucester to love her and after to wed her.' Necromancers were punished here. In the reign of Edward III. a man was taken practising magic with a dead man's hand, and carried to Tothill, where his dead man's hand was burned before his face.

Here was held the ordeal of battle. Stow relates one such trial. The dispute was about a manor in the Isle of Harty. The plaintiffs, two in number, appointed their champion, and the defendant his. The latter was a 'Master of Defence,' which does not seem quite fair upon the other, who was only a 'big, broad, strong set fellow.' Before the day appointed for the fight an agreement was arrived at between the parties ; only, 'for the defendant's assurance,' the order for the fight should be observed, the plaintiffs not putting in an appearance, so that the case should be

U

BLACK DOG ALLEY, WESTMINSTER

judged against them in default. The lists were twenty-one yards square, set with scaffolds crowded with people—for who would not go out to see two men trying to kill each other? The Master of Defence, to whom the proceedings were an excellent advertisement, rode through London at seven in the morning in splendid attire, having the gauntlet borne before him; he entered Westminster Hall, but made no long stay there, going back to King Street, and so through the Sanctuary and Tothill Street to the lists, where he waited for the Judge. At ten the Court of Common Pleas removed to the lists. Then the combatants stood face to face, bare-footed, bare-legged, bare-headed, with their doublet sleeves turned back—ready for the fight; and all hearts beat faster, and the ladies caught their breath and gasped, and their colour came and went. Then the Judge gave order that every person must keep his place and give no help or encouragement by word or by weapon to the combatants. Next—this was the last of the tedious preliminaries: when would they begin?—each champion took oath—'This hear you Justices, that I this day neither eate, drunk, nor have upon me neither bone, stone, nor glasse, or any enchantment, sorcerie, or witchcraft, where-through the power of the word of God might be increased or diminished and the devil's power increased; and that my appeal is true, so help me God, and His saints, and by this booke.'

Alas! instead of giving the word to fight it out, the Lord Chief Justice remarked that the plaintiffs were not present; that there could be no fight without them; and that the estate consequently went to the defendant. Then with sad faces and heavy hearts the company dispersed. No fight, after all—nobody killed! To be sure, the Master of Defence invited the 'big broad strong set fellow' to play with him half a score blows; but the latter refused, saying he had come to fight and not to play.

A great Fair was held in these Fields on St. Edward's Day

(October 12) and for fifteen days afterwards. It was instituted by Henry III., in the hope of doing some mischief to the City of London. The Fair continued, but after the first year it seems to have done no harm to the trade of London. It continued, in fact, into the present century, when it was an ordinary fair of booths and shows, with Richardson's Theatre—like Greenwich Fair or Portsdown Fair. All these Fairs were alike. The two latter I can remember. Unfortunately my visits to these renowned Fairs took place in the afternoon; the real Fun of the Fair, I believe, took place in the evening. I remember a great

THE WESTMINSTER SNUFFBOX

crowd pushing and fighting and springing rattles on each other; and I remember the performers outside Richardson's marching about in magnificent costumes; the band playing; the clown tumbling; the columbine, a true fairy if ever there was one, gracefully pirouetting; then all forming into line for a dance; and after the dance the play in the tent behind. Such a Fair was that of Tothill Fields, at night the resort of all the ruffians of Westminster and Lambeth and half London. At least, however, while they were at the Fair they were out of other mischief. The exact site on which this Fair was held does not appear; but since it continued for the first quarter of this century at least, we may look for the

U 2

place which was the last to be built upon. In Crutchley's map of 1834 there are fields between the Vauxhall Bridge Road and James Street—that is, north-west of Rochester Row. There are also fields south of Vauxhall Bridge Road towards Chelsea. The former site seems the more probable.

Of course so fine a situation as Tothill Fields for the favourite diversions of a sporting people could not be neglected. Hither resorted all the lovers of those old English games, cock-fighting, bear-baiting, bull-baiting, cock-throwing, dog-fighting and prize-fighting. There were horse-races. These sports were continued well into this century. The Earl of Albemarle in his ' Recollections ' speaks of these sports. The Westminster boys of his time haunted the houses called the Seven Chimneys or the Five Houses—they were the old pest-houses—which were the resort of the bull-baiters, the dog-fanciers, and other gentry of cognate pursuits. Among them was the unfortunate Heberfield, commonly known as ' Slender Billy,' who seems to have been a good-tempered, easy-going person, without the least tincture of morals. The following is the strange and shameful story of his end :—

He got into trouble for assisting the escape of a certain French general who was on parole : took him probably to the south coast—Lyme Regis, Rousdon, or Charmouth—and introduced him to a smuggler who ran him across. He was caught, tried, and sentenced to imprisonment in Newgate. Unhappily for him, the Bank of England was just then suffering heavy losses from forgeries. They badly wanted to hang somebody—no matter who—somebody in order to deter others from forging notes. The story is quite amazing, as Lord Albemarle tells it. Can we conceive the Governing Body of the Bank of England meeting together and resolving to entrap some miserable wretch into passing the forged notes, so that by getting him hanged others would be deterred ? This is what Lord Albemarle says they did :—

' The Solicitors of the Bank accordingly took into their pay a confederate of Heberfield's named Barry. Through this man's agency Heberfield was easily inveigled into passing forged notes provided by the Solicitors of the Bank themselves. On the evidence of Barry, Heberfield was found guilty and sentenced to death. He was hanged at Newgate for forgery on January 12, 1812.'

The saddest of all the memories connected with Tothill Fields is that of the triumphal entry of Cromwell into London after the ' crowning mercy ' of Worcester. He brought with him the miserable prisoners he had taken on that field. There were four thousand of them in all. They camped at Mile End Green when Cromwell drove into London ; the next day they were marched right through the City and along the Strand to Westminster, and so to Tothill Fields. On the way they received alms, oatmeal and biscuit, from any who were moved of their pity to bestow something upon them. So they lay in the marshy fields, where many died, until they were sold as slaves to the merchants of Guinea. In Mr. J. E. Smith's ' History of the Church of St. John the Evangelist ' there is an entry which tells its own story. It is from the Church-wardens' Accounts of 1652-53 :—

' Paid to Thomas Wright for 67 load of soyle laid on the graves in Tothill Fields, wherein 1200 Scotch prisoners, taken at the ffight at Worcester, were buried, and for other paines taken with his teame of horsse about amending the Sanctuary Highway when General Ireton was buried. XXXS.'

How many of the remaining two thousand eight hundred ever got home again ? Chance once threw into my hands a tract which showed the hard treatment and the barbarities to which Monmouth's convicts in Barbadoes were subjected : most of these were men of respectable family, to whom money might be sent for their exemption from work in the fields, or even for their redemption. But these other poor fellows were absolutely friendless and penniless. And they were going to the Guinea Coast, the Gold Coast, the white man's grave !

One hopes that the mortality on their arrival was swifter and more extensive than even the mortality in Tothill Fields, because death was certainly the best thing that could happen to them.

When these papers first appeared I received a letter of expostulation from a reader. He said that the streets of Westminster were not all so disreputable as I seemed to think. He said :—

'Westminster only became a slum within this hundred years. The old Westminster workhouse had been the mansion of Sir John Pye. Sir Francis Burdett was born in Orchard Street, and Admiral Kempenfeldt who went down in the " Royal George " had his house there, and not so very long ago a pear tree bloomed annually in his garden. The father of Henry Boys, organist of St. John's, about 1830 to 1840, was a bullion worker and carried on his business for many years and up to the thirties in Great St. Anne's Lane. My grandmother was born 1770 in Peter Street, at the corner of Duck Lane. She told me that all that neighbourhood was very respectable in her girlhood, Duck Lane being the only exception. She attributed the downfall of the locality to the cheap houses that were built at that time in New Peter Street. Towards the end of the century there was only one shop in Strutton Ground : all the rest being public-houses. My mother was born in 1802 in Marlborough House, Peter Street : then the premises of the Cudbear Company. She used to recall Brown's Gardens in her young days, that were between St. Peter Street and the Horseferry Road. They were nursery gardens. Palmer's village was a collection of houses for workmen, built about the beginning of this century or the end of last, between Emanuel Hospital and Brewer's Green, and accessible through an archway leading from the latter.'

I am glad to print this protest. I have however given my authorities for what I have stated. It is quite possible that respectable streets and good houses existed side by side with the slums. There are always respectable streets and great houses in every neighbourhood, just as among associations of the greatest villains there are always some with redeeming traits. Among the residents of Westminster our friend might have mentioned Lord Grey of Wilton, Cornelius Van Dun, Yeoman of the Guard to four sovereigns, Oliver Cromwell, John Milton and Dick Turpin.

Hear, however, further from Mr. William Bardwell, writing in 1839 :—

'Another of the peculiarities which this district presents is the number of middle-men it contains : these generally possess themselves of a house or houses, with gardens, large or small as it may happen ; here they erect, in open defiance of all building or sewers' acts, a number of tenements of the most wretched description, and to which the only access is by a passage through one of the front houses ; in process of time these become lanes, or courts, or alleys, or places, or buildings or yards. These tenements are divided into separate rooms, and let weekly by the middle-man, who subsists upon his beneficial interest in the concern ; and so numerous are the houses of this description in the district, that considerably more than one half of the number proposed to be removed are let to weekly lodgers ; but these places, most of them old, and very slightly built, frequently with boards held together by iron hoops, are so utterly destitute of every convenience, that the heretofore pleasant gardens of Tothill are most terrible nuisances.

'It is in these narrow streets, and in these close and insalubrious lanes, courts, and alleys, where squalid misery and poverty struggle with filth and wretchedness, where vice reigns unchecked, and in the atmosphere of which the worst diseases are generated and diffused. That uncleanness and impurity are an unerring index, pointing out the situation where the malignancy of epidemics more or less exists, is a truth known and admitted from the earliest ages.

' Dr. Wright, the assiduous and highly-intelligent medical officer to the parish, stated before the same Committee, " that fever is exceedingly prevalent, and had been very general in the months of April and May." The Doctor had upwards of thirty cases of typhus fever in one court containing four houses ; most of which cases it is probable would have terminated fatally had the sufferers not been removed from that locality ; " That fever is propagated and continued in these miserable courts long after the ravages of epidemics have ceased in more open parts."

' Mr. Cubitt also has stated, that " the ground between the Almonry and the western end of Palmer's village is occupied by the worst possible description of inhabitants. The land is exceedingly badly drained, or rather not drained ; and there being no proper outlets for the water, a great deal of bad air must pass off by evaporation from the quantity of stagnant water upon the surface and in the cesspools." '

Here we make an end : it is not a Survey of Westminster to which you have been invited ; it is but this side and that side of the many-sided life of this remarkable City, which is, as was pointed out at the beginning, unlike any other city in the world, in having no citizens, but only residents or tenants ; no municipal life ; which welcomed all the scum, riffraff and *ribauderie* of the country, and gave them harbour ; which has always belonged to the Church, yet has never been expected to have any morals ; always its streets and courts have been crammed with thieves and drabs, gamesters, sporting men, cheats and bullies ; and beside the streets always stood the stately Monastery, the quiet cloister, the noble Church, the splendid Court, the gallant following of king and noble, and the gathering of grave and responsible knights and burgesses assembled to carry on the affairs of the country. I have invited you to restore Thorney as it was long ago, the stepping-stone and halting-place of all the trade of the island, busy and noisy ; the life of the Benedictine in his monastery ; the consecration of the Anchorite; the strange life of the mediæval Sanctuary; the Palace of the Plantagenets; the Palace of the Stuarts; the Masques of James I.; the Parliamentary side of the last century; and the streets and slums. A great many things have been purposely omitted from these pages which belong to Westminster and have taken place there. For instance, there is the School with its long line of scholars, afterwards famous. Nothing has been said about the School. There is, again, the Abbey Church. Very little has been said about the buildings; the additions, alterations, restorations: nothing at all has been said about the monuments which crowd its aisles and transepts.

THE WESTMINSTER TOBACCO BOX

There is Westminster Hall: very little, indeed, has been said here of the things done within its walls: the Coronation Banquets; the Trials; the Receptions. Nothing has been said concerning the executions and the tournaments which have taken place in Palace Yard, Old and New. Nothing has been said about the New Houses of Parliament. These things, and a great many more which the reader can remember for himself, have been omitted from these pages, partly because they belong to the history of this country and may be found in all Histories ; they happened in Westminster and they belong to Great Britain : partly because they have already been so well treated that it is unnecessary and would be even presumptuous for me to attempt them ; and partly because the space at my disposal is limited, though the materials are practically inexhaustible. These chapters are not to be considered as a History of Westminster, or a Survey : they are pictures of the City with its Palace, its Abbey, its Sanctuary, and its slums, from a time when London did not exist until the present day.

APPENDIX

THE COURT OF CHARLES II.

THE popular imagination pictures the Court of Charles the Second as a place of no ceremony or state or dignity whatever ; where the King strolled about the courts and where there was singing of boys, laughter of women, tinkling of guitars, playing of cards, making merriment without stint or restraint, a Bohemia of Courts. We have been taught to think thus of King Charles's Court by the historian who has seized on one or two scenes and episodes—for instance, the last Sunday evening of Charles's life ; by the writer of romance ; by the chronicler of scandal ; by the Restoration poets and the Restoration dramatists.

This view of Whitehall after the Restoration is, to say the least, incomplete. Charles had a Court, like every other sovereign : he had a Court with officers many and distinguished : there were Court ceremonies which he had to go through : that part of his private life which is now paraded as if it was his public life was conducted with some regard to public opinion. What his Court really was, may be learned from a little book by Thomas de Laune, Gentleman, called 'The Present State of London,' published in the year 1681, for George Lurkin, Enoch Prosser, and John How, at the *Rose and Crown*. Since we have seen what were the chief offices of the Confessor's Court and of Richard the Second's Court, it may be useful to learn, from this book, the offices and management of a Stuart's Court.

I. *Its Government, Ecclesiastical, Civil and Military*

1. *Ecclesiastical.*—The Dean of the King's Chapel was generally a Bishop. The Chapel itself is a Royal Peculiar, exempt from episcopal visitation. The Dean chose the Sub-Dean or *Precentor Capellæ* ; thirty-six gentlemen of the Chapel, of whom twelve were priests and

twenty-four singing clerks, twelve children, three organists, four vergers, a sergeant, two yeomen, and a Groom of the Chapel. The King had his private oratory where every day one of the chaplains read the service of the day. Twelve times a year the King, attended by his principal nobility, offered a sum of money in gold, called the Byzantine gift, because it was formerly coined at Byzantium, in recognition of the Grace of God which made him King. James the First used a coin with the legend—on one side—'Quid retribuam Domino pro omnibus quæ retribuit mihi?'—and on the other side—' Cor contritum et humiliatum non despiciet Deus.'

In addition there were forty-eight Chaplains in Ordinary, of whom four every month waited at Court.

The Lord High Almoner, usually the Bishop of London, disposed of the King's alms : he received all *deodands* and *bona felonum de se* to be applied to that purpose : Under him were a Sub-Almoner, two Yeomen and two Grooms of the Almonry. There was also a Clerk of the Closet whose duty was to resolve doubts on spiritual matters. In the reign of good King Charles the duties of this officer were probably light.

II. *The Civil Government*

The chief officer was the Lord Steward. He had authority over all the officers of the Court except those of the Chapel, the Chamber, and the Stable. He was Judge of all offences committed within the precincts of the Court and within the Verge. In the King's Presence the Lord Steward carried a white staff : when he went abroad the White Staff was borne before him by a footman bareheaded. His salary was 100*l.* a year with sixteen Dishes daily and allowances of wine, beer, &c. The Lord Chamberlain had the supervision of all officers belonging to the King's Chamber, such as the officers of the wardrobe, of the Revels, of the music, of the plays, of the Hunt ; the messengers, Trumpeters, Heralds, Poursuivants, Apothecaries, Chyrurgeons, Barbers, Chaplains, &c.

The third great officer was the Master of the Horse. His duties are signified by his title, which was formerly *comes stabuli* or Constable.

Under these principal officers were the Treasurer of the Household, the Comptroller, the Cofferer, the Master of the Household, the two Clerks of the Green Cloth, the sergeants, messengers, &c.

In the Compting House was held the Court of Green Cloth, which sat every day with authority to maintain the Peace within a circle of twelve miles radius. It was so called from the colour of the cloth spread upon the table.

The chief Clerk was an official of great power and dignity : he received the King's guests ; kept the accounts ; looked after the provisions and had charge of the Pantry, Buttery and Cellar. There were clerks under him. The Knight Harbinger with three Gentlemen Harbingers and seven Yeomen Harbingers provided lodgings for the King's Guests, Ambassadors, officers and servants.

The Knight Marshal was Judge in all cases in which a servant of the King was concerned : he was also one of the Judges in the Court of the Marshalsea. He had six Provost Marshals or Vergers in scarlet coats to wait upon him.

The Servants in ordinary were the Gentlemen of the Bedchamber, and the Groom of the Stole, the Vice-Chamberlain, the Keeper of the Privy Purse, the Treasurer of the Chamber, the Master of the Robes, the twelve Grooms of the Bedchamber, the six Pages of the Bedchamber, the four Gentlemen Ushers of the Privy Chamber, the forty-eight Gentlemen of the Privy Chamber, the six Grooms of the Privy Chamber, the Library Keeper, Black Rod, the eight Gentlemen Ushers of the Presence Chamber, the fourteen Grooms of the Great Chamber, six gentlemen waiters, four cupbearers, four carvers, four servers, four esquires of the Body, the eight servers of the Chamber, the Groom Porter, sixteen sergeants at arms, four other sergeants at arms who attended on the Speaker and on the Lord Lieutenant of Ireland. There were four Physicians in Ordinary, a Master and Treasurer of the Jewel House, three Yeomen of the Jewel House, a Master of the Ceremonies with an assistant and a marshal ; three Kings at Arms, six Heralds, and four Poursuivants at Arms ; a Geographer, a Historiographer, a Hydrographer, a Cosmographer, a Poet Laureate, and a Notary.

These were the Officers of the Wardrobe : the Great Wardrobe, the standing wardrobes at Hampton, Windsor and other places, and the Removing Wardrobe which was carried about with the King. For the wardrobes were one Yeoman, two Grooms, and three Pages.

For the Office of Tents and Pavilions were two Masters, four Yeomen, one Groom, one Clerk Comptroller and one Clerk of the Tents. The Master of the Revels ordered the plays and masques &c. He had one Yeoman and one Groom. Attached to the Master of the Robes were workmen, each in his own craft. The Royal Falconer had thirty-three officers under him. The Master of Buckhounds had thirty-four assistants : the Master of the otter hounds had five under him. So had the Master of the Harriers. The Master of the Ordnance had a Lieutenant, a master Armourer and seventeen under officers. There were forty-two messengers of the Chamber. There were sixty-four Musicians in ordinary ; fifteen trumpeters and kettle drummers ; seven drummers and fifes ; two Apothecaries ; two Chyrurgeons ; two Barbers ; three Printers ; one Printer of Oriental tongues. There were bookseller, stationer, bookbinder, silkman, woollen draper, post-master, and a Master of Cock-fighting.

There were two Embroiderers, one Serjeant Skinner, two Keepers of the Privy Lodging, two Gentlemen, and two Yeomen of the Bows ; one Cross-bow maker ; one Fletcher ; one Cormorant keeper ; one Hand-gun maker ; one master and marker of Tennis ; one Mistress Semstress, and one Laundress ; one Perspective-maker, one Master-Fencer, one Haberdasher of Hats, one Combmaker, one Sergeant Painter, one Painter, one Limner, one Picture-Drawer, one Silver-Smith, one Goldsmith, one Jeweller, one Peruque-maker, one Keeper of Pheasants and Turkies. Joyner, Copier of Pictures, Watch-maker, Cabinet-maker, Lock-Smith, of each one. Game of Bears and Bulls, one Master, one Sergeant, one Yeoman. Two Operators for the Teeth. Two Coffer-bearers for the Back-stairs, one Yeoman of the Leash, fifty-five Watermen. Upholsterer, Letter Carrier, Foreign Post, Coffee Maker, of each one.

Ten Officers belonging to Gardens, Bowling-Greens, Tennis-Court, Pall-Mall, Keeper of the Theatre at Whitehall. Cutler, Spurrier, Girdler, Corn-Cutter, Button-maker, Embosser, Enameler, of each one. Writer, Flourisher, and Embellisher, Scenographer, or Designer of Prospects, Letter-Founder, of each one. Comedians, Seventeen Men, and Eight Women, Actors.

Gunner, Gilder, Cleaner of Pictures, Scene Keeper, Coffer-maker, Wax-Chandler, of each one. Keeper of Birds and Fowl in St. James's-Park, one. Keeper of the Volery, Coffee-club-maker, Sergeant-Painter, of each one ; with divers other officers and servants under the Lord Chamberlain to serve his Majesty upon occasion.

As to the Officers under the Master of the Horse, there are Twelve Querries so called of the French Escayer, derived from Escury, a Stable. Their office is to attend the King on Hunting or Progress, or on any occasion of Riding Abroad, to help His Majesty up and down from his Horse, &c. Four of these are called Querries of the Crown-Stable, and the others are called Querries of the Hunting-Stable. The Fee to each of these is only 20*l.* yearly, according to the Ancient Custom ; but they have allowance for Diet, to each 100*l.* yearly, besides Lodgings, and two Horse-Liveries.

Next is the Chief Avener, from Avena, Oats, whose yearly Fee is 40*l.* There is, moreover, one Clerk of the Stable, four Yeomen-Riders, four Child-Riders, Yeomen of the Stirrup, Sergeant-Marshal, and Yeomen-Farriers, four Groom-Farriers, Sergeants of the Carriage, three Surveyors, a Squire and Yeomen-Sadlers, four Yeomen-Granators, four Yeomen-Purveyors, a Yeoman-Pickman, a Yeoman-Bitmaker, four Coach-men, eight Litter-men, a Yeoman of the Close Wagon, sixty-four Grooms of the Stable, whereof thirty are called Grooms of the Crown Stable, and thirty-four of the Hunting and Pad-Stable. Twenty-six Footmen in their Liveries, to run by the King's Horse. All these Places are in the Gift of the Masters of the Horse.

There is besides these an antient Officer, called Clerk of the Market, who within the Verge of the King's Household, is to keep a Standard of all Weights and Measures, and to burn all that are false. From the Pattern of this Standard, all the Weights and Measures of the Kingdom are to be taken.

There are divers other considerable Officers, not Subordinate to the Three Great Officers, as the Master of the Great Wardrobe, Post-Master, Master of the Ordinance, Warden of the Mint, &c.

Upon the King are also attending in his Court the Lords of the Privy Council, Secretaries of State, the Judges, the College of Civilians, the King's Council at Law, the King's Serjeants at Law, the Masters of Requests, Clerks of the Signet, Clerks of the Council, Keeper of the Paper-Office, or Papers of State, &c.

There is always a Military Force to preserve the King's Person, which are His Guards of Horse and Foot. The Guards of Horse are in Number 600 Men, well armed and equipped ; who are generally Young Gentlemen of considerable Families, who are there made fit for Military Commands. They are divided into Three Troops, viz. : the Kings Troop, distinguished by their Blew Ribbons and Carbine Belts, their Red Hooses, and Houlster-Caps, Embroidered with His Majesties Cypher and Crown. The Queens Troops by Green Ribbons, Carbine Belts, covered with Green Velvet, and Gold Lace, also Green Hooses and Houlster Caps, Embroidered with the same Cypher and Crown. And the Dukes Troop by Yellow Ribbons, and Carbine Belts, and Yellow Hooses, Embroidered as the others. In which Troops, are 200 Gentlemen, besides Officers. Each of these Three Troops is divided into Four Squadrons or Divisions, two of which consisting of one hundred Gentlemen, and Commanded by one Principal Commissioned Officer, two Brigadiers, and two Sub-Brigadiers, with two Trumpets mount the Guards one day in six, and are Relieved in their turns. Their Duty is always by Parties from the Guard, to attend the Person of the King, the Queen, the Duke, and the Duchess, wheresoever they go near home, but if out of town, they are attended by Detachments of the said Three Troops.

Besides these, there is a more strict Duty and Attendance Weekly on the King's Person on Foot, wheresoever he walks, from His Rising to His going to Bed, by one of the Three Captains, who always waits immediately next the King's own Person, before all others, carrying in his hand an Ebony-staff or Truncheon, with a Gold head, Engraved with His Majesty's Cypher and Crown. Near him also attends a Principal Commissioned Officer, with an Ebony-staff, and Silver head, who is ready to Relieve the Captain on occasion; and at the same time also, two Brigadiers, having also Ebony-staves, headed with Ivory, and Engraven as the others.

There is added a Troop of Grenadiers to each Troop of Guards, one Division of which mounts with a Division of the Troop to which they belong; they never go out on small Parties from the Guard, only perform Centry-Duty on Foot, and attend the King also on Foot when he walks abroad, but always March with great Detachments. The King's Troop consists of a Captain, two Lieutenants, three Sergeants, three Corporals, two Drums, two Hautbois, and eighty private Souldiers mounted. The Queens Troop, of a Captain, two Lieutenants, two Sergeants, two Corporals, two Hautbois, and sixty private Souldiers mounted. The Dukes Troop consists of the like number with the Queens.

The Captains of His Majesties Guards always Command as Eldest Colonels of Horse; the Lieutenants as Eldest Lieutenant-Colonels of Horse; the Cornets and Guidons, as Eldest Majors of Horse; the Quartermasters, as Youngest Captains of Horse; the Brigadiers as Eldest Lieutenants of Horse; and amongst themselves every Officer, according to the Date of His Commission, takes precedency, when on Detachments, but not when the Three Troops march with their Colours, for then the Officer of the Eldest Troop, commands those of equal Rank with him in the others, though their Commission be of Elder Date.

Next immediately after the Three Troops of Guards, His Majestys Regiment of Horse, Commanded by the Earl of Oxford takes place, and the Colonel of it is to have precedency, after the Captains of the

Guards, and before all other Colonels of Horse, whatsoëver change may be of the Colonel ; and all the Officers thereof, in their proper Degree, are to take place according to the Dates of their Commissions. As to the Foot, the King's Regiment, Commanded by the Honorable Colonel John Russel, takes place of all other Regiments, and the Colonel thereof is always to precede as the first Colonel. The Colestream Regiment, Commanded by the Earl of Craven, takes the next ; the Duke of Yorks Regiment next, then His Majestys Holland Regiment, Commanded by the Earl of Mulgrave, and all other Colonels, according to the Dates of their Commissions. All other Regiments of Horse and Foot, not of the Guards, take place according to their Respective Seniority, from the time they were first Raised, and no Regiment loses its precedency by the Death of its Colonel.

At the Kings House, there is a guard for his Person, both above and below stairs. In the Presence Chamber, the Band of Gentlemen Pensioners wait, instituted by King Henry the VII., and chosen out of the best and antientest Families in England, to be a Guard to His Majesties Person, and also to be a Nursery to breed up hopeful Gentlemen, and fit them for Employments, Civil and Military, as well abroad as at home ; as Deputies of Ireland, Embassadors in Foreign Parts, Counsellors of State, Captains of the Guard, Governors of Places, Commanders in the Wars, both by Sea and Land, of all which these have been Examples. They are to attend the King's Person to and from His Chappel, only as far as the Privy Chamber : also in all other Solemnity, as Coronations, publick Audience of Embassadors, &c. They are 40 in number, over whom there is a Captain, usually some Peer of the Realm, a Lieutenant, a Standard-Bearer, and a Clerk of the Check. They wait half at a time quarterly. Those in quarter wait daily five at a time upon the King in the House, and when He walks abroad. Upon extraordinary occasions, all of them are Summoned. Their ordinary Arms are Gilt Pole-Axes. Their Arms on Horse-back in time of War, are Cuirassiers Arms, with Sword and Pistol. These are only under their own Officers, and are always Sworn by the Clerk of the Check, who is to take notice of such as are absent when they should be upon their duty. Their Standard in time of war, is a Cross Gules in a Field Argent, also 4 bends.

In the first Room above Stairs, called the Guard-Chamber, attend the Yeomen of the Guard of His Majesties body ; whereof there were wont to be 250 Men of the best quality under Gentry, and of

X

larger Stature than ordinary (for every one was to be Six Foot high) there are at present 100 Yeomen in dayly waiting, and 70 more not in waiting, and as any of the 100 die, his place is filled up out of the 70. These wear Scarlet Coats Down to the Knee, and Scarlet Breeches, both richly guarded with black Velvet, and rich Badges upon their Coats both before and behind, moreover, black Velvet round broad Crown'd Caps, with Ribbons of the King's Colour ; one half of them of late bear in their hands Harquebuzes, and the other half Partizans, with large Swords by their Sides ; they have Wages and Diet allowed them. Their office is to wait upon the King in His standing Houses, 40 by Day, and 20 to Watch by Night ; about the City to wait upon the Kings Person abroad by Water or Land.

The Kings Palace Royal (*ratione Regiæ dignitatis*) is exempted from all Jurisdiction of any Court, Civil, or Ecclesiastick, but only to the Lord Steward, and in his absence, to the Treasurer and Comptroller of the Kings Household, with the Steward of the Marshalsea, who by vertue of their Office, without Commission, may Hear and Determin all Treasons, Fellonies, Breaches of the Peace, Committed within the Kings Court or Palace. The Orders and Rules for the Demeanor of all Officers and Servants, are hung upon Tables in several Rooms at the Court, and Signed with the Kings own hand, worthy to be read of all Strangers.

The Court or House where the King resides, is accounted a Place so Sacred, that if any Man presume to strike another there, and only draw Blood, his Right Hand shall be cut off, and he committed to perpetual Imprisonment, and Fined. All occasions of striking are also there forbidden.

The Court of England, for Magnificence, Order, Number and Quality of Officers, rich Furniture, Entertainment and Civility to Strangers, and for plentiful Tables, might compare with the best in Christendom, and far excels most Courts abroad. It hath for a long time been a Pattern of Hospitality and Charity, to the Nobility and Gentry of England. All Noblemen or Gentlemen, Subjects or Strangers, were freely entertained at the plentiful Tables of His Majesties Officers. Divers Dishes were provided every day extraordinary for the King's Honour. Two hundred and fourty Gallons of Beer a day, were allowed at the Buttery-Bar for the Poor, besides all the broken Meat, Bread, &c., gathered into Baskets, and given to the Poor, at the Court-Gates, by Two Grooms, and Two Yeomen of the Almonry, who have Salaries of His Majesty for that Service. The Lord Almoner hath the Privilege to give the Kings Dish, to whatsoever Poor Man he pleases ; that is, the first Dish at Dinner which is set upon the Kings Table, or in stead thereof fourpence a day (which anciently was equivalent to four Shillings now) ; next he distributes to 24 poor men, named by the Parishioners of the Parish adjacent to the Kings Place of Residence, to each of them fourpence in money, a Two-penny Loaf, and a Gallon of Beer, or instead thereof three pence in Money, equally to be divided among them every Morning at seven of the Clock at the Court-Gate. The Sub-Almoner is to Scatter new-coined Two-pences in the Towns and Places where the King passes through in his Progresses, to a certain Sum by the Year. Besides, there are many poor Pensioners, either because so old that they are unfit for Service, or the Widows of any of the Kings Servants that dyed poor, who have a Competency duly paid them : Besides, there are distributed among the Poor the larger Offerings which the King gives in Collar Days.

The magnificent and abundant plenty of the King's Tables, hath caused amazement in Foreigners. In the Reign of King Charles I. there were daily in his Court 86 Tables well furnished each Meal, whereof the Kings Tables had 28 Dishes, the Queens 24, 4 other Tables 16 Dishes each, 3 other 10 Dishes, 12 other 7 Dishes, 17 other 5 Dishes, 3 other 4, 32 had 3, and 13 had each two ; in all about 500 Dishes each Meal, with Bread, Beer, Wine, and all other things necessary. There was spent yearly in the Kings House of gross Meat 1500 Oxen, 7000 Sheep, 1200 Veals, 300 Porkers, 400 Sturks or young Beefs, 6800 Lambs, 300 Flitches of Bacon, and 26 Boars. Also 140 dozen of Geese, 250 dozen of Capons, 470 dozen of Hens, 750 dozen of Pullets, 1470 dozen of Chickens, for Bread 36400 Bushels of Wheat, and for Drink 600 Tun of Wine, and 1700 Tun of Beer. Moreover, of Butter 46,640, together with the Fish, and Fowl, Venison, Fruit, Spice proportionably. This prodigious plenty in the Kings Court caused Foreigners to put a higher value upon the King, and was much for the Honour of the Kingdom. The King's Servants being Men of Quality, by His Majestys special Order went to Westminster-Hall in Term Time, to invite Gentlemen, to eat of the King's Acates or Viands, and in Parliament-time, to invite the Parliament-men thereto.

On the Thursday before Easter, called Maundy Thursday, the King, or his Lord Almoner, was wont to wash the Feet of as many poor Men, as His Majesty had reigned years, and then to wipe them with a Towel (according to the Pattern of our Saviour), and then to give everyone of them two Yards and a half of Woollen Cloth, to make a Suit of Cloaths ; also Linnen Cloth for two Shirts, and a pair of Stockings, and a pair of Shoes, three Dishes of Fish in Wooden Platters, one of Salt Salmon, a second of Green Fish or Cod, a third of Pickle-Herrings, Red Herrings, and Red Sprats, a Gallon of Beer, a Quart Pottle of Wine, and four six-penny Loaves of Bread, also a Red-Leather-Purse with as many single Pence as the King is years old, and in fact another Purse as many Shillings as the King hath reigned Years. The Queen doth the like to divers poor Women.

The Form of Government is by the wisdom of many Ages, so contrived and regulated, that it is almost impossible to mend it. The Account (which is of so many Natures, and is therefore very difficult, must pass through many hands, and is therefore very exact) is so wisely contrived and methodized, that without the Combination of everyone of these following Officers, viz., the Cofferer, a Clerk of the Green-Cloth, a Clerk Comptroller, a Clerk of the Kitchin, of the Spicery or Avery, or a particular Clerk, together with the con junction of a Purveyor and Waiter in the Office, it is impossible to defraud the King of a Loaf of Bread, of a Pint of Wine, a Quart of Beer, or Joint of Meat, or Money, or anything else.

INDEX

PRINTED BY
SPOTTISWOODE AND CO., NEW-STREET SQUARE
LONDON

[*July*, 1895.

A List of Books Published by
CHATTO & WINDUS
214, Piccadilly, London, W.

ABOUT (EDMOND).—THE FELLAH : An Egyptian Novel. Translated by Sir RANDAL ROBERTS. Post 8vo, illustrated boards, **2s.**

ADAMS (W. DAVENPORT), WORKS BY.
A DICTIONARY OF THE DRAMA : The Plays, Playwrights, Players, and Playhouses of the United Kingdom and America. Cr. 8vo, half-bound, **12s. 6d.** [*Preparing.*
QUIPS AND QUIDDITIES. Selected by W. D. ADAMS. Post 8vo, cloth limp, **2s. 6d.**

AGONY COLUMN (THE) OF "THE TIMES," from 1800 to 1870. Edited, with an Introduction, by ALICE CLAY. Post 8vo, cloth limp, **2s. 6d.**

AIDE (HAMILTON), WORKS BY. Post 8vo, illustrated boards, **2s.** each.
CARR OF CARRLYON. | CONFIDENCES.

ALBERT (MARY).—BROOKE FINCHLEY'S DAUGHTER. Post 8vo, picture boards, **2s.**; cloth limp, **2s. 6d.**

ALDEN (W. L.).—A LOST SOUL. Fcap. 8vo, cloth boards, **1s. 6d.**

ALEXANDER (MRS.), NOVELS BY. Post 8vo, illustrated boards, **2s.** each.
MAID, WIFE, OR WIDOW? | VALERIE'S FATE.

ALLEN (F. M.).—GREEN AS GRASS. Crown 8vo, cloth, **3s. 6d.**

ALLEN (GRANT), WORKS BY.
THE EVOLUTIONIST AT LARGE. Crown 8vo, cloth extra, **6s.**
POST-PRANDIAL PHILOSOPHY. Crown 8vo, art linen, **3s. 6d.**

Crown 8vo, cloth extra, **3s. 6d.** each ·post 8vo, illustrated boards, **2s.** each.

PHILISTIA.	THE DEVIL'S DIE.	THE DUCHESS OF
BABYLON.	THIS MORTAL COIL.	POWYSLAND.
STRANGE STORIES.	THE TENTS OF SHEM.	BLOOD ROYAL.
BECKONING HAND.	THE GREAT TABOO.	IVAN GREET'S MASTER-
FOR MAIMIE'S SAKE.	DUMARESQ'S DAUGH-	PIECE.
IN ALL SHADES.	TER.	THE SCALLYWAG.

DR. PALLISER'S PATIENT. Fcap. 8vo, cloth extra, **1s. 6d.**
AT MARKET VALUE. Two Vols., crown 8vo, cloth, **10s.** net.
UNDER SEALED ORDERS. Three Vols., crown 8vo, cloth, **15s.** net.

ANDERSON (MARY).—OTHELLO'S OCCUPATION. Cr. 8vo, cl., **3s. 6d.**

ARNOLD (EDWIN LESTER), STORIES BY.
THE WONDERFUL ADVENTURES OF PHRA THE PHŒNICIAN. With 12 Illusts. by H. M. PAGET. Crown 8vo, cloth extra, **3s. 6d.**; post 8vo, illust. boards, **2s.**
THE CONSTABLE OF ST. NICHOLAS. With Front. by S. WOOD Cr. 8vo, cl., **3s. 6d.**

ARTEMUS WARD'S WORKS. With Portrait and Facsimile. Crown 8vo, cloth extra.—Also a POPULAR EDITION, post 8vo, picture boards, **2s.**
THE GENIAL SHOWMAN : Life and Adventures of ARTEMUS WARD. By EDWARD P. HINGSTON. With a Frontispiece. Crown 8vo, cloth extra, **3s. 6d.**

ASHTON (JOHN), WORKS BY. Crown 8vo, cloth extra, **7s. 6d.** each.
HISTORY OF THE CHAP-BOOKS OF THE 18th CENTURY. With 334 Illusts.
SOCIAL LIFE IN THE REIGN OF QUEEN ANNE. With 85 Illustrations.
HUMOUR, WIT, AND SATIRE OF SEVENTEENTH CENTURY. With 82 Illusts.
ENGLISH CARICATURE AND SATIRE ON NAPOLEON THE FIRST. 115 Illusts
MODERN STREET BALLADS. With 57 Illustrations.

BACTERIA, YEAST FUNGI, AND ALLIED SPECIES, A SYNOPSIS
OF. By W. B. GROVE, B.A.   With 87 Illustrations, Crown 8vo, cloth extra, **3s. 6**.

BARDSLEY (REV. C. W.), WORKS BY.
ENGLISH SURNAMES: Their Sources and Significations. Cr. 8vo. cloth, **7s. 6d.**
CURIOSITIES OF PURITAN NOMENCLATURE.   Crown 8vo, cloth extra, **6s.**

BARING GOULD (S., Author of "John Herring," &c.), NOVELS BY.
Crown 8vo, cloth extra, **3s. 6d.** each; post 8vo, illustrated boards, **2s.** each.
RED SPIDER. | EVE.

BARR (ROBERT : LUKE SHARP), STORIES BY. Cr. 8vo, cl., **3s. 6d.** ea.
IN A STEAMER CHAIR.   With Frontispiece and Vignette by DEMAIN HAMMOND.
FROM WHOSE BOURNE, &c.   With 47 Illustrations.

BARRETT (FRANK), NOVELS BY.
Post 8vo, illustrated boards, **2s.** each; cloth. **2s. 6d.** each.
FETTERED FOR LIFE.   A PRODIGAL'S PROGRESS.
THE SIN OF OLGA ZASSOULICH.   JOHN FORD; and HIS HELPMATE.
BETWEEN LIFE AND DEATH.   A RECOILING VENGEANCE.
FOLLY MORRISON. | HONEST DAVIE. LIEUT. BARNABAS. | FOUND GUILTY.
LITTLE LADY LINTON.   FOR LOVE AND HONOUR.
THE WOMAN OF THE IRON BRACELETS. Crown 8vo. cloth. **3s. 6d.**

BEACONSFIELD, LORD. By T. P. O'CONNOR, M.P. Cr. 8vo, cloth, 5s.

BEAUCHAMP (S).—GRANTLEY GRANGE. Post 8vo, illust. boards, **2s.**

BEAUTIFUL PICTURES BY BRITISH ARTISTS : A Gathering from
the Picture Galleries, engraved on Steel. Imperial 4to. cloth extra, gilt edges, **21s.**

BECHSTEIN (LUDWIG).—AS PRETTY AS SEVEN, and other German
Stories.   With Additional Tales by the Brothers GRIMM, and 98 Illustrations by
RICHTER.   Square 8vo, cloth extra, **6s. 6d.**; gilt edges, **7s. 6d.**

BESANT (Sir WALTER), NOVELS BY.
Cr. 8vo, cl. ex., **3s. 6d.** each; post 8vo. illust. bds., **2s.** each; cl. limp, **2s. 6d.** each.
ALL SORTS AND CONDITIONS OF MEN. With Illustrations by FRED. BARNARD.
THE CAPTAINS' ROOM, &c.   With Frontispiece by E. J. WHEELER.
ALL IN A GARDEN FAIR.   With 6 Illustrations by Harry Furniss.
DOROTHY FORSTER.   With Frontispiece by CHARLES GREEN.
UNCLE JACK, and other Stories. | CHILDREN OF GIBEON.
THE WORLD WENT VERY WELL THEN. With 12 Illustrations by A. FORESTIER.
HERR PAULUS: His Rise, his Greatness, and his Fall.
FOR FAITH AND FREEDOM.   With Illustrations by A. FORESTIER and F. WADDY.
TO CALL HER MINE, &c.   With 9 Illustrations by A. FORESTIER.
THE BELL OF ST. PAUL'S.
THE HOLY ROSE, &c.   With Frontispiece by F. BARNARD.
ARMOREL OF LYONESSE: A Romance of To-day. With 12 Illusts. by F. BARNARD.
ST. KATHERINE'S BY THE TOWER.   With 12 page Illustrations by C. GREEN.
VERBENA CAMELLIA STEPHANOTIS, &c. | THE IVORY GATE: A Novel.
THE REBEL QUEEN.
BEYOND THE DREAMS OF AVARICE.   Crown 8vo, cloth extra, **6s.**
IN DEACON'S ORDERS, &c.   With Frontispiece. Crown 8vo, cloth, **6s.**
FIFTY YEARS AGO. With 144 Plates and Woodcuts. Crown 8vo, cloth extra, **5s.**
THE EULOGY OF RICHARD JEFFERIES. With Portrait.   Cr. 8vo, cl. extra, **6s.**
LONDON. With 125 Illustrations. New Edition. Demy 8vo, cloth extra, **7s. 6d.**
SIR RICHARD WHITTINGTON. Frontispiece. Crown 8vo, art linen, **3s. 6d.**
GASPARD DE COLIGNY. With a Portrait. Crown 8vo, art linen, **3s. 6d.**
AS WE ARE: AS WE MAY BE: Social Essays. Crown 8vo, linen, **6s.** [Shortly.

BESANT (Sir WALTER) AND JAMES RICE, NOVELS BY.
Cr. 8vo, cl. ex., **3s. 6d.** each; post 8vo, illust. bds., **2s.** each; cl. limp, **2s. 6d.** each.
READY-MONEY MORTIBOY.   BY CELIA'S ARBOUR.
MY LITTLE GIRL.   THE CHAPLAIN OF THE FLEET
WITH HARP AND CROWN.   THE SEAMY SIDE.
THIS SON OF VULCAN.   THE CASE OF MR. LUCRAFT, &c.
THE GOLDEN BUTTERFLY.   'TWAS IN TRAFALGAR'S BAY, &c.
THE MONKS OF THELEMA.   THE TEN YEARS' TENANT, &c.
*** There is also a LIBRARY EDITION of the above Twelve Volumes, handsomely
set in new type on a large crown 8vo page. and bound in cloth extra, **6s.** each; and
a POPULAR EDITION of THE GOLDEN BUTTERFLY, medium 8vo, 6d.; cloth, 1s.;
and a NEW EDITION, printed in large type, crown 8vo, figured cloth binding, 3s. 6d

BEERBOHM (JULIUS).—WANDERINGS IN PATAGONIA ; or, Life among the Ostrich Hunters. With Illustrations. Crown 8vo. cloth extra. **3s. 6d.**

BELLEW (FRANK).—THE ART OF AMUSING : A Collection of Graceful Arts, Games, Tricks, Puzzles, and Charades. 300 Illusts. Cr. 8vo. cl. ex. **4s. 6d.**

BENNETT (W. C., LL. D.)—SONGS FOR SAILORS. Post 8vo, cl. limp. **2s.**

BEWICK (THOMAS) AND HIS PUPILS. By AUSTIN DOBSON. With 95 Illustrations. Square 8vo, cloth extra, **6s.**

BIERCE (AMBROSE).—IN THE MIDST OF LIFE : Tales of Soldiers and Civilians. Crown 8vo, cloth extra, **6s. :** post 8vo, illustrated boards, **2s.**

BILL NYE'S HISTORY OF THE UNITED STATES. With 146 Illustrations by F. OPPER. Crown 8vo, cloth extra, **3s. 6d.**

BLACKBURN'S (HENRY) ART HANDBOOKS.

ACADEMY NOTES, 1875, 1877-86, 1889, 1890, 1892-1895, Illustrated, each **1s.**
ACADEMY NOTES, 1875-79. Complete in One Vol., with 600 Illusts. Cloth, **6s.**
ACADEMY NOTES, 1880-84. Complete in One Vol., with 700 Illusts. Cloth, **6s.**
ACADEMY NOTES, 1890-94. Complete in One Vol., with 800 Illusts. Cloth, **7s. 6d.**
GROSVENOR NOTES, 1877. 6d.
GROSVENOR NOTES, separate years, from 1878-1890, each **1s.**
GROSVENOR NOTES, Vol. I., **1877-82.** With 300 Illusts. Demy 8vo, cloth, **6s.**

GROSVENOR NOTES, Vol. II., **1883-87.** With 300 Illusts. Demy 8vo, cloth, **6s.**
GROSVENOR NOTES, Vol. III., **1888-90.** With 230 Illusts. Demy 8vo, cloth, **3s. 6d.**
THE NEW GALLERY, 1888-1895. With numerous Illustrations, each **1s.**
THE NEW GALLERY, Vol. I., **1888-1892.** With 250 Illustrations. Demy 8vo, cloth, **6s.**
ENGLISH PICTURES at the NATIONAL GALLERY. With 114 Illustrations. **1s.**
OLD MASTERS AT THE NATIONAL GALLERY. With 128 Illustrations. **1s. 6d.**
ILLUSTRATED CATALOGUE TO THE NATIONAL GALLERY. 242 Illusts., cl., **3s.**

THE PARIS SALON, 1894. With Facsimile Sketches. **3s.**

BLIND (MATHILDE). POEMS BY.
THE ASCENT OF MAN. Crown 8vo, cloth, **5s.**
DRAMAS IN MINIATURE. With a Frontispiece by F. MADOX BROWN. Cr. 8vo, **5s.**
SONGS AND SONNETS. Fcap. 8vo, vellum and gold, **5s.**
BIRDS OF PASSAGE : Songs. Crown 8vo, linen. **6s.** net.

BOURNE (H. R. FOX), WORKS BY.
ENGLISH MERCHANTS : Memoirs in Illustration of the Progress of British Commerce. With numerous Illustrations. Crown 8vo, cloth extra, **7s. 6d.**
ENGLISH NEWSPAPERS: The History of Journalism. Two Vols., demy 8vo, cl., **25s.**
THE OTHER SIDE OF THE EMIN PASHA RELIEF EXPEDITION. Cr. 8vo. **6s.**

BOWERS (GEORGE).—LEAVES FROM A HUNTING JOURNAL. Oblong folio, half-bound. **21s.**

BOYLE (FREDERICK), WORKS BY. Post 8vo, illustrated boards. **2s.** each.
CHRONICLES OF NO-MAN'S LAND. | CAMP NOTES. | SAVAGE LIFE.

BRAND (JOHN).—OBSERVATIONS ON POPULAR ANTIQUITIES ; chiefly illustrating the Origin of our Vulgar Customs, Ceremonies, and Superstitions. With the Additions of Sir HENRY ELLIS, and Illusts. Cr. 8vo. cloth extra, **7s. 6d.**

BREWER (REV. DR.), WORKS BY.
THE READER'S HANDBOOK OF ALLUSIONS, REFERENCES, PLOTS, AND STORIES. Seventeenth Thousand. Crown 8vo. cloth extra, **7s. 6d.**
AUTHORS AND THEIR WORKS, WITH THE DATES: Being the Appendices to "The Reader's Handbook," separately printed. Crown 8vo, cloth limp, **2s.**
A DICTIONARY OF MIRACLES. Crown 8vo, cloth extra, **7s. 6d.**

BREWSTER (SIR DAVID), WORKS BY. Post 8vo, cl. ex., **4s. 6d.** each.
MORE WORLDS THAN ONE: Creed of Philosopher and Hope of Christian. Plates.
THE MARTYRS OF SCIENCE: GALILEO, TYCHO BRAHE, and KEPLER. With Portraits.
LETTERS ON NATURAL MAGIC. With numerous Illustrations.

BRILLAT-SAVARIN.—GASTRONOMY AS A FINE ART. Translated by R. E. ANDERSON, M.A. Post 8vo, half-bound. **2s.**

BURTON (RICHARD F.).—THE BOOK OF THE SWORD. With over 400 Illustrations. Demy 4to, cloth extra. **32s.**

BURTON (ROBERT).—THE ANATOMY OF MELANCHOLY. With Translations of the Quotations. Demy 8vo, cloth extra, **7s. 6d.**
MELANCHOLY ANATOMISED. Abridgment of BURTON'S ANAT. Post 8vo, **2s. 6d.**

BRET HARTE'S COLLECTED WORKS. Revised by the Author.
LIBRARY EDITION. In Eight Volumes, crown 8vo, cloth extra, **6s.** each.
Vol.   I. COMPLETE POETICAL AND DRAMATIC WORKS. With Steel Portrait.
Vol.   II. LUCK OF ROARING CAMP—BOHEMIAN PAPERS—AMERICAN LEGENDS.
Vol. III. TALES OF THE ARGONAUTS—EASTERN SKETCHES.
Vol. IV. GABRIEL CONROY. | Vol. V. STORIES—CONDENSED NOVELS, &c.
Vol.   VI. TALES OF THE PACIFIC SLOPE.
Vol. VII. TALES OF THE PACIFIC SLOPE—II. With Portrait by JOHN PETTIE, R.A.
Vol.VIII. TALES OF THE PINE AND THE CYPRESS.
THE SELECT WORKS OF BRET HARTE, in Prose and Poetry. With Introductory
Essay by J. M. BELLEW. Portrait of Author, and 50 Illusts. Cr. 8vo, cl. ex., **7s. 6d.**
BRET HARTE'S POETICAL WORKS. Hand-made paper & buckram. Cr. 8vo, **4s.6d.**
THE QUEEN OF THE PIRATE ISLE. With 28 original Drawings by KATE
GREENAWAY, reproduced in Colours by EDMUND EVANS. Small 4to, cloth, **5s.**
Crown 8vo, cloth extra, **3s. 6d.** each ; post 8vo, picture boards, **2s.** each.
A WAIF OF THE PLAINS. With 60 Illustrations by STANLEY L. WOOD.
A WARD OF THE GOLDEN GATE. With 59 Illustrations by STANLEY L. WOOD.
Crown 8vo, cloth extra, **3s. 6d.** each.
A SAPPHO OF GREEN SPRINGS, &c. With Two Illustrations by HUME NISBET.
COLONEL STARBOTTLE'S CLIENT, AND SOME OTHER PEOPLE. Frontisp.
SUSY: A Novel. With Frontispiece and Vignette by J. A. CHRISTIE.
SALLY DOWS, &c. With 47 Illustrations by W. D. ALMOND, &c.
A PROTÉGÉE OF JACK HAMLIN'S. With 26 Illustrations by W. SMALL, &c.
THE BELL-RINGER OF ANGEL'S, &c. 39 Illusts. by DUDLEY HARDY, &c.
CLARENCE: A Story of the War. With Illustrations.   [*Shortly*.
Post 8vo, illustrated boards, **2s.** each.
GABRIEL CONROY. | **THE LUCK OF ROARING CAMP,** &c.
AN HEIRESS OF RED DOG, &c. | **CALIFORNIAN STORIES.**
Post 8vo, illustrated boards, **2s.** each ; cloth limp, **2s. 6d.** each.
FLIP. | **MARUJA.** | **A PHYLLIS OF THE SIERRAS.**
Fcap. 8vo, picture cover, **1s.** each.
SNOW-BOUND AT EAGLE'S. | **JEFF BRIGGS'S LOVE STORY.**

BRYDGES (HAROLD).—UNCLE SAM AT HOME. Post 8vo, illustrated boards, **2s.** ; cloth limp, **2s. 6d.**

BUCHANAN (ROBERT), WORKS BY. Crown 8vo, cloth extra, **6s.** each.
SELECTED POEMS OF ROBERT BUCHANAN. With Frontispiece by T. DALZIEL.
THE EARTHQUAKE; or, Six Days and a Sabbath.
THE CITY OF DREAM: An Epic Poem. With Two Illustrations by P. MACNAB.
THE WANDERING JEW: A Christmas Carol. Second Edition.
THE OUTCAST: A Rhyme for the Time. With 15 Illustrations by RUDOLF BLIND,
PETER MACNAB, and HUME NISBET. Small demy 8vo, cloth extra, **8s.**
ROBERT BUCHANAN'S COMPLETE POETICAL WORKS. With Steel-plate Por-
trait. Crown 8vo, cloth extra, **7s. 6d.**
Crown 8vo, cloth extra, **3s. 6d.** each ; post 8vo, illustrated boards, **2s.** each.
THE SHADOW OF THE SWORD. | **LOVE ME FOR EVER.** Frontispiece.
A CHILD OF NATURE. Frontispiece. | **ANNAN WATER.** | **FOXGLOVE MANOR.**
GOD AND THE MAN. With 11 Illus- | **THE NEW ABELARD.**
trations by FRED. BARNARD. | **MATT:** A Story of a Caravan. Frontisp.
THE MARTYRDOM OF MADELINE. | **THE MASTER OF THE MINE.** Front.
With Frontispiece by A. W. COOPER. | **THE HEIR OF LINNE.**
Crown 8vo, cloth extra, **3s. 6d.** each.
WOMAN AND THE MAN. | **RED AND WHITE HEATHER.**
RACHEL DENE. Crown 8vo, cloth extra, **3s. 6d.**   [*Sept.*
LADY KILPATRICK. Crown 8vo, cloth extra, **6s.**   [*Shortly*
THE CHARLATAN. By ROBERT BUCHANAN and H. MURRAY. Two Vols., **10s.** net.

CAINE (T. HALL), NOVELS BY. Crown 8vo, cloth extra, **3s. 6d.** each;
post 8vo, illustrated boards. **2s.** each ; cloth limp, **2s. 6d.** each.
SHADOW OF A CRIME. | **A SON OF HAGAR.** | **THE DEEMSTER.**

CAMERON (COMMANDER V. LOVETT).—THE CRUISE OF THE
"BLACK PRINCE" PRIVATEER. Post 8vo. picture boards, **2s.**

CAMERON (MRS. H. LOVETT), NOVELS BY. Post 8vo, illust. bds., **2s.** each.
JULIET'S GUARDIAN. | **DECEIVERS EVER.**

CARRUTH (HAYDEN).—THE ADVENTURES OF JONES. With 17
Illustrations. Fcap. 8vo, cloth, **2s.**

CARLYLE (JANE WELSH), LIFE OF. By Mrs. ALEXANDER IRELAND.
With Portrait and Facsimile Letter. Small demy 8vo, cloth extra, **7s. 6d.**

CARLYLE (THOMAS) on the CHOICE of BOOKS. Post 8vo, 1s. 6d.
CORRESPONDENCE OF THOMAS CARLYLE AND R. W. EMERSON, 1834 to 1872.
Edited by C. E. NORTON. With Portraits. Two Vols., crown 8vo. cloth, **24s.**

CHAPMAN'S (GEORGE) WORKS.—Vol. I., Plays.—Vol. II., Poems and
Minor Translations, with Essay by A. C. SWINBURNE.—Vol. III., Translations of
the Iliad and Odyssey. Three Vols., crown 8vo, cloth, **6s.** each.

CHAPPLE (J. M.).—THE MINOR CHORD : Story of Prima Donna. **3s. 6d.**

**CHATTO (W. A.) AND J. JACKSON. — A TREATISE ON WOOD
ENGRAVING.** With 450 fine Illustrations. Large 4to. half-leather, **28s.**

CHAUCER FOR CHILDREN : A Golden Key. By Mrs. H. R. HAWEIS.
With 8 Coloured Plates and 30 Woodcuts. Small 4to, cloth extra, **3s. 6d.**
CHAUCER FOR SCHOOLS. By Mrs. H. R. HAWEIS. Demy 8vo, cloth limp. **2s. 6d.**

CHESS, THE LAWS AND PRACTICE OF. With Analysis of Openings.
By HOWARD STAUNTON. Edited by R. B. WORMALD. Crown 8vo, cloth, **5s.**
THE MINOR TACTICS OF CHESS : A Treatise on the Deployment of the Forces.
By F. K. YOUNG and E. C. HOWELL. Long fcap. 8vo, cloth, **2s. 6d.**

CLARE (A.).—FOR THE LOVE OF A LASS. Post 8vo, 2s. ; cl., 2s. 6d.

CLIVE (MRS. ARCHER), NOVELS BY. Post 8vo, illust. boards **2s.** each.
PAUL FERROLL. | WHY PAUL FERROLL KILLED HIS WIFE.

CLODD (EDWARD, F.R.A.S.).—MYTHS AND DREAMS. Cr.8vo,**3s.6d.**

COBBAN (J. MACLAREN), NOVELS BY.
THE CURE OF SOULS. Post 8vo, illustrated boards, **2s.**
THE RED SULTAN. Crown 8vo, cl. extra. **3s. 6d.** ; post 8vo, illustrated bds., **2s.**
THE BURDEN OF ISABEL. Crown 8vo, cloth extra, **3s. 6d.**

**COLEMAN (JOHN).—PLAYERS AND PLAYWRIGHTS I HAVE
KNOWN.** Two Vols., demy 8vo, cloth, **24s.**

COLERIDGE (M. E.) —SEVEN SLEEPERS OF EPHESUS. 1s. 6d.

COLLINS (C. ALLSTON).—THE BAR SINISTER. Post 8vo, 2s.

COLLINS (JOHN CHURTON, M.A.), BOOKS BY.
ILLUSTRATIONS OF TENNYSON. Crown 8vo, cloth extra ,**6s.**
JONATHAN SWIFT : A Biographical and Critical Study. Crown 8vo, cloth extra **8s.**

COLLINS (MORTIMER AND FRANCES), NOVELS BY.
Crown 8vo. cloth extra, **3s. 6d.** each ; post 8vo, illustrated boards. **2s.** each.
FROM MIDNIGHT TO MIDNIGHT. | BLACKSMITH AND SCHOLAR.
TRANSMIGRATION. | YOU PLAY ME FALSE. | A VILLAGE COMEDY.
Post 8vo, illustrated boards, **2s.** each.
SWEET ANNE PAGE. | FIGHT WITH FORTUNE. | SWEET & TWENTY. | FRANCES.

COLLINS (WILKIE), NOVELS BY.
Cr. 8vo, cl. ex., **3s. 6d.** each ; post 8vo, illust. bds., **2s.** each ; cl. limp, **2s. 6d.** each.
ANTONINA. With a Frontispiece by Sir JOHN GILBERT, R.A.
BASIL. Illustrated by Sir JOHN GILBERT, R.A., and J. MAHONEY.
HIDE AND SEEK. Illustrated by Sir JOHN GILBERT, R.A., and J. MAHONEY.
AFTER DARK. Illustrations by A. B. HOUGHTON. | THE TWO DESTINIES.
THE DEAD SECRET. With a Frontispiece by Sir JOHN GILBERT, R.A.
QUEEN OF HEARTS. With a Frontispiece by Sir JOHN GILBERT, R.A.
THE WOMAN IN WHITE. With Illusts. by Sir J. GILBERT, R.A., and F. A. FRASER.
NO NAME. With Illustrations by Sir J. E. MILLAIS, R.A., and A. W. COOPER.
MY MISCELLANIES. With a Steel-plate Portrait of WILKIE COLLINS.
ARMADALE. With Illustrations by G. H. THOMAS.
THE MOONSTONE. With Illustrations by G. Du MAURIER and F. A. FRASER.
MAN AND WIFE. With Illustrations by WILLIAM SMALL.
POOR MISS FINCH. Illustrated by G. Du MAURIER and EDWARD HUGHES.
MISS OR MRS.? With Illusts. by S. L. FILDES, R.A., and HENRY WOODS, A.R.A.
THE NEW MAGDALEN. Illustrated by G. Du MAURIER and C. S. REINHARDT.
THE FROZEN DEEP. Illustrated by G. Du MAURIER and J. MAHONEY.
THE LAW AND THE LADY. Illusts. by S. L. FILDES, R.A., and SYDNEY HALL.
THE HAUNTED HOTEL. Illustrated by ARTHUR HOPKINS.
THE FALLEN LEAVES. | HEART AND SCIENCE. | THE EVIL GENIUS.
JEZEBEL'S DAUGHTER. | "I SAY NO." | LITTLE NOVELS.
THE BLACK ROBE. | A ROGUE'S LIFE. | THE LEGACY OF CAIN.
BLIND LOVE. With Preface by S r WALTER BESANT. Illusts. by A. FORESTIER.
    Popular Editions. Medium 8vo, **6d.** each ; cloth **1s.** each.
       THE WOMAN IN WHITE. | THE MOONSTONE.

COLMAN'S (GEORGE) HUMOROUS WORKS: "Broad Grins," "My Nightgown and Slippers," &c. With Life and Frontis. Cr. 8vo, cl. extra, **7s. 6d.**

COLQUHOUN (M. J.).—EVERY INCH A SOLDIER. Post 8vo, bds., **2s.**

CONVALESCENT COOKERY: A Family Handbook. By CATHERINE RYAN. Crown 8vo, **1s.**; cloth limp. **1s. 6d.**

CONWAY (MONCURE D.), WORKS BY.
DEMONOLOGY AND DEVIL-LORE. 65 Illustrations. Two Vols. 8vo, cloth, **28s.**
GEORGE WASHINGTON'S RULES OF CIVILITY. Fcap.8vo, Jap. vellum, **2s. 6d.**

COOK (DUTTON), NOVELS BY.
PAUL FOSTER'S DAUGHTER. Cr. 8vo, cl. ex., **3s. 6d.**; post 8vo, illust. boards, **2s.**
LEO. Post 8vo. illustrated boards. **2s.**

COOPER (EDWARD H.)—GEOFFORY HAMILTON. Cr. 8vo, **3s. 6d.**

CORNWALL.—POPULAR ROMANCES OF THE WEST OF ENG-LAND; or, The Drolls, Traditions, and Superstitions of Old Cornwall. Collected by ROBERT HUNT, F.R.S. Two Steel-plates by GEO.CRUIKSHANK. Cr.8vo. cl., **7s. 6d.**

COTES (V. CECIL).—TWO GIRLS ON A BARGE. With 44 Illustrations by F. H. TOWNSEND. Post 8vo, cloth, **2s. 6d.**

CRADDOCK (C. EGBERT), STORIES BY.
PROPHET OF THE GREAT SMOKY MOUNTAINS. Post 8vo, illustrated boards, **2s.**
HIS VANISHED STAR. Crown 8vo, cloth extra. **3s. 6d.**

CRELLIN (H. N.), BOOKS BY.
ROMANCES of the OLD SERAGLIO. 28 Illusts. by S. L. WOOD. Cr. 8vo,cl., **3s. 6d.**
TALES OF THE CALIPH. Crown 8vo, cloth. **2s.**
THE NAZARENES: A Drama. Crown 8vo, **1s.**

CRIM (MATT.).—ADVENTURES OF A FAIR REBEL. Crown 8vo, cloth extra, with a Frontispiece, **3s. 6d.**; post 8vo, illustrated boards, **2s.**

CROKER (MRS. B. M.), NOVELS BY. Crown 8vo, cloth extra, **3s. 6d.** each; post 8vo, illustrated boards, **2s.** each; cloth limp, **2s. 6d.** each.
PRETTY MISS NEVILLE. | DIANA BARRINGTON.
A BIRD OF PASSAGE. | PROPER PRIDE.
A FAMILY LIKENESS. | "TO LET."
MR. JERVIS. Three Vols., crown 8vo, cloth. **15s.** net.
VILLAGE TALES AND JUNGLE TRAGEDIES. Crown 8vo, cloth, **3s. 6d.**

CRUIKSHANK'S COMIC ALMANACK. Complete in TWO SERIES: The FIRST from 1835 to 1843; the SECOND from 1844 to 1853. A Gathering of the BEST HUMOUR of THACKERAY, HOOD, MAYHEW, ALBERT SMITH, A'BECKETT, ROBERT BROUGH, &c. With numerous Steel Engravings and Woodcuts by CRUIK-SHANK, HINE, LANDELLS, &c. Two Vols., crown 8vo, cloth gilt, **7s. 6d.** each.
THE LIFE OF GEORGE CRUIKSHANK. By BLANCHARD JERROLD. With 84 Illustrations and a Bibliography. Crown 8vo, cloth extra, **6s.**

CUMMING (C. F. GORDON), WORKS BY. Demy 8vo, cl. ex., **8s. 6d.** each.
IN THE HEBRIDES. With Autotype Facsimile and 23 Illustrations.
IN THE HIMALAYAS AND ON THE INDIAN PLAINS. With 42 Illustrations.
TWO HAPPY YEARS IN CEYLON. With 28 Illustrations.
VIA CORNWALL TO EGYPT. With Photogravure Frontis. Demy 8vo, cl., **7s. 6d.**

CUSSANS (JOHN E.).—A HANDBOOK OF HERALDRY; with Instructions for Tracing Pedigrees and Deciphering Ancient MSS., &c ; 408 Woodcuts and 2 Coloured Plates. Fourth edition, revised, crown 8vo. cloth extra. **6s.**

CYPLES(W.)—HEARTS of GOLD. Cr.8vo,cl.,**3s.6d.**; post 8vo,bds.**2s.**

DANIEL (GEORGE).—MERRIE ENGLAND IN THE OLDEN TIME. With Illustrations by ROBERT CRUIKSHANK. Crown 8vo, cloth extra. **3s. 6d.**

DAUDET (ALPHONSE).—THE EVANGELIST; or, Port Salvation. Crown 8vo, cloth extra, **3s. 6d.**; post 8vo, illustrated boards, **2s.**

DAVIDSON (HUGH COLEMAN).—MR. SADLER'S DAUGHTERS. With a Frontispiece by STANLEY WOOD. Crown 8vo, cloth extra, **3s. 6d.**

DAVIES (DR. N. E. YORKE), WORKS BY. Cr. 8vo, **1s.** ea.; cl., **1s. 6d.** ea.
ONE THOUSAND MEDICAL MAXIMS AND SURGICAL HINTS.
NURSERY HINTS: A Mother's Guide in Health and Disease.
FOODS FOR THE FAT: A Treatise on Corpulency, and a Dietary for its Cure.
AIDS TO LONG LIFE. Crown 8vo, **2s.**; cloth limp, **2s. 6d.**

DAVIES' (SIR JOHN) COMPLETE POETICAL WORKS. Collected and Edited, with Memorial-Introduction and Notes, by the Rev. A. B. GROSART, D.D. Two Vols., crown 8vo, cloth boards, **12s.**

DAWSON (ERASMUS, M.B.).—THE FOUNTAIN OF YOUTH. Crown 8vo, cloth extra, **3s. 6d.** ; post 8vo, illustrated boards, **2s.**

DE GUERIN (MAURICE), THE JOURNAL OF. Edited by G. S. TREBUTIEN. With a Memoir by SAINTE-BEUVE. Translated from the 20th French Edition by JESSIE P. FROTHINGHAM. Fcap, 8vo, half-bound, **2s. 6d.**

DE MAISTRE (XAVIER).—A JOURNEY ROUND MY ROOM. Translated by Sir HENRY ATTWELL. Post 8vo, cloth limp, **2s. 6d.**

DE MILLE (JAMES).—A CASTLE IN SPAIN. With a Frontispiece. Crown 8vo, cloth extra, **3s. 6d.**; post 8vo, illustrated boards, **2s.**

DERBY (THE).—THE BLUE RIBBON OF THE TURF. With Brief Accounts of THE OAKS. By LOUIS HENRY CURZON. Cr. 8vo, cloth limp, **2s. 6d.**

DERWENT (LEITH), NOVELS BY. Cr.8vo,cl.,**3s.6d.** ea.; post 8vo,bds.,**2s.**ea.
OUR LADY OF TEARS. | CIRCE'S LOVERS.

DEWAR (T. R.).—A RAMBLE ROUND THE GLOBE. With 220 Illustrations. Crown 8vo, cloth extra, **7s. 6d.**

DICKENS (CHARLES), NOVELS BY. Post 8vo, illustrated boards, **2s.** each.
SKETCHES BY BOZ. | NICHOLAS NICKLEBY. | OLIVER TWIST.

> **THE SPEECHES OF CHARLES DICKENS,** 1841–1870. With a New Bibliography Edited by RICHARD HERNE SHEPHERD. Crown 8vo, cloth extra. **6s.**
> **ABOUT ENGLAND WITH DICKENS.** By ALFRED RIMMER. With 57 Illustrations by C. A. VANDERHOOF, ALFRED RIMMER, and others. Sq. 8vo, cloth extra, **7s. 6d.**

DICTIONARIES.

> **A DICTIONARY OF MIRACLES:** Imitative, Realistic, and Dogmatic. By the Rev. E. C. BREWER, LL.D. Crown 8vo. cloth extra, **7s. 6d.**
> **THE READER'S HANDBOOK OF ALLUSIONS, REFERENCES, PLOTS, AND STORIES.** By the Rev. E. C. BREWER, LL.D. With an ENGLISH BIBLIOGRAPHY. Seventeenth Thousand. Crown 8vo. cloth extra **7s. 6d.**
> **AUTHORS AND THEIR WORKS, WITH THE DATES.** Cr. 8vo, cloth limp, **2s.**
> **FAMILIAR SHORT SAYINGS OF GREAT MEN.** With Historical and Explanatory Notes. By SAMUEL A. BENT, A.M. Crown 8vo, cloth extra, **7s. 6d.**
> **SLANG DICTIONARY:** Etymological, Historical, and Anecdotal. Cr. 8vo, cl., **6s. 6d.**
> **WOMEN OF THE DAY:** A Biographical Dictionary. By F. HAYS. Cr. 8vo, cl., **5s.**
> **WORDS, FACTS, AND PHRASES:** A Dictionary of Curious, Quaint, and Out-of-the-Way Matters. By ELIEZER EDWARDS. Crown 8vo, cloth extra, **7s. 6d.**

DIDEROT.—THE PARADOX OF ACTING. Translated, with Notes, by WALTER HERRIES POLLOCK. With a Preface by HENRY IRVING. Crown 8vo, parchment, **4s. 6d.**

DOBSON (AUSTIN), WORKS BY.

> **THOMAS BEWICK & HIS PUPILS.** With 95 Illustrations. Square 8vo, cloth, **6s.**
> **FOUR FRENCHWOMEN.** With 4 Portraits. Crown 8vo, buckram, gilt top, **6s.**
> **EIGHTEENTH CENTURY VIGNETTES.** Two SERIES. Cr. 8vo, buckram, **6s.** each.

DOBSON (W. T.)—POETICAL INGENUITIES AND ECCENTRICITIES. Post 8vo, cloth limp, **2s. 6d.**

DONOVAN (DICK), DETECTIVE STORIES BY.
Post 8vo, illustrated boards, **2s.** each; cloth limp, **2s. 6d.** each.

THE MAN-HUNTER.	WANTED!	A DETECTIVE'S TRIUMPHS.
CAUGHT AT LAST!	IN THE GRIP OF THE LAW.
TRACKED AND TAKEN.	FROM INFORMATION RECEIVED.
WHO POISONED HETTY DUNCAN?	LINK BY LINK.	DARK DEEDS.
SUSPICION AROUSED.	THE LONG ARM OF THE LAW. [*Shortly.*

Crown 8vo, cloth, **3s. 6d.** each ; post 8vo, boards, **2s.** each ; cloth, **2s. 6d.** each.
THE MAN FROM MANCHESTER. With 23 Illustrations.
TRACKED TO DOOM. With 6 full-page Illustrations by GORDON BROWNE.

DOYLE (A. CONAN).—THE FIRM OF GIRDLESTONE : A Romance of the Unromantic. Crown 8vo, cloth extra, **3s. 6d.**

DRAMATISTS, THE OLD. With Vignette Portraits. Cr. 8vo, cl. ex., **6s.** per Vol.
　BEN JONSON'S WORKS. With Notes Critical and Explanatory, and a Bio-
　　graphical Memoir by WM. GIFFORD. Edited by Col. CUNNINGHAM. Three Vols.
　CHAPMAN'S WORKS. Complete in Three Vols. Vol. I. contains the Plays
　　complete; Vol. II., Poems and Minor Translations, with an Introductory Essay
　　by A. C. SWINBURNE; Vol. III., Translations of the Iliad and Odyssey.
　MARLOWE'S WORKS. Edited, with Notes, by Col. CUNNINGHAM. One Vol.
　MASSINGER'S PLAYS. From GIFFORD's Text. Edit by Col. CUNNINGHAM. One Vol.

DUNCAN (SARA JEANNETTE: Mrs. EVERARD COTES), WORKS BY.
　　　　　　Crown 8vo, cloth extra, **7s. 6d.** each.
　A SOCIAL DEPARTURE: How Orthodocia and I Went round the World by Our-
　　selves. With 111 Illustrations by F. H. TOWNSEND.
　AN AMERICAN GIRL IN LONDON. With 80 Illustrations by F. H. TOWNSEND.
　THE SIMPLE ADVENTURES OF A MEMSAHIB. Illustrated by F. H. TOWNSEND.
　　　　　　Crown 8vo, cloth extra, **3s. 6d.** each.
　A DAUGHTER OF TO-DAY. | VERNON'S AUNT. 47 Illusts. by HAL HURST.

DYER (T. F. THISELTON, M.A.).—FOLK-LORE OF PLANTS. **6s.**

EARLY ENGLISH POETS. Edited, with Introductions and Annota-
　tions, by Rev. A. B. GROSART, D.D. Crown 8vo, cloth boards, **6s.** per Volume.
　FLETCHER'S (GILES) COMPLETE POEMS. One Vol.
　DAVIES' (SIR JOHN) COMPLETE POETICAL WORKS. Two Vols.
　HERRICK'S (ROBERT) COMPLETE COLLECTED POEMS. Three Vols.
　SIDNEY'S (SIR PHILIP) COMPLETE POETICAL WORKS. Three Vols.

EDGCUMBE (Sir E. R. PEARCE).—ZEPHYRUS: A Holiday in Brazil
　and on the River Plate. With 41 Illustrations. Crown 8vo, cloth extra, **5s.**

EDISON, THE LIFE & INVENTIONS OF THOMAS A. By W. K. L. and
　A. DICKSON. With 200 Illustrations by R. F. OUTCALT, &c. Demy 4to, cloth gilt, **18s.**

EDWARDES (MRS. ANNIE), NOVELS BY.
　A POINT OF HONOUR. Post 8vo, illustrated boards, **2s.**
　ARCHIE LOVELL. Crown 8vo, cloth extra. **3s. 6d.**; post 8vo, illust. boards, **2s.**

EDWARDS (ELIEZER).—WORDS, FACTS, AND PHRASES: A
　Dictionary of Quaint Matters. Crown 8vo, cloth, **7s. 6d.**

EDWARDS (M. BETHAM-), NOVELS BY.
　KITTY. Post 8vo, cloth, **2s.**; cloth, **2s. 6d.** | FELICIA. Post 8vo, **2s.**

EGERTON (REV. J. C.).—SUSSEX FOLK AND SUSSEX WAYS.
　With Introduction by Rev. Dr. H. WACE, and 4 Illustrations. Cr. 8vo, cloth ex., **5s.**

EGGLESTON (EDWARD).—ROXY: A Novel. Post 8vo, illust. bds., **2s.**

ENGLISHMAN'S HOUSE, THE: A Practical Guide to all interested in
　Selecting or Building a House; with Estimates of Cost, Quantities, &c. By C. J.
　RICHARDSON. With Coloured Frontispiece and 600 Illusts. Crown 8vo, cloth, **7s. 6d.**

EWALD (ALEX. CHARLES, F.S.A.), WORKS BY.
　THE LIFE AND TIMES OF PRINCE CHARLES STUART, Count of Albany
　　(THE YOUNG PRETENDER). With a Portrait. Crown 8vo, cloth extra, **7s. 6d.**
　STORIES FROM THE STATE PAPERS. With an Autotype. Crown 8vo, cloth, **6s.**

EYES, OUR: How to Preserve Them. By JOHN BROWNING. **1s.**

FAMILIAR SHORT SAYINGS OF GREAT MEN. By SAMUEL ARTHUR
　BENT, A.M. Fifth Edition, Revised and Enlarged. Crown 8vo, cloth extra, **7s. 6d.**

FARADAY (MICHAEL), WORKS BY. Post 8vo, cloth extra, **4s. 6d.** each.
　THE CHEMICAL HISTORY OF A CANDLE: Lectures delivered before a Juvenile
　　Audience. Edited by WILLIAM CROOKES F.C.S. With numerous Illustrations.
　**ON THE VARIOUS FORCES OF NATURE, AND THEIR RELATIONS TO
　EACH OTHER.** Edited by WILLIAM CROOKES. F.C.S. With Illustrations.

FARRER (J. ANSON), WORKS BY.
　MILITARY MANNERS AND CUSTOMS. Crown 8vo, cloth extra, **6s.**
　WAR: Three Essays, reprinted from "Military Manners." Cr. 8vo. **1s.**; cl., **1s. 6d.**

FENN (G. MANVILLE), NOVELS BY.
　　Crown 8vo, cloth extra, **3s. 6d.** each; post 8vo, illustrated boards, **2s.** each.
　THE NEW MISTRESS. | WITNESS TO THE DEED.
　　　　　　Crown 8vo, cloth extra, **3s. 6d.** each.
　THE TIGER LILY: A Tale of Two Passions. | THE WHITE VIRGIN.

FIN-BEC.—THE CUPBOARD PAPERS: Observations on the Art of
　Living and Dining. Post 8vo, cloth limp, **2s. 6d.**

FIREWORKS, THE COMPLETE ART OF MAKING; or, The Pyro-technist's Treasury. By THOMAS KENTISH. With 267 Illustrations. Cr. 8vo, cl., **5s.**

FIRST BOOK, MY. By WALTER BESANT, JAMES PAYN, W. CLARK RUS-SELL, GRANT ALLEN, HALL CAINE, GEORGE R. SIMS, RUDYARD KIPLING, A. CONAN DOYLE, M. E. BRADDON, F. W. ROBINSON, H. RIDER HAGGARD, R. M. BALLANTYNE, I. ZANGWILL, MORLEY ROBERTS, D. CHRISTIE MURRAY, MARIE CORELLI. J. K. JEROME, JOHN STRANGE WINTER, BRET HARTE, "Q.," ROBERT BUCHANAN, and R. L. STEVENSON. With a Prefatory Story by JEROME K. JEROME, and 185 Illustrations. Small demy 8vo, cloth extra, **7s. 6d.**

FITZGERALD (PERCY), WORKS BY.
THE WORLD BEHIND THE SCENES. Crown 8vo, cloth extra, **3s. 6d.**
LITTLE ESSAYS: Passages from Letters of CHARLES LAMB. Post 8vo, cl., **2s. 6d.**
A DAY'S TOUR: Journey through France and Belgium. With Sketches. Cr. 4to. **1s.**
FATAL ZERO. Crown 8vo, cloth extra, **3s. 6d.**; post 8vo, illustrated boards, **2s.**

Post 8vo, illustrated boards. **2s.** each.
BELLA DONNA. | LADY OF BRANTOME. | THE SECOND MRS. TILLOTSON.
POLLY. | NEVER FORGOTTEN. | SEVENTY-FIVE BROOKE STREET
LIFE OF JAMES BOSWELL (of Auchinleck). Two Vols., demy 8vo, cloth, **24s.**
THE SAVOY OPERA. With 60 Illustrations and Portraits. Cr. 8vo, cloth, **3s. 6d.**

FLAMMARION (CAMILLE), WORKS BY.
POPULAR ASTRONOMY: A General Description of the Heavens. Translated by J. ELLARD GORE, F.R.A.S. With 3 Plates and 288 Illusts. Medium 8vo, cloth, **16s.**
URANIA: A Romance. With 87 Illustrations. Crown 8vo, cloth extra, **5s.**

FLETCHER'S (GILES, B.D.) COMPLETE POEMS: Christ's Victorie in Heaven, Christ's Victorie on Earth, Christ's Triumph over Death, and Minor Poems. With Notes by Rev. A. B. GROSART, D.D. Crown 8vo, cloth boards, **6s.**

FONBLANQUE (ALBANY).—FILTHY LUCRE. Post 8vo, illust. bds., **2s.**

FRANCILLON (R. E.), NOVELS BY.
Crown 8vo. cloth extra, **3s. 6d.** each; post 8vo, illustrated boards. **2s.** each.
ONE BY ONE. | A REAL QUEEN. | KING OR KNAVE?
ROPES OF SAND. Illustrated. | A DOG AND HIS SHADOW.

Post 8vo, illustrated boards, **2s.** each.
QUEEN COPHETUA. | OLYMPIA. | ROMANCES OF THE LAW.

JACK DOYLE'S DAUGHTER. Crown 8vo, cloth, **3s. 6d.**
ESTHER'S GLOVE. Fcap. 8vo. picture cover, **1s.**

FREDERIC (HAROLD), NOVELS BY. Post 8vo, illust. bds., **2s.** each.
SETH'S BROTHER'S WIFE. | THE LAWTON GIRL.

FRENCH LITERATURE, A HISTORY OF. By HENRY VAN LAUN. Three Vols., demy 8vo, cloth boards, **7s. 6d.** each.

FRISWELL (HAIN).—ONE OF TWO: A Novel. Post 8vo, illust. bds., **2s.**

FROST (THOMAS), WORKS BY. Crown 8vo, cloth extra, **3s. 6d.** each.
CIRCUS LIFE AND CIRCUS CELEBRITIES. | LIVES OF THE CONJURERS.
THE OLD SHOWMEN AND THE OLD LONDON FAIRS.

FRY'S (HERBERT) ROYAL GUIDE TO THE LONDON CHARITIES. Edited by JOHN LANE. Published Annually. Crown 8vo, cloth, **1s. 6d.**

GARDENING BOOKS. Post 8vo. **1s.** each; cloth limp, **1s. 6d.** each.
A YEAR'S WORK IN GARDEN AND GREENHOUSE. By GEORGE GLENNY.
HOUSEHOLD HORTICULTURE. By TOM and JANE JERROLD. Illustrated.
THE GARDEN THAT PAID THE RENT. By TOM JERROLD.
MY GARDEN WILD. By FRANCIS G. HEATH. Crown 8vo, cloth extra, **6s.**

GARDNER (MRS. ALAN).—RIFLE AND SPEAR WITH THE RAJPOOTS: Being the Narrative of a Winter's Travel and Sport in Northern India. With numerous Illustrations by the Author and F. H. TOWNSEND. Demy 4to, half-bound. **21s.**

GARRETT (EDWARD).—THE CAPEL GIRLS: A Novel. Crown 8vo, cloth extra, **3s. 6d.**; post 8vo, illustrated boards, **2s.**

GAULOT (PAUL).—THE RED SHIRTS: A Story of the Revolution. Translated by J. A. J. DE VILLIERS. Crown 8vo, cloth, **3s. 6d.**

GENTLEMAN'S MAGAZINE, THE. 1s. Monthly. With Stories, Articles upon Literature, Science, and Art, and **"TABLE TALK"** by SYLVANUS URBAN.
₊ *Bound Volumes for recent years kept in stock, 8s. 6d. each. Cases for binding, 2s.*

GENTLEMAN'S ANNUAL, THE. Published Annually in November. 1s.

GERMAN POPULAR STORIES. Collected by the Brothers GRIMM and Translated by EDGAR TAYLOR. With Introduction by JOHN RUSKIN, and 22 Steel Plates after GEORGE CRUIKSHANK. Square 8vo. cloth, 6s. 6d.; gilt edges, 7s. 6d.

GIBBON (CHARLES), NOVELS BY.
Crown 8vo, cloth extra, 3s. 6d. each; post 8vo, illustrated boards, 2s. each.
ROBIN GRAY. | THE GOLDEN SHAFT.
LOVING A DREAM.

Post 8vo, illustrated boards, 2s. each.
THE FLOWER OF THE FOREST. | IN LOVE AND WAR.
THE DEAD HEART. | A HEART'S PROBLEM.
FOR LACK OF GOLD. | BY MEAD AND STREAM.
WHAT WILL THE WORLD SAY? | THE BRAES OF YARROW.
FOR THE KING. | A HARD KNOT. | FANCY FREE. | OF HIGH DEGREE.
QUEEN OF THE MEADOW. | IN HONOUR BOUND.
IN PASTURES GREEN. | HEART'S DELIGHT. | BLOOD-MONEY.

GIBNEY (SOMERVILLE).—SENTENCED! Cr. 8vo, 1s.; cl., 1s. 6d.

GILBERT (WILLIAM), NOVELS BY. Post 8vo, illustrated boards, 2s. each.
DR. AUSTIN'S GUESTS. | JAMES DUKE, COSTERMONGER.
THE WIZARD OF THE MOUNTAIN.

GILBERT (W. S.), ORIGINAL PLAYS BY. Three Series, 2s. 6d. each.
The FIRST SERIES contains: The Wicked World—Pygmalion and Galatea—Charity—The Princess—The Palace of Truth—Trial by Jury.
The SECOND SERIES: Broken Hearts—Engaged—Sweethearts—Gretchen—Dan'l Druce—Tom Cobb—H.M.S. "Pinafore"—The Sorcerer—Pirates of Penzance.
The THIRD SERIES: Comedy and Tragedy—Foggerty's Fairy—Rosencrantz and Guildenstern—Patience—Princess Ida—The Mikado—Ruddigore—The Yeomen of the Guard—The Gondoliers—The Mountebanks—Utopia.

EIGHT ORIGINAL COMIC OPERAS written by W. S. GILBERT. Containing: The Sorcerer—H.M.S. "Pinafore"—Pirates of Penzance—Iolanthe—Patience—Princess Ida—The Mikado—Trial by Jury. Demy 8vo. cloth limp, 2s. 6d.
THE "GILBERT AND SULLIVAN" BIRTHDAY BOOK: Quotations for Every Day in the Year, Selected from Plays by W. S. GILBERT set to Music by Sir A. SULLIVAN. Compiled by ALEX. WATSON. Royal 16mo, Jap. leather, 2s. 6d.

GLANVILLE (ERNEST), NOVELS BY.
Crown 8vo, cloth extra, 3s. 6d. each; post 8vo, illustrated boards, 2s. each.
THE LOST HEIRESS: A Tale of Love, Battle, and Adventure. With 2 Illusts.
THE FOSSICKER: A Romance of Mashonaland. With 2 Illusts. by HUME NISBET.
A FAIR COLONIST.

GLENNY (GEORGE).—A YEAR'S WORK IN GARDEN and GREEN-HOUSE: Practical Advice to Amateur Gardeners as to the Management of the Flower, Fruit and Frame Garden. Post 8vo. 1s.; cloth limp, 1s. 6d.

GODWIN (WILLIAM).—LIVES OF THE NECROMANCERS. Post 8vo. cloth limp, 2s.

GOLDEN TREASURY OF THOUGHT, THE: An Encyclopædia of QUOTATIONS. Edited by THEODORE TAYLOR. Crown 8vo. cloth gilt, 7s. 6d.

GONTAUT, MEMOIRS OF THE DUCHESSE DE (Gouvernante to the Children of France), 1773-1836. With Photogravure Frontispieces. Two Vols., small demy 8vo, cloth extra, 21s.

GOODMAN (E. J.).—FATE OF HERBERT WAYNE. Cr. 8vo, 3s. 6d.

GRAHAM (LEONARD). — THE PROFESSOR'S WIFE: A Story. Fcap. 8vo, picture cover, 1s.

GREEKS AND ROMANS, THE LIFE OF THE, described from Antique Monuments. By ERNST GUHL and W. KONER. Edited by Dr. F. HUEFFER. With 545 Illustrations. Large crown 8vo. cloth extra, 7s. 6d.

GREVILLE (HENRY), NOVELS BY:
NIKANOR. Translated by ELIZA E. CHASE. Post 8vo, illustrated boards, 2s.
A NOBLE WOMAN. Crown 8vo, cloth extra, 5s.; post 8vo, illustrated boards, 2s.

GREENWOOD (JAMES), WORKS BY. Cr. 8vo, cloth extra, **3s. 6d.** each.
　　THE WILDS OF LONDON. | LOW-LIFE DEEPS.

GRIFFITH (CECIL).—CORINTHIA MARAZION: A Novel. Crown 8vo, cloth extra, **3s. 6d.**; post 8vo, illustrated boards, **2s.**

GRUNDY (SYDNEY).—THE DAYS OF HIS VANITY: A Passage in the Life of a Young Man. Crown 8vo, cloth extra, **3s. 6d.**; post 8vo, boards, **2s.**

HABBERTON (JOHN, Author of " Helen's Babies "), **NOVELS BY.** Post 8vo, illustrated boards **2s.** each; cloth limp, **2s. 6d.** each.
　　BRUETON'S BAYOU. | COUNTRY LUCK.

HAIR, THE: Its Treatment in Health, Weakness, and Disease. Translated from the German of Dr. J. PINCUS. Crown 8vo. **1s.**; cloth, **1s. 6d.**

HAKE (DR. THOMAS GORDON), POEMS BY. Cr. 8vo, cl. ex., **6s.** each.
　　NEW SYMBOLS. | LEGENDS OF THE MORROW. | THE SERPENT PLAY.
　　MAIDEN ECSTASY. Small 4to, cloth extra, **8s.**

HALL (MRS. S. C.).—SKETCHES OF IRISH CHARACTER. With numerous Illustrations on Steel and Wood by MACLISE, GILBERT, HARVEY, and GEORGE CRUIKSHANK. Small demy 8vo, cloth extra, **7s. 6d.**

HALLIDAY (ANDREW).—EVERY-DAY PAPERS. Post 8vo, 2s.

HANDWRITING, THE PHILOSOPHY OF. With over 100 Facsimiles and Explanatory Text. By DON FELIX DE SALAMANCA. Post 8vo, cloth limp. **2s. 6d.**

HANKY-PANKY: Easy Tricks, White Magic, Sleight of Hand, &c. Edited by W. H. CREMER. With 200 Illustrations. Crown 8vo, cloth extra. **4s. 6d.**

HARDY (LADY DUFFUS).— PAUL WYNTER'S SACRIFICE. 2s.

HARDY (THOMAS).—UNDER THE GREENWOOD TREE. Crown 8vo, cloth extra, with Portrait and 15 Illustrations, **3s. 6d.**; post 8vo, illustrated boards, **2s.**; cloth limp, **2s. 6d.**

HARPER (CHARLES G.), WORKS BY. Demy 8vo, cloth extra, **16s.** each.
　　THE BRIGHTON ROAD. With Photogravure Frontispiece and 90 Illustrations.
　　FROM PADDINGTON TO PENZANCE: The Record of a Summer Tramp. 105 Illusts.

HARWOOD (J. BERWICK). — THE TENTH EARL. Post 8vo, illustrated boards, **2s.**

HAWEIS (MRS. H. R.), WORKS BY. Square 8vo, cloth extra, **6s.** each.
　　THE ART OF BEAUTY. With Coloured Frontispiece and 91 Illustrations.
　　THE ART OF DECORATION. With Coloured Frontispiece and 74 Illustrations.
　　THE ART OF DRESS. With 32 Illustrations. Post 8vo, **1s.**; cloth, **1s. 6d.**
　　CHAUCER FOR SCHOOLS. Demy 8vo, cloth limp, **2s. 6d.**
　　CHAUCER FOR CHILDREN. 38 Illusts. (8 Coloured). Sm. 4to, cl. extra, **3s. 6d.**

HAWEIS (Rev. H. R., M.A.). —AMERICAN HUMORISTS: WASHINGTON IRVING. OLIVER WENDELL HOLMES, JAMES RUSSELL LOWELL, ARTEMUS WARD, MARK TWAIN, and BRET HARTE. Third Edition. Crown 8vo, cloth extra. **6s.**

HAWLEY SMART. — WITHOUT LOVE OR LICENCE: A Novel. Crown 8vo, cloth extra, **3s. 6d.**; post 8vo, illustrated boards, **2s.**

HAWTHORNE (JULIAN), NOVELS BY.
Crown 8vo, cloth extra, **3s. 6d.** each; post 8vo, illustrated boards, **2s.** each.
　　GARTH. | ELLICE QUENTIN. | BEATRIX RANDOLPH. | DUST.
　　SEBASTIAN STROME. | DAVID POINDEXTER.
　　FORTUNE'S FOOL. | THE SPECTRE OF THE CAMERA.
　　　　　Post 8vo, illustrated boards, **2s.** each.
　　MISS CADOGNA. | LOVE—OR A NAME.
　　MRS. GAINSBOROUGH'S DIAMONDS. Fcap. 8vo. illustrated cover, **1s.**

HAWTHORNE (NATHANIEL).—OUR OLD HOME. Annotated with Passages from the Author's Note-books, and Illustrated with 31 Photogravures. Two Vols., crown 8vo. buckram, gilt top, **15s.**

HEATH (FRANCIS GEORGE).—MY GARDEN WILD, AND WHAT I GREW THERE. Crown 8vo, cloth extra, gilt edges, **6s.**

HELPS (SIR ARTHUR), WORKS BY. Post 8vo, cloth limp, **2s. 6d.** each
　　ANIMALS AND THEIR MASTERS. | SOCIAL PRESSURE.
　　IVAN DE BIRON: A Novel. Cr. 8vo, cl. extra, **3s. 6d.**; post 8vo, illust. bds., **2s.**

HENDERSON (ISAAC).—AGATHA PAGE: A Novel. Crown 8vo, cloth extra, **3s. 6d.**

HENTY (G. A.), NOVELS BY. Crown 8vo, cloth extra, **3s. 6d.** each.
RUJUB THE JUGGLER. 8 Illusts. by STANLEY L. WOOD. PRESENTATION ED., **5s.**
DOROTHY'S DOUBLE.

HERMAN (HENRY).—A LEADING LADY. Post 8vo, illustrated boards, **2s.**; cloth extra, **2s. 6d.**

HERRICK'S (ROBERT) HESPERIDES, NOBLE NUMBERS, AND COMPLETE COLLECTED POEMS. With Memorial-Introduction and Notes by the Rev. A. B. GROSART, D.D.; Steel Portrait, &c. Three Vols., crown 8vo, cl. bds., **18s.**

HERTZKA (Dr. THEODOR). — FREELAND: A Social Anticipation. Translated by ARTHUR RANSOM. Crown 8vo, cloth extra, **6s.**

HESSE-WARTEGG (CHEVALIER ERNST VON).—TUNIS: The Land and the People. With 22 Illustrations. Crown 8vo, cloth extra, **3s. 6d.**

HILL (HEADON).—ZAMBRA THE DETECTIVE. Post 8vo, illustrated boards, **2s.**; cloth, **2s. 6d.**

HILL (JOHN), WORKS BY.
TREASON-FELONY. Post 8vo, **2s.** | THE COMMON ANCESTOR. Cr. 8vo, **3s. 6d.**

HINDLEY (CHARLES), WORKS BY.
TAVERN ANECDOTES AND SAYINGS: Including Reminiscences connected with Coffee Houses, Clubs, &c. With Illustrations. Crown 8vo, cloth, **3s. 6d.**
THE LIFE AND ADVENTURES OF A CHEAP JACK. Cr. 8vo. cloth ex., **3s. 6d.**

HOEY (MRS. CASHEL).—THE LOVER'S CREED. Post 8vo, **2s.**

HOLLINGSHEAD (JOHN).—NIAGARA SPRAY. Crown 8vo, **1s.**

HOLMES (GORDON, M.D.).—THE SCIENCE OF VOICE PRODUCTION AND VOICE PRESERVATION. Crown 8vo, **1s.**

HOLMES (OLIVER WENDELL), WORKS BY.
THE AUTOCRAT OF THE BREAKFAST-TABLE. Illustrated by J. GORDON THOMSON. Post 8vo, cloth limp **2s. 6d.**—Another Edition, post 8vo, cloth, **2s.**
THE AUTOCRAT OF THE BREAKFAST-TABLE and THE PROFESSOR AT THE BREAKFAST-TABLE. In One Vol. Post 8vo, half-bound, **2s.**

HOOD'S (THOMAS) CHOICE WORKS, in Prose and Verse. With Life of the Author, Portrait, and 200 Illustrations. Crown 8vo, cloth extra, **7s. 6d.**
HOOD'S WHIMS AND ODDITIES. With 85 Illusts. Post 8vo, half-bound, **2s.**

HOOD (TOM).—FROM NOWHERE TO THE NORTH POLE: A Noah's Arkæological Narrative. With 25 Illustrations by W. BRUNTON and E. C. BARNES. Square 8vo, cloth extra, gilt edges, **6s.**

HOOK'S (THEODORE) CHOICE HUMOROUS WORKS; including his Ludicrous Adventures, Bons Mots, Puns, and Hoaxes. With Life of the Author, Portraits, Facsimiles, and Illustrations. Crown 8vo, cloth extra, **7s. 6d.**

HOOPER (MRS. GEO.).—THE HOUSE OF RABY. Post 8vo, bds., **2s.**

HOPKINS (TIGHE). — "'TWIXT LOVE AND DUTY:" A Novel. Post 8vo, illustrated boards, **2s.**

HORNE (R. HENGIST).—ORION: An Epic Poem. With Photographic Portrait by SUMMERS. Tenth Edition. Crown 8vo, cloth extra, **7s.**

HUNGERFORD (MRS., Author of "Molly Bawn"), NOVELS BY.
Post 8vo, illustrated boards, **2s.** each; cloth limp, **2s. 6d.** each.
A MAIDEN ALL FORLORN. | IN DURANCE VILE. | A MENTAL STRUGGLE.
MARVEL. | A MODERN CIRCE.
LADY VERNER'S FLIGHT. Cr. 8vo, cloth, **3s. 6d.**; post 8vo, illust. boards, **2s.**
THE RED-HOUSE MYSTERY. Crown 8vo, cloth extra, **3s. 6d.**
THE THREE GRACES. Two Vols., **10s.** nett.

HUNT (MRS. ALFRED), NOVELS BY.
Crown 8vo, cloth extra, **3s. 6d.** each; post 8vo, illustrated boards, **2s.** each.
THE LEADEN CASKET. | SELF-CONDEMNED. | THAT OTHER PERSON.
THORNICROFT'S MODEL. Post 8vo, illustrated boards, **2s.**
MRS. JULIET. Crown 8vo, cloth extra, **3s. 6d.**

HUNT'S (LEIGH) ESSAYS: A TALE FOR A CHIMNEY CORNER, &c. Edited by EDMUND OLLIER. Post 8vo, printed on laid paper and half-bd., **2s.**

HUTCHISON (W. M.).— HINTS ON COLT-BREAKING. With 25 Illustrations. Crown 8vo, cloth extra, **3s. 6d.**

HYDROPHOBIA : An Account of M. Pasteur's System ; Technique of his Method, and Statistics. By Renaud Suzor, M.B. Crown 8vo. cloth extra, **6s.**

HYNE (C. J. CUTCLIFFE).— HONOUR OF THIEVES. Crown 8vo, cloth extra, **3s. 6d.**

IDLER (THE) : A Monthly Magazine. Profusely Illustr. **6d.** Monthly. The first Six Vols. now ready, cl. extra, **5s.** each : Cases for Binding, **1s. 6d.** each.

INDOOR PAUPERS. By One of Them. Crown 8vo, **1s.** ; cloth, **1s. 6d.**

INGELOW (JEAN).— FATED TO BE FREE. Post 8vo, illustrated bds., **2s.**

INNKEEPER'S HANDBOOK (THE) AND LICENSED VICTUALLER'S MANUAL. By J. Trevor-Davies. Crown 8vo, **1s.** ; cloth. **1s. 6d.**

IRISH WIT AND HUMOUR, SONGS OF. Collected and Edited by A. Perceval Graves. Post 8vo, cloth limp, **2s. 6d.**

JAMES (C. T. C.). — A ROMANCE OF THE QUEEN'S HOUNDS. Post 8vo, picture cover, **1s.** ; cloth limp, **1s. 6d.**

JAMESON (WILLIAM). — MY DEAD SELF. Post 8vo, illustrated boards, **2s.** ; cloth, **2s. 6d.**

JAPP (ALEX. H., LL.D.).— DRAMATIC PICTURES, &c. Cr. 8vo, **5s.**

JAY (HARRIETT), NOVELS BY. Post 8vo, illustrated boards, **2s.** each.
    THE DARK COLLEEN. | **THE QUEEN OF CONNAUGHT.**

JEFFERIES (RICHARD), WORKS BY. Post 8vo, cloth limp, **2s. 6d.** each.
    NATURE NEAR LONDON. | **THE LIFE OF THE FIELDS.** | **THE OPEN AIR.**
    ** Also the Hand-made Paper Edition, crown 8vo, buckram, gilt top, **6s.** each.
    THE EULOGY OF RICHARD JEFFERIES. By Sir Walter Besant. With a Photograph Portrait. Crown 8vo, cloth extra, **6s.**

JENNINGS (HENRY J.), WORKS BY.
    CURIOSITIES OF CRITICISM. Post 8vo, cloth limp, **2s. 6d.**
    LORD TENNYSON : A Biographical Sketch. Post 8vo, **1s.** ; cloth, **1s. 6d.**

JEROME (JEROME K.), BOOKS BY.
    STAGELAND. With 64 Illusts. by J. Bernard Partridge. Fcap. 4to, pict. cov., **1s.**
    JOHN INGERFIELD, &c. With 9 Illusts. by A. S. Boyd and John Gulich. Fcap. 8vo, picture cover. **1s. 6d.**

JERROLD (DOUGLAS).— THE BARBER'S CHAIR ; and THE HEDGE-HOG LETTERS. Post 8vo, printed on laid paper and half-bound. **2s.**

JERROLD (TOM), WORKS BY. Post 8vo, **1s.** each ; cloth limp, **1s. 6d.** each.
    THE GARDEN THAT PAID THE RENT.
    HOUSEHOLD HORTICULTURE : A Gossip about Flowers. Illustrated.

JESSE (EDWARD).— SCENES AND OCCUPATIONS OF A COUNTRY LIFE. Post 8vo, cloth limp, **2s.**

JONES (WILLIAM, F.S.A.), WORKS BY. Cr. 8vo, cl. extra, **7s. 6d.** each.
    FINGER-RING LORE : Historical, Legendary, and Anecdotal. With nearly 300 Illustrations. Second Edition, Revised and Enlarged.
    CREDULITIES, PAST AND PRESENT. Including the Sea and Seamen, Miners, Talismans, Word and Letter Divination, Exorcising and Blessing of Animals, Birds, Eggs, Luck, &c. With an Etched Frontispiece.
    CROWNS AND CORONATIONS : A History of Regalia. With 100 Illustrations.

JONSON'S (BEN) WORKS. With Notes Critical and Explanatory, and a Biographical Memoir by William Gifford. Edited by Colonel Cunningham. Three Vols., crown 8vo, cloth extra, **6s.** each.

JOSEPHUS, THE COMPLETE WORKS OF. Translated by Whiston. Containing "The Antiquities of the Jews" and "The Wars or the Jews." With 52 Illustrations and Maps. Two Vols., demy 8vo, half-bound. **12s. 6d.**

KEMPT (ROBERT).— PENCIL AND PALETTE : Chapters on Art and Artists. Post 8vo, cloth limp, **2s. 6d.**

KERSHAW (MARK).—COLONIAL FACTS & FICTIONS: Humorous Sketches. Post 8vo. illustrated boards. **2s.**; cioth, **2s. 6d.**

KEYSER (ARTHUR).—CUT BY THE MESS: A Novel. Crown 8vo, picture cover, **1s.**; cloth limp, **1s. 6d.**

KING (R. ASHE), NOVELS BY. Cr. 8vo, cl., **3s. 6d.** ea.; post 8vo, bds., **2s.** ea.
A DRAWN GAME. | "THE WEARING OF THE GREEN."
PASSION'S SLAVE. Post 8vo, illustrated boards, **2s.** each. | BELL BARRY.

KNIGHT (WILLIAM, M.R.C.S., and EDWARD, L.R.C.P.).—THE PATIENT'S VADE MECUM: How to Get Most Benefit from Medical Advice. Crown 8vo, **1s.**; cloth limp, **1s. 6d.**

KNIGHTS (THE) OF THE LION: A Romance of the Thirteenth Century. Edited, with an Introduction, by the MARQUESS of LORNE, K.T. Cr 8vo, cl. ex. **6s.**

LAMB'S (CHARLES) COMPLETE WORKS, in Prose and Verse, including "Poetry for Children" and "Prince Dorus." Edited, with Notes and Introduction, by R. H. SHEPHERD. With Two Portraits and Facsimile of a page of the "Essay on Roast Pig." Crown 8vo, half-bound, **7s. 6d.**
THE ESSAYS OF ELIA. Post 8vo, printed on laid paper and half-bound, **2s.**
LITTLE ESSAYS: Sketches and Characters by CHARLES LAMB, selected from his Letters by PERCY FITZGERALD. Post 8vo, cloth limp, **2s. 6d.**
THE DRAMATIC ESSAYS OF CHARLES LAMB. With Introduction and Notes by BRANDER MATTHEWS, and Steel-plate Portrait. Fcap. 8vo, hf.-bd., **2s. 6d.**

LANDOR (WALTER SAVAGE).—CITATION AND EXAMINATION OF WILLIAM SHAKSPEARE, &c., before Sir THOMAS LUCY, touching Deer-stealing, 19th September, 1582. To which is added, **A CONFERENCE OF MASTER EDMUND SPENSER** with the Earl of Essex, touching the State of Ireland, 1595. Fcap. 8vo, half-Roxburghe, **2s. 6d.**

LANE (EDWARD WILLIAM). — THE THOUSAND AND ONE NIGHTS, commonly called in England THE ARABIAN NIGHTS' ENTERTAIN-MENTS. Translated from the Arabic, with Notes. Illustrated by many hundred Engravings from Designs by HARVEY. Edited by EDWARD STANLEY POOLE. With a Preface by STANLEY LANE-POOLE. Three Vols., demy 8vo, cloth extra, **7s. 6d.** each.

LARWOOD (JACOB), WORKS BY.
THE STORY OF THE LONDON PARKS. With Illusts. Cr. 8vo, cl. extra, **3s. 6d.**
ANECDOTES OF THE CLERGY. Post 8vo, laid paper, half-bound, **2s.**
Post 8vo, cloth limp, **2s. 6d.** each.
FORENSIC ANECDOTES. | THEATRICAL ANECDOTES.

LEHMANN (R. C.), WORKS BY. Post 8vo, pict. cover, **1s.** ea.; cloth, **1s.6d.** ea.
HARRY FLUDYER AT CAMBRIDGE.
CONVERSATIONAL HINTS FOR YOUNG SHOOTERS: A Guide to Polite Talk.

LEIGH (HENRY S.), WORKS BY.
CAROLS OF COCKAYNE. Printed on hand-made paper, bound in buckram, **5s.**
JEUX D'ESPRIT. Edited by HENRY S. LEIGH. Post 8vo, cloth limp, **2s. 6d.**

LEPELLETIER (EDMOND).—MADAME SANS-GENE. Translated from the French by J. A. J. DE VILLIERS. Crown 8vo, cloth extra, **3s. 6d.**

LEYS (JOHN).—THE LINDSAYS: A Romance. Post 8vo, illust. bds., **2s.**

LINDSAY (HARRY).—RHODA ROBERTS: A Welsh Mining Story. Crown 8vo, cloth, **3s. 6d.**

LINTON (E. LYNN), WORKS BY. Post 8vo, cloth limp, **2s. 6d.** each.
WITCH STORIES. | OURSELVES: ESSAYS ON WOMEN.
Crown 8vo, cloth extra, **3s. 6d.** each; post 8vo, illustrated boards, **2s.** each.
PATRICIA KEMBALL. | IONE. | UNDER WHICH LORD?
ATONEMENT OF LEAM DUNDAS. | "MY LOVE!" | SOWING THE WIND.
THE WORLD WELL LOST. | PASTON CAREW, Millionaire & Miser.
Post 8vo, illustrated boards, **2s.** each.
THE REBEL OF THE FAMILY. | WITH A SILKEN THREAD.
THE ONE TOO MANY. Crown 8vo, cloth extra, **3s. 6d.**
FREESHOOTING: Extracts from Works of Mrs. LINTON. Post 8vo, cloth, **2s. 6d.**

LUCY (HENRY W.).—GIDEON FLEYCE: A Novel. Crown 8vo, cloth extra, **3s. 6d.**; post 8vo, illustrated boards, **2s.**

MACALPINE (AVERY), NOVELS BY.
TERESA ITASCA.   Crown 8vo, cloth extra. **1s.**
BROKEN WINGS.   With 6 Illusts. by W. J. HENNESSY.   Crown 8vo, cloth extra, **6s.**

McCARTHY (JUSTIN, M.P.), WORKS BY.
A HISTORY OF OUR OWN TIMES, from the Accession of Queen Victoria to the General Election of 1880.   Four Vols. demy 8vo, cloth extra, **12s.** each.—Also a POPULAR EDITION, in Four Vols., crown 8vo, cloth extra, **6s.** each.—And a JUBILEE EDITION, with an Appendix of Events to the end of 1886, in Two Vols., large crown 8vo, cloth extra, **7s. 6d.** each.
A SHORT HISTORY OF OUR OWN TIMES.   One Vol., crown 8vo, cloth extra, **6s.** —Also a CHEAP POPULAR EDITION, post 8vo, cloth limp, **2s. 6d.**
A HISTORY OF THE FOUR GEORGES.   Four Vols. demy 8vo, cloth extra, **12s.** each.   [Vols. I. & II. *ready.*

Cr. 8vo, cl. extra, **3s. 6d.** each: post 8vo, illust. bds., **2s.** each : cl. limp, **2s. 6d.** each.

THE WATERDALE NEIGHBOURS.	DONNA QUIXOTE.
MY ENEMY'S DAUGHTER.	THE COMET OF A SEASON.
A FAIR SAXON.	MAID OF ATHENS.
LINLEY ROCHFORD.	CAMIOLA: A Girl with a Fortune.
DEAR LADY DISDAIN.	THE DICTATOR.
MISS MISANTHROPE.	RED DIAMONDS.

"THE RIGHT HONOURABLE."   By JUSTIN McCARTHY, M.P., and Mrs. CAMPBELL PRAED.   Crown 8vo, cloth extra, **6s.**

McCARTHY (JUSTIN HUNTLY), WORKS BY.
THE FRENCH REVOLUTION.   Four Vols., 8vo, **12s.** each.   [Vols. I. & II. *ready.*
AN OUTLINE OF THE HISTORY OF IRELAND.   Crown 8vo, **1s.** ; cloth, **1s. 6d.**
IRELAND SINCE THE UNION : Irish History, 1798-1886.   Crown 8vo, cloth, **6s.**

HAFIZ IN LONDON : Poems.   Small 8vo, gold cloth, **3s. 6d.**

OUR SENSATION NOVEL.   Crown 8vo, picture cover, **1s.** ; cloth limp, **1s. 6d.**
DOOM! An Atlantic Episode.   Crown 8vo, picture cover, **1s.**
DOLLY : A Sketch.   Crown 8vo, picture cover, **1s.** ; cloth limp, **1s. 6d.**
LILY LASS: A Romance.   Crown 8vo, picture cover, **1s.** ; cloth limp, **1s. 6d.**
THE THOUSAND AND ONE DAYS.   2 Photogravures.   Two Vols., cr. 8vo, **12s.**
A LONDON LEGEND.   Three Vols., crown 8vo, **15s.** net.

MACCOLL (HUGH), NOVELS BY.
MR. STRANGER'S SEALED PACKET.   Post 8vo, illustrated boards, **2s.**
EDNOR WHITLOCK.   Crown 8vo, cloth extra, **6s.**

MACDONALD (GEORGE, LL.D.), WORKS BY.
WORKS OF FANCY AND IMAGINATION.   Ten Vols., 16mo, cl., gilt edges, in cloth case. **21s.**   Or the Vols. may be had separately, in grolier cl., at **2s. 6d.** each.
Vol.   I. WITHIN AND WITHOUT.—THE HIDDEN LIFE.
,,   II. THE DISCIPLE.—THE GOSPEL WOMEN.—BOOK OF SONNETS.—ORGAN SONGS.
,,   III. VIOLIN SONGS.—SONGS OF THE DAYS AND NIGHTS.—A BOOK OF DREAMS.— ROADSIDE POEMS.—POEMS FOR CHILDREN.
,,   IV. PARABLES.—BALLADS.—SCOTCH SONGS.
,, V. & VI. PHANTASTES: A Faerie Romance. | Vol. VII. THE PORTENT.
,, VIII. THE LIGHT PRINCESS.—THE GIANT'S HEART.—SHADOWS.
,,   IX. CROSS PURPOSES.—THE GOLDEN KEY.—THE CARASOYN.—LITTLE DAYLIGHT.
,,   X. THE CRUEL PAINTER.—THE WOW o' RIVVEN.—THE CASTLE.—THE BROKEN SWORDS.—THE GRAY WOLF.—UNCLE CORNELIUS.
POETICAL WORKS OF GEORGE MACDONALD.   Collected and arranged by the Author.   2 vols., crown 8vo, buckram, **12s.**
A THREEFOLD CORD.   Edited by GEORGE MACDONALD.   Post 8vo, cloth, **5s.**
HEATHER AND SNOW: A Novel.   Crown 8vo, cloth extra, **3s. 6d.**
PHANTASTES: A Faerie Romance.   With 25 Illustrations by J. BELL.   Crown 8vo, cloth extra, **3s. 6d.**
LILITH: A Romance.   Crown 8vo, cloth extra, **6s.**   [*Shortly.*

MACDONELL (AGNES).—QUAKER COUSINS.   Post 8vo, boards, 2s.

MACGREGOR (ROBERT).—PASTIMES AND PLAYERS : Notes on
Popular Games.   Post 8vo. cloth limp, **2s. 6d.**

MACKAY (CHARLES, LL.D.).—INTERLUDES AND UNDERTONES;
or, Music at Twilight.   Crown 8vo, cloth extra, **6s.**

MACLISE PORTRAIT GALLERY (THE) OF ILLUSTRIOUS LITER-ARY CHARACTERS: 85 PORTRAITS; with Memoirs — Biographical, Critical, Bibliographical, and Anecdotal—illustrative of the Literature of the former half of the Present Century, by WILLIAM BATES, B.A. Crown 8vo, cloth extra, **7s. 6d.**

MACQUOID (MRS.), WORKS BY. Square 8vo, cloth extra, **6s.** each.
IN THE ARDENNES. With 50 Illustrations by THOMAS R. MACQUOID.
PICTURES AND LEGENDS FROM NORMANDY AND BRITTANY. 34 Illustrations.
THROUGH NORMANDY. With 92 Illustrations by T. R. MACQUOID, and a Map.
THROUGH BRITTANY. With 35 Illustrations by T. R. MACQUOID, and a Map.
ABOUT YORKSHIRE. With 67 Illustrations by T. R. MACQUOID.

Post 8vo, illustrated boards, **2s.** each.
THE EVIL EYE, and other Stories. | **LOST ROSE.**

MAGICIAN'S OWN BOOK, THE: Performances with Eggs, Hats, &c. Edited by W. H. CREMER. With 200 Illustrations. Crown 8vo, cloth extra. **4s. 6d.**

MAGIC LANTERN, THE, and its Management: including full Practical Directions. By T. C. HEPWORTH. 10 Illustrations. Cr. 8vo. **1s.**; cloth. **1s. 6d.**

MAGNA CHARTA: An Exact Facsimile of the Original in the British Museum, 3 feet by 2 feet, with Arms and Seals emblazoned in Gold and Colours, **5s.**

MALLOCK (W. H.), WORKS BY.
THE NEW REPUBLIC. Post 8vo, picture cover, **2s.**; cloth limp, **2s. 6d.**
THE NEW PAUL & VIRGINIA: Positivism on an Island. Post 8vo, cloth, **2s. 6d.**
POEMS. Small 4to, parchment, **8s.**
IS LIFE WORTH LIVING? Crown 8vo, cloth extra, **6s.**
A ROMANCE OF THE NINETEENTH CENTURY. Crown 8vo, cloth, **6s.**; post 8vo, illustrated boards. **2s.**

MALLORY (SIR THOMAS).—MORT D'ARTHUR: The Stories of King Arthur and of the Knights of the Round Table. (A Selection.) Edited by B. MONTGOMERIE RANKING. Post 8vo, cloth limp, **2s.**

MARK TWAIN, WORKS BY. Crown 8vo, cloth extra, **7s. 6d.** each.
THE CHOICE WORKS OF MARK TWAIN. Revised and Corrected throughout by the Author. With Life, Portrait, and numerous Illustrations.
ROUGHING IT, and **INNOCENTS AT HOME.** With 200 Illusts. by F. A. FRASER.
MARK TWAIN'S LIBRARY OF HUMOUR. With 197 Illustrations.

Crown 8vo, cloth extra (illustrated), **7s. 6d.** each; post 8vo, illust. boards, **2s.** each.
THE INNOCENTS ABROAD; or, New Pilgrim's Progress. With 234 Illustrations. (The Two-Shilling Edition is entitled **MARK TWAIN'S PLEASURE TRIP.**)
THE GILDED AGE. By MARK TWAIN and C. D. WARNER. With 212 Illustrations.
THE ADVENTURES OF TOM SAWYER. With 111 Illustrations.
A TRAMP ABROAD. With 314 Illustrations.
THE PRINCE AND THE PAUPER. With 190 Illustrations.
LIFE ON THE MISSISSIPPI. With 300 Illustrations.
ADVENTURES OF HUCKLEBERRY FINN. With 174 Illusts. by E. W. KEMBLE.
A YANKEE AT THE COURT OF KING ARTHUR. With 220 Illusts. by BEARD.

Post 8vo, illustrated boards, **2s.** each.
THE STOLEN WHITE ELEPHANT. | **MARK TWAIN'S SKETCHES.**

Crown 8vo, cloth extra, **3s. 6d.** each.
THE AMERICAN CLAIMANT. With 81 Illustrations by HAL HURST, &c.
TOM SAWYER ABROAD. With 26 Illustrations by DAN BEARD.
PUDD'NHEAD WILSON. With Portrait and Six Illustrations by LOUIS LOEB.
THE £1,000,000 BANK-NOTE. Cr. 8vo, cloth, **3s. 6d.**; post 8vo, picture bds., **2s.**

MARKS (H. S., R.A.), PEN AND PENCIL SKETCHES BY. With 4 Photogravures and 126 Illustrations. Two Vols., demy 8vo, cloth, **32s.**

MARLOWE'S WORKS. Including his Translations. Edited, with Notes and Introductions, by Col. CUNNINGHAM. Crown 8vo. cloth extra. **6s.**

MARRYAT (FLORENCE), NOVELS BY. Post 8vo, illust. boards, **2s.** each.
A HARVEST OF WILD OATS. | **FIGHTING THE AIR.**
OPEN! SESAME! | **WRITTEN IN FIRE.**

MASSINGER'S PLAYS. From the Text of WILLIAM GIFFORD. Edited by Col. CUNNINGHAM. Crown 8vo, cloth extra, **6s.**

MASTERMAN (J.).—HALF-A-DOZEN DAUGHTERS : A Novel. Post 8vo, illustrated boards, **2s.**

MATTHEWS (BRANDER).—A SECRET OF THE SEA, &c. Post 8vo, illustrated boards, **2s.** ; cloth limp, **2s. 6d.**

MAYHEW (HENRY).—LONDON CHARACTERS & THE HUMOROUS SIDE OF LONDON LIFE. With Illustrations. Crown 8vo, cloth, **3s. 6d.**

MEADE (L. T.), NOVELS BY.
A SOLDIER OF FORTUNE. Crown 8vo, cloth, **3s. 6d.**
IN AN IRON GRIP. Two Vols., crown 8vo, cloth, **10s.** net.
THE VOICE OF THE CHARMER. Three Vo's., **15s.** net.   [*Short'y.*

MERRICK (LEONARD).—THE MAN WHO WAS GOOD. Post 8vo, illustrated boards, **2s.**

MEXICAN MUSTANG (ON A), through Texas to the Rio Grande. By A. E. SWEET and J. ARMOY KNOX. With 265 Illusts. Cr. 8vo, cloth extra, **7s. 6d.**

MIDDLEMASS (JEAN), NOVELS BY. Post 8vo, illust. boards, **2s.** each.
TOUCH AND GO. | MR. DORILLION.

MILLER (MRS. F. FENWICK).—PHYSIOLOGY FOR THE YOUNG; or, The House of Life. With Illustrations. Post 8vo, cloth limp, **2s. 6d.**

MILTON (J. L.), WORKS BY. Post 8vo, **1s.** each ; cloth, **1s. 6d.** each.
THE HYGIENE OF THE SKIN. With Directions for Diet, Soaps, Baths, &c.
THE BATH IN DISEASES OF THE SKIN.
THE LAWS OF LIFE, AND THEIR RELATION TO DISEASES OF THE SKIN.
THE SUCCESSFUL TREATMENT OF LEPROSY. Demy 8vo, **1s.**

MINTO (WM.)—WAS SHE GOOD OR BAD? Cr. 8vo, **1s.** ; cloth, **1s. 6d.**

MITFORD (BERTRAM), NOVELS BY. Crown 8vo, cloth extra, **3s. 6d.** each.
THE GUN-RUNNER: A Romance of Zululand. With Frontispiece by S. L. WOOD.
THE LUCK OF GERARD RIDGELEY. With a Frontispiece by STANLEY L. WOOD.
THE KING'S ASSEGAI. With Six full-page Illustrations by STANLEY L. WOOD.
RENSHAW FANNING'S QUEST. With a Frontispiece by STANLEY. L. WOOD.

MOLESWORTH (MRS.), NOVELS BY.
HATHERCOURT RECTORY. Post 8vo, illustrated boards, **2s.**
THAT GIRL IN BLACK. Crown 8vo, cloth, **1s. 6d.**

MOORE (THOMAS), WORKS BY.
THE EPICUREAN; and ALCIPHRON. Post 8vo, half-bound, **2s.**
PROSE AND VERSE. With Suppressed Passages from the MEMOIRS OF LORD BYRON. Edited by R. H. SHEPHERD. With Portrait. Cr 8vo, cl. ex., **7s. 6d.**

MUDDOCK (J. E.), STORIES BY.
STORIES WEIRD AND WONDERFUL. Post 8vo, illust. boards, **2s.**; cloth, **2s. 6d.**
THE DEAD MAN'S SECRET; or, The Valley of Gold. With Frontispiece by F. BARNARD. Crown 8vo, cloth extra, **5s.** ; post 8vo, illustrated boards, **2s.**
FROM THE BOSOM OF THE DEEP. Post 8vo, illustrated boards, **2s.**
MAID MARIAN AND ROBIN HOOD: A Romance of Old Sherwood Forest. With 12 Illustrations by STANLEY L. WOOD. Crown 8vo, cloth extra, **3s. 6d.**

MURRAY (D. CHRISTIE), NOVELS BY.
Crown 8vo, cloth extra. **3s. 6d.** each : post 8vo. illustrated boards. **2s.** each.

A LIFE'S ATONEMENT.	THE WAY OF THE WORLD.	A BIT OF HUMAN NATURE.
JOSEPH'S COAT.	A MODEL FATHER.	FIRST PERSON SINGULAR.
COALS OF FIRE.	OLD BLAZER'S HERO.	BOB MARTIN'S Little GIRL.
VAL STRANGE.	CYNIC FORTUNE.	TIME'S REVENGES.
HEARTS.	BY THE GATE OF THE SEA.	A WASTED CRIME.

Crown 8vo, cloth extra, **3s. 6d.** each.
IN DIREST PERIL.
MOUNT DESPAIR, &c. With Frontispiece by G. GRENVILLE MANTON.
THE MAKING OF A NOVELIST: An Experiment in Autobiography. With a Collotype Portrait and Vignette. Crown 8vo, art linen. **6s.**

MURRAY (D. CHRISTIE) & HENRY HERMAN, WORKS BY.
Crown 8vo, cloth extra, **3s. 6d.** each ; post 8vo, illustrated boards, **2s.** each.
ONE TRAVELLER RETURNS. | PAUL JONES'S ALIAS. | THE BISHOPS' BIBLE.

MURRAY (HENRY), NOVELS BY. Post 8vo, illust. bds., **2s.** ea.; cl., **2s. 6d.** ea.
A GAME OF BLUFF. | A SONG OF SIXPENCE.

NEWBOLT (HENRY).—TAKEN FROM THE ENEMY. Fcap. 8vo, cloth boards, **1s. 6d.**

NISBET (HUME), BOOKS BY.
"BAIL UP!" Crown 8vo, cloth extra, **3s. 6d.**; post 8vo, illustrated boards, **2s.**
DR. BERNARD ST. VINCENT. Post 8vo, illustrated boards, **2s.**
LESSONS IN ART. With 21 Illustrations. Crown 8vo, cloth extra, **2s. 6d.**
WHERE ART BEGINS. With 27 Illustrations. Square 8vo, cloth extra, **7s. 6d.**

NORRIS (W. E.), NOVELS BY.
ST. ANN'S. Cr. 8vo, cl. ex., **3s. 6d.** | BILLY BELLEW. Two Vols. cr. 8vo, **10s.** net

O'HANLON (ALICE), NOVELS BY. Post 8vo, illustrated boards, **2s.** each.
THE UNFORESEEN. | CHANCE? OR FATE?

OHNET (GEORGES), NOVELS BY. Post 8vo, illustrated boards, **2s.** each.
DOCTOR RAMEAU. | A LAST LOVE.
A WEIRD GIFT. Crown 8vo, cloth, **3s. 6d.**, post 8vo, picture boards. **2s.**

OLIPHANT (MRS.), NOVELS BY. Post 8vo, illustrated boards, **2s.** each.
THE PRIMROSE PATH. | WHITELADIES.
THE GREATEST HEIRESS IN ENGLAND.

O'REILLY (HARRINGTON).—LIFE AMONG THE AMERICAN IN-DIANS: Fifty Years on the Trail. 100 Illusts. by P. FRENZENY. Crown 8vo. **3s. 6d.**

O'REILLY (MRS.).—PHŒBE'S FORTUNES. Post 8vo, illust. bds., **2s.**

OUIDA, NOVELS BY. Cr. 8vo, cl., **3s. 6d.** each; post 8vo. illust. bds., **2s.** each.

HELD IN BONDAGE.	FOLLE-FARINE.	MOTHS.	PIPISTRELLO.
TRICOTRIN.	A DOG OF FLANDERS.	A VILLAGE COMMUNE.
STRATHMORE.	PASCAREL.	SIGNA.	IN MAREMMA.	WANDA.
CHANDOS.	TWO WOODEN SHOES.	BIMBI.	SYRLIN.
CECIL CASTLEMAINE.	IN A WINTER CITY.	FRESCOES.	OTHMAR.
UNDER TWO FLAGS.	ARIADNE.	PRINCESS NAPRAXINE.
PUCK.	IDALIA.	FRIENDSHIP.	GUILDEROY.	RUFFINO.

Square 8vo, cloth extra, **5s.** each.
BIMBI. With Nine Illustrations by EDMUND H. GARRETT.
A DOG OF FLANDERS, &c. With Six Illustrations by EDMUND H. GARRETT.
SANTA BARBARA, &c. Square 8vo, cloth, **6s.**; crown 8vo, cloth, **3s. 6d.**; post 8vo, illustrated boards, **2s.**
TWO OFFENDERS. Square 8vo, cloth extra, **6s.**; crown 8vo, cloth extra, **3s. 6d.**
WISDOM, WIT, AND PATHOS, selected from the Works of OUIDA by F. SYDNEY MORRIS. Post 8vo, cloth extra, **5s.** CHEAP EDITION, illustrated boards. **2s.**

PAGE (H. A.), WORKS BY.
THOREAU: His Life and Aims. With Portrait. Post 8vo, cloth limp, **2s. 6d.**
ANIMAL ANECDOTES. Arranged on a New Principle. Crown 8vo, cloth extra. **5s.**

PAYN (JAMES), NOVELS BY.
Crown 8vo, cloth extra. **3s. 6d.** each; post 8vo, illustrated boards. **2s.** each.

LOST SIR MASSINGBERD.	FROM EXILE.	HOLIDAY TASKS.
WALTER'S WORD. [ED.	THE CANON'S WARD.
LESS BLACK THAN WE'RE PAINT-	THE TALK OF THE TOWN.
BY PROXY.	FOR CASH ONLY.	GLOW-WORM TALES.
HIGH SPIRITS.	THE MYSTERY OF MIRBRIDGE.
UNDER ONE ROOF.	THE WORD AND THE WILL.
A CONFIDENTIAL AGENT.	THE BURNT MILLION.
A GRAPE FROM A THORN.	SUNNY STORIES.	A TRYING PATIENT

Post 8vo, illustrated boards, **2s.** each.

HUMOROUS STORIES.	FOUND DEAD.
THE FOSTER BROTHERS.	GWENDOLINE'S HARVEST.
THE FAMILY SCAPEGRACE.	A MARINE RESIDENCE.
MARRIED BENEATH HIM.	MIRK ABBEY.
BENTINCK'S TUTOR.	SOME PRIVATE VIEWS.
A PERFECT TREASURE.	NOT WOOED, BUT WON.
A COUNTY FAMILY.	TWO HUNDRED POUNDS REWARD.
LIKE FATHER, LIKE SON.	THE BEST OF HUSBANDS.
A WOMAN'S VENGEANCE.	HALVES.
CARLYON'S YEAR.	CECIL'S TRYST.	FALLEN FORTUNES.
MURPHY'S MASTER.	WHAT HE COST HER.
AT HER MERCY.	KIT: A MEMORY.
THE CLYFFARDS OF CLYFFE.	A PRINCE OF THE BLOOD.

IN PERIL AND PRIVATION. 17 Illustrations. Crown 8vo. cloth, **3s. 6d.**
NOTES FROM THE "NEWS." Crown 8vo, portrait cover, **1s.**; cloth, **1s. 6d.**

PANDURANG HARI; or, Memoirs of a Hindoo. With Preface by Sir
BARTLE FRERE. Crown 8vo, cloth, **3s. 6d.**; post 8vo, illustrated boards, **2s.**

PASCAL'S PROVINCIAL LETTERS. A New Translation, with Historical Introduction and Notes by T. M'CRIE, D.D. Post 8vo, cloth limp. **2s.**

PAUL (MARGARET A.).—GENTLE AND SIMPLE. With Frontis-
piece by HELEN PATERSON. Crown 8vo, cloth, **3s. 6d.**; post 8vo, illust. boards. **2s.**

PENNELL (H. CHOLMONDELEY), WORKS BY. Post 8vo, cl., **2s. 6d.** each.
PUCK ON PEGASUS. With Illustrations.
PEGASUS RE-SADDLED. With Ten full-page Illustrations by G. DU MAURIER.
THE MUSES OF MAYFAIR. Vers de Société, Selected by H. C. PENNELL.

PHELPS (E. STUART), WORKS BY. Post 8vo **1s.** each; cloth **1s. 6d.** each.
BEYOND THE GATES. | **OLD MAID'S PARADISE.** | **BURGLARS IN PARADISE.**
JACK THE FISHERMAN. Illustrated by C. W. REED. Cr. 8vo, **1s.**; cloth, **1s. 6d.**

PIRKIS (C. L.), NOVELS BY.
TROOPING WITH CROWS. Fcap. 8vo, picture cover, **1s.**
LADY LOVELACE. Post 8vo, illustrated boards, **2s.**

PLANCHE (J. R.), WORKS BY.
THE PURSUIVANT OF ARMS. With Six Plates, and 209 Illusts. Cr. 8vo, cl. **7s. 6d.**
SONGS AND POEMS, 1819-1879. Introduction by Mrs. MACKARNESS. Cr. 8vo, cl., **6s.**

PLUTARCH'S LIVES OF ILLUSTRIOUS MEN. With Notes and Life
of Plutarch by J. and WM. LANGHORNE. Portraits. Two Vols., demy 8vo, **10s. 6d.**

POE'S (EDGAR ALLAN) CHOICE WORKS, in Prose and Poetry. Introduction by CHAS. BAUDELAIRE, Portrait, and Facsimiles. Cr. 8vo, cloth, **7s. 6d.**
THE MYSTERY OF MARIE ROGET, &c. Post 8vo, illustrated boards, **2s.**

POPE'S POETICAL WORKS. Post 8vo, cloth limp, 2s.

PRAED (MRS. CAMPBELL), NOVELS BY. Post 8vo, illust. bds., **2s.** ea.
THE ROMANCE OF A STATION. | **THE SOUL OF COUNTESS ADRIAN.**
OUTLAW AND LAWMAKER. Crown 8vo, cloth, **3s. 6d.**; post 8vo, boards, **2s.**
CHRISTINA CHARD. Crown 8vo, cloth extra, **3s. 6d.**

PRICE (E. C.), NOVELS BY.
Crown 8vo, cloth extra, **3s. 6d.** each; post 8vo, illustrated boards. **2s.** each.
VALENTINA. | **THE FOREIGNERS.** | **MRS. LANCASTER'S RIVAL.**
GERALD. Post 8vo, illustrated boards. **2s.**

PRINCESS OLGA.—RADNA : A Novel. Crown 8vo, cloth extra, **6s.**

PROCTOR (RICHARD A., B.A.), WORKS BY.
FLOWERS OF THE SKY. With 55 Illusts. Small crown 8vo, cloth extra, **3s. 6d.**
EASY STAR LESSONS. With Star Maps for Every Night in the Year. Cr. 8vo, **6s.**
FAMILIAR SCIENCE STUDIES. Crown 8vo, cloth extra, **6s.**
SATURN AND ITS SYSTEM. With 13 Steel Plates. Demy 8vo, cloth ex., **10s. 6d.**
MYSTERIES OF TIME AND SPACE. With Illustrations. Cr. 8vo, cloth extra, **6s.**
THE UNIVERSE OF SUNS. With numerous Illustrations. Cr. 8vo, cloth ex., **6s.**
WAGES AND WANTS OF SCIENCE WORKERS. Crown 8vo, **1s. 6d.**

PRYCE (RICHARD).—MISS MAXWELL'S AFFECTIONS. Frontis-
piece by HAL LUDLOW. Crown 8vo, cloth, **3s. 6d.**; post 8vo, illust. boards., **2s.**

RAMBOSSON (J.). — POPULAR ASTRONOMY. With Coloured
Plate and numerous Illustrations. Crown 8vo, cloth extra, **7s. 6d.**

**RANDOLPH (LIEUT.-COL. GEORGE, U.S.A.).—AUNT ABIGAIL
DYKES:** A Novel. Crown 8vo, cloth extra, **7s. 6d.**

RIDDELL (MRS. J. H.), NOVELS BY.
WEIRD STORIES. Crown 8vo, cloth extra, **3s. 6d.**; post 8vo, illustrated bds., **2s.**
Post 8vo, illustrated boards, **2s.** each.
THE UNINHABITED HOUSE. | **FAIRY WATER.**
THE PRINCE OF WALES'S GARDEN | **HER MOTHER'S DARLING.**
PARTY. | **THE NUN'S CURSE.**
MYSTERY IN PALACE GARDENS. | **IDLE TALES.**

RIVES (AMELIE).—BARBARA DERING : A Sequel to "The Quick or
the Dead " Crown 8vo, cloth extra, **3s. 6d.**; post 8vo, illustrated boards, **2s.**

READE (CHARLES), NOVELS BY.

Crown 8vo, cloth extra, illustrated, **3s. 6d.** each; post 8vo, illust. bds., **2s.** each.

PEG WOFFINGTON. Illustrated by S. L. FILDES, R.A.—Also a POCKET EDITION, set in Elzevir style, fcap. 8vo, half-leather, **2s. 6d.**—And a LIBRARY EDITION of PEG WOFFINGTON and CHRISTIE JOHNSTONE, in One Vol., cr. 8vo, cloth, **3s. 6d.**

CHRISTIE JOHNSTONE. Illustrated by WILLIAM SMALL.—Also a POCKET EDITION, set in New Type, in Elzevir style, fcap. 8vo, half-leather, **2s. 6d.**

IT IS NEVER TOO LATE TO MEND. Illustrated by G. J. PINWELL.—Also the Cheap POPULAR EDITION, medium 8vo, portrait cover, **6d.**; cloth, **1s.**

COURSE OF TRUE LOVE NEVER DID RUN SMOOTH. Illust. HELEN PATERSON.

THE AUTOBIOGRAPHY OF A THIEF, &c. Illustrated by MATT STRETCH.

LOVE ME LITTLE, LOVE ME LONG. Illustrated by M. ELLEN EDWARDS.

THE DOUBLE MARRIAGE. Illusts. by Sir JOHN GILBERT, R.A., and C. KEENE.

THE CLOISTER AND THE HEARTH. Illustrated by CHARLES KEENE.—Also the ELZEVIR EDITION, with Introduction by BESANT, 4 vols., post 8vo, cloth gilt, **14s.**

HARD CASH. Illustrated by F. W. LAWSON.

GRIFFITH GAUNT. Illustrated by S. L. FILDES, R.A., and WILLIAM SMALL.

FOUL PLAY. Illustrated by GEORGE DU MAURIER.

PUT YOURSELF IN HIS PLACE. Illustrated by ROBERT BARNES.

A TERRIBLE TEMPTATION. Illustrated by EDWARD HUGHES and A. W. COOPER.

A SIMPLETON. Illustrated by KATE CRAUFURD.

THE WANDERING HEIR. Illust. by H. PATERSON, S. L. FILDES, C. GREEN, &c.

A WOMAN-HATER. Illustrated by THOMAS COULDERY.

SINGLEHEART AND DOUBLEFACE. Illustrated by P. MACNAB.

GOOD STORIES OF MEN AND OTHER ANIMALS. Illust. by E. A. ABBEY, &c.

THE JILT, and other Stories. Illustrated by JOSEPH NASH.

A PERILOUS SECRET. Illustrated by FRED. BARNARD.

READIANA. With a Steel-plate Portrait of CHARLES READE.

POPULAR EDITIONS, medium 8vo, **6d.** each; cloth, **1s.** each.

THE CLOISTER AND THE HEARTH. | **IT IS NEVER TOO LATE TO MEND.**
PEG WOFFINGTON; and **CHRISTIE JOHNSTONE.**

BIBLE CHARACTERS: Studies of David, Paul, &c. Fcap. 8vo, leatherette, **1s.**

SELECTIONS FROM THE WORKS OF CHARLES READE. Post 8vo, cloth, **2s. 6d.**

RIMMER (ALFRED), WORKS BY. Square 8vo, cloth gilt, **7s. 6d.** each.

OUR OLD COUNTRY TOWNS. With 55 Illustrations.

RAMBLES ROUND ETON AND HARROW. With 50 Illustrations.

ABOUT ENGLAND WITH DICKENS. With 58 Illusts. by C. A. VANDERHOOF, &c.

ROBINSON CRUSOE. By DANIEL DEFOE. (MAJOR'S EDITION.) With

37 Illustrations by GEORGE CRUIKSHANK. Post 8vo, half-bound, **2s.**

ROBINSON (F. W.), NOVELS BY.

WOMEN ARE STRANGE. Post 8vo, illustrated boards, **2s.**

THE HANDS OF JUSTICE. Cr. 8vo, cloth ex., **3s. 6d.**; post 8vo, illust. bds., **2s.**

ROBINSON (PHIL), WORKS BY. Crown 8vo, cloth extra, **6s.** each.

THE POETS' BIRDS. | **THE POETS' BEASTS.**

THE POETS AND NATURE: REPTILES, FISHES, AND INSECTS.

ROCHEFOUCAULD'S MAXIMS AND MORAL REFLECTIONS. With

Notes, and an Introductory Essay by SAINTE-BEUVE. Post 8vo, cloth limp, **2s.**

ROLL OF BATTLE ABBEY, THE : A List of the Principal Warriors

who came from Normandy with William the Conqueror. Handsomely printed, **5s.**

ROSENGARTEN (A.).—HANDBOOK OF ARCHITECTURAL STYLES.

Translated by W. COLLETT-SANDARS. With 639 Illusts. Cr. 8vo, cloth extra, **7s. 6d.**

ROWLEY (HON. HUGH), WORKS BY. Post 8vo, cloth, **2s. 6d.** each.

PUNIANA: RIDDLES AND JOKES. With numerous Illustrations.

MORE PUNIANA. Profusely Illustrated.

RUSSELL (W. CLARK), BOOKS AND NOVELS BY :

Cr. 8vo, cloth extra, **6s.** each; post 8vo, illust. boards, **2s.** each; cloth limp, **2s. 6d.** ea.

ROUND THE GALLEY-FIRE. | **A BOOK FOR THE HAMMOCK.**
IN THE MIDDLE WATCH. | **MYSTERY OF THE "OCEAN STAR."**
A VOYAGE TO THE CAPE. | **THE ROMANCE OF JENNY HARLOWE.**

Cr. 8vo, cl. extra, **3s. 6d.** ea.; post 8vo, illust. boards, **2s.** ea.; cloth limp, **2s. 6d.** ea.

OCEAN TRAGEDY. | **SHIPMATE LOUISE.** | **ALONE ON WIDE WIDE SEA.**

ON THE FO'K'SLE HEAD. Post 8vo, illust. boards, **2s.**; cloth limp, **2s. 6d.**

THE GOOD SHIP "MOHOCK." Two Vols., crown 8vo, **10s.** net.

THE PHANTOM DEATH, &c. With Frontispiece. Crown 8vo, **3s. 6d.**

THE CONVICT SHIP. Three Vols., crown 8vo, **15s.** net.

IS HE THE MAN? Crown 8vo, cloth, **3s. 6d.**

RUNCIMAN (JAMES), STORIES BY. Post 8vo, bds., **2s.** ea.; cl., **2s. 6d.** ea.
SKIPPERS AND SHELLBACKS. | GRACE BALMAIGN'S SWEETHEART.
SCHOOLS AND SCHOLARS.

RUSSELL (DORA), NOVELS BY.
A COUNTRY SWEETHEART. Crown 8vo, cloth extra, **3s. 6d.** [*Sept.*
THE DRIFT OF FATE. Three Vols., crown 8vo, **15s.** net.

SAINT AUBYN (ALAN), NOVELS BY.
Crown 8vo, cloth extra, **3s. 6d.** each; post 8vo, illust. boards, **2s.** each.
A FELLOW OF TRINITY. Note by OLIVER WENDELL HOLMES and Frontispiece.
THE JUNIOR DEAN. | MASTER OF ST. BENEDICT'S. | TO HIS OWN MASTER.
Fcap. 8vo, cloth boards, **1s. 6d.** each.
THE OLD MAID'S SWEETHEART. | MODEST LITTLE SARA.
Crown 8vo, cloth extra, **3s. 6d.** each
ORCHARD DAMEREL. | IN THE FACE OF THE WORLD.
THE TREMLETT DIAMONDS. Two Vols., **10s.** net.

SALA (G. A.).—GASLIGHT AND DAYLIGHT. Post 8vo, boards, **2s.**

SANSON.—SEVEN GENERATIONS OF EXECUTIONERS: Memoirs
of the Sanson Family (1688 to 1847). Crown 8vo, cloth extra, **3s. 6d.**

SAUNDERS (JOHN), NOVELS BY.
Crown 8vo, cloth extra, **3s. 6d.** each; post 8vo, illustrated boards, **2s.** each.
GUY WATERMAN. | THE LION IN THE PATH. | THE TWO DREAMERS.
BOUND TO THE WHEEL. Crown 8vo, cloth extra, **3s. 6d.**

SAUNDERS (KATHARINE), NOVELS BY.
Crown 8vo, cloth extra, **3s. 6d.** each; post 8vo. illustrated boards, **2s.** each.
MARGARET AND ELIZABETH. | HEART SALVAGE.
THE HIGH MILLS. | SEBASTIAN.
JOAN MERRYWEATHER. Post 8vo, illustrated boards, **2s.**
GIDEON'S ROCK. Crown 8vo, cloth extra, **3s. 6d.**

SCOTLAND YARD, Past and Present: Experiences of 37 Years. By
Ex-Chief-Inspector CAVANAGH. Post 8vo, illustrated boards. **2s.**; cloth, **2s. 6d.**

SECRET OUT, THE: One Thousand Tricks with Cards; with Entertaining Experiments in Drawing-room or "White Magic." By W. H. CREMER.
With 300 Illustrations. Crown 8vo, cloth extra, **4s. 6d.**

SEGUIN (L. G.), WORKS BY.
THE COUNTRY OF THE PASSION PLAY (OBERAMMERGAU) and the Highlands
of Bavaria. With Map and 37 Illustrations. Crown 8vo, cloth extra, **3s. 6d.**
WALKS IN ALGIERS. With 2 Maps and 16 Illusts. Crown 8vo, cloth extra, **6s.**

SENIOR (WM.).—BY STREAM AND SEA. Post 8vo, cloth, **2s. 6d.**

SERGEANT (A.).—DR. ENDICOTT'S EXPERIMENT. 2 vols., **10s.** net.

SHAKESPEARE FOR CHILDREN: LAMB'S TALES FROM SHAKE-
SPEARE. With Illusts., coloured and plain, by J. MOYR SMITH. Cr. 4to. **3s. 6d.**

SHARP (WILLIAM).—CHILDREN OF TO-MORROW: A Novel.
Crown 8vo, cloth extra, **6s.**

SHELLEY (PERCY BYSSHE), THE COMPLETE WORKS IN VERSE
AND PROSE. Edited, Prefaced, and Annotated by R. HERNE SHEPHERD.
Five Vols., crown 8vo, cloth boards, **3s. 6d.** each.
POETICAL WORKS, in Three Vols.:
Vol. I. Introduction by the Editor; Posthumous Fragments of Margaret Nicholson; Shelley's Corre-
spondence with Stockdale; The Wandering Jew; Queen Mab, with the Notes; Alastor,
and other Poems; Rosalind and Helen; Prometheus Unbound; Adonais, &c.
Vol. II. Laon and Cythna; The Cenci; Julian and Maddalo; Swellfoot the Tyrant; The Witch of
Atlas; Epipsychidion: Hellas.
Vol. III. Posthumous Poems; The Masque of Anarchy; and other Pieces.
PROSE WORKS, in Two Vols.:
Vol. I. The Two Romances of Zastrozzi and St. Irvyne; the Dublin and Marlow Pamphlets; A Refuta-
tion of Deism; Letters to Leigh Hunt, and some Minor Writings and Fragments.
Vol. II. The Essays; Letters from Abroad; Translations and Fragments, Edited by Mrs. SHELLEY.
With a Bibliography of Shelley, and an Index of the Prose Works.

SHERARD (R. H.).—ROGUES: A Novel. Crown 8vo, **1s.**; cloth, **1s. 6d.**

SHERIDAN (GENERAL P. H.), PERSONAL MEMOIRS OF. With
Portraits and Facsimiles. Two Vols., demy 8vo, cloth, **24s.**

SHERIDAN'S (RICHARD BRINSLEY) COMPLETE WORKS. With Life and Anecdotes. Including his Dramatic Writings, his Works in Prose and Poetry, Translations, Speeches and Jokes. 10 Illusts. Cr. 8vo, hf.-bound, **7s. 6d.**
THE RIVALS, THE SCHOOL FOR SCANDAL, and other Plays. Post 8vo, printed on laid paper and half-bound, **2s.**
SHERIDAN'S COMEDIES: THE RIVALS and **THE SCHOOL FOR SCANDAL.** Edited, with an Introduction and Notes to each Play, and a Biographical Sketch, by BRANDER MATTHEWS. With Illustrations. Demy 8vo, half-parchment, **12s. 6d.**

SIDNEY'S (SIR PHILIP) COMPLETE POETICAL WORKS, including all those in "Arcadia." With Portrait, Memorial-Introduction, Notes, &c. by the Rev. A. B. GROSART, D.D. Three Vols., crown 8vo, cloth boards, **18s.**

SIGNBOARDS: Their History. With Anecdotes of Famous Taverns and Remarkable Characters. By JACOB LARWOOD and JOHN CAMDEN HOTTEN. With Coloured Frontispiece and 94 Illustrations. Crown 8vo, cloth extra, **7s. 6d.**

SIMS (GEO. R.), WORKS BY. Post 8vo, illust. bds., **2s.** ea ; cl. limp, **2s. 6d.** ea.

ROGUES AND VAGABONDS.	TALES OF TO-DAY.
THE RING O' BELLS.	DRAMAS OF LIFE. With 60 Illustrations.
MARY JANE'S MEMOIRS.	MEMOIRS OF A LANDLADY.
MARY JANE MARRIED.	MY TWO WIVES.
TINKLETOP'S CRIME.	SCENES FROM THE SHOW.
ZEPH: A Circus Story, &c.	

Crown 8vo, picture cover, **1s.** each ; cloth, **1s. 6d.** each.
HOW THE POOR LIVE ; and HORRIBLE LONDON.
THE DAGONET RECITER AND READER: being Readings and Recitations in Prose and Verse, selected from his own Works by GEORGE R. SIMS.
THE CASE OF GEORGE CANDLEMAS. | DAGONET DITTIES.
DAGONET ABROAD. Crown 8vo, cloth, **3s. 6d.**   [*Shortly.*

SISTER DORA: A Biography. By MARGARET LONSDALE. With Four Illustrations. Demy 8vo, picture cover, **4d.** ; cloth, **6d.**

SKETCHLEY (ARTHUR). — A MATCH IN THE DARK. Post 8vo, illustrated boards, **2s.**

SLANG DICTIONARY (THE): Etymological, Historical, and Anecdotal. Crown 8vo, cloth extra, **6s. 6d.**

SMITH (J. MOYR), WORKS BY.
THE PRINCE OF ARGOLIS. With 130 Illusts. Post 8vo, cloth extra. **3s. 6d.**
THE WOOING OF THE WATER WITCH. Illustrated. Post 8vo, cloth, **6s.**

SOCIETY IN LONDON. Crown 8vo, 1s. ; cloth, 1s. 6d.

SOCIETY IN PARIS: The Upper Ten Thousand. A Series of Letters from Count PAUL VASILI to a Young French Diplomat. Crown 8vo, cloth, **6s.**

SOMERSET (LORD HENRY). — SONGS OF ADIEU. Small 4to, Japanese vellum, **6s.**

SPALDING (T. A., LL.B.).—ELIZABETHAN DEMONOLOGY: An Essay on the Belief in the Existence of Devils. Crown 8vo, cloth extra, **5s.**

SPEIGHT (T. W.), NOVELS BY.
Post 8vo, illustrated boards, **2s.** each.

THE MYSTERIES OF HERON DYKE.	THE GOLDEN HOOP.
BY DEVIOUS WAYS, &c.	BACK TO LIFE.
HOODWINKED; and THE SANDY-	THE LOUDWATER TRAGEDY.
CROFT MYSTERY.	BURGO'S ROMANCE.

QUITTANCE IN FULL.
Post 8vo, cloth limp, **1s. 6d.** each.
A BARREN TITLE. | WIFE OR NO WIFE?
THE SANDYCROFT MYSTERY. Crown 8vo, picture cover, **1s.**
A SECRET OF THE SEA. Crown 8vo, cloth extra, **3s. 6d.**
THE GREY MONK. Three Vols , **15s. net.**

SPENSER FOR CHILDREN. By M. H. TOWRY. With Illustrations by WALTER J. MORGAN. Crown 4to, cloth extra, **3s. 6d.**

STARRY HEAVENS (THE): A POETICAL BIRTHDAY BOOK. Royal 16mo, cloth extra, **2s. 6d.**

STEDMAN (E. C.), WORKS BY. Crown 8vo, cloth extra, **9s.** each.
VICTORIAN POETS. | THE POETS OF AMERICA.

STERNDALE (R. ARMITAGE).—THE AFGHAN KNIFE: A Novel. Crown 8vo, cloth extra. **3s. 6d.**: post 8vo, illustrated boards. **2s.**

STEVENSON (R. LOUIS), WORKS BY.   Post 8vo, cl. limp, **2s. 6d.** each
TRAVELS WITH A DONKEY. With a Frontispiece by WALTER CRANE.
AN INLAND VOYAGE. With a Frontispiece by WALTER CRANE.
Crown 8vo, buckram, gilt top, **6s.** each.
FAMILIAR STUDIES OF MEN AND BOOKS.
THE SILVERADO SQUATTERS. With Frontispiece by J. D. STRONG.
THE MERRY MEN. | UNDERWOODS: Poems.
MEMORIES AND PORTRAITS.
VIRGINIBUS PUERISQUE, and other Papers. | BALLADS. | PRINCE OTTO.
ACROSS THE PLAINS, with other Memories and Essays.
NEW ARABIAN NIGHTS. Crown 8vo, buckram, gilt top, **6s.;** post 8vo, illustrated boards, **2s.**
THE SUICIDE CLUB; and THE RAJAH'S DIAMOND. (From NEW ARABIAN NIGHTS.) With 8 Illustrations by W. J. HENNESSY. Crown 8vo, cloth, **5s.**
FATHER DAMIEN: An Open Letter to the Rev. Dr. Hyde. Crown 8vo, handmade and brown paper, **1s.**
THE EDINBURGH EDITION OF THE WORKS OF ROBERT LOUIS STEVENSON. 20 Vols., demy 8vo. This Edition (which is limited to 1,000 copies) is sold only in Sets, the price of which may be learned from the Booksellers. The Vols. are appearing at the rate of one a month, beginning Nov. 1894.

STODDARD (C. WARREN).—SUMMER CRUISING IN THE SOUTH SEAS. Illustrated by WALLIS MACKAY. Crown 8vo, cloth extra, **3s. 6d.**

STORIES FROM FOREIGN NOVELISTS. With Notices by HELEN and ALICE ZIMMERN. Crown 8vo, cloth extra, **3s. 6d.**: post 8vo, illustrated boards, **2s.**

STRANGE MANUSCRIPT (A) FOUND IN A COPPER CYLINDER. Cr. 8vo, cloth extra, with 19 Illusts. by GILBERT GAUL, **5s.**; post 8vo, illust. bds., **2s.**

STRANGE SECRETS. Told by CONAN DOYLE, PERCY FITZGERALD, FLORENCE MARRYAT, &c. Post 8vo, illustrated boards, **2s.**

STRUTT (JOSEPH).—THE SPORTS AND PASTIMES OF THE PEOPLE OF ENGLAND; including the Rural and Domestic Recreations, May Games, Mummeries, Shows, &c., from the Earliest Period to the Present Time. Edited by WILLIAM HONE. With 140 Illustrations. Crown 8vo, cloth extra, **7s. 6d.**

SWIFT'S (DEAN) CHOICE WORKS, in Prose and Verse. With Memoir, Portrait, and Facsimiles of the Maps in "Gulliver's Travels." Cr. 8vo, cl., **7s. 6d.**
GULLIVER'S TRAVELS, and A TALE OF A TUB. Post 8vo, half-bound, **2s.**
JONATHAN SWIFT: A Study. By J. CHURTON COLLINS. Crown 8vo, cloth extra, **8s.**

SWINBURNE (ALGERNON C.), WORKS BY.

SELECTIONS FROM POETICAL WORKS OF A. C. SWINBURNE. Fcap. 8vo, 6s.
ATALANTA IN CALYDON. Crown 8vo, 6s.
CHASTELARD: A Tragedy. Crown 8vo, 7s.
POEMS AND BALLADS. FIRST SERIES. Crown 8vo or fcap. 8vo, 9s.
POEMS AND BALLADS. SECOND SERIES. Crown 8vo, 9s.
POEMS & BALLADS. THIRD SERIES. Cr. 8vo, 7s.
SONGS BEFORE SUNRISE. Crown 8vo, 10s. 6d.
BOTHWELL: A Tragedy. Crown 8vo, 12s. 6d.
SONGS OF TWO NATIONS. Crown 8vo, 6s.
GEORGE CHAPMAN. (See Vol. II. of G. CHAPMAN'S Works.) Crown 8vo, 6s.
ESSAYS AND STUDIES. Crown 8vo, 12s.
ERECHTHEUS: A Tragedy. Crown 8vo, 6s.

A NOTE ON CHARLOTTE BRONTE. Cr. 8vo, 6s.
SONGS OF THE SPRINGTIDES. Crown 8vo, 6s.
STUDIES IN SONG. Crown 8vo. 7s.
MARY STUART: A Tragedy. Crown 8vo, 8s.
TRISTRAM OF LYONESSE. Crown 8vo, 9s.
A CENTURY OF ROUNDELS. Small 4to, 8s.
A MIDSUMMER HOLIDAY. Crown 8vo, 7s.
MARINO FALIERO: A Tragedy. Crown 8vo, 6s.
A STUDY OF VICTOR HUGO. Crown 8vo, 6s.
MISCELLANIES. Crown 8vo, 12s.
LOCRINE: A Tragedy. Crown 8vo, 6s.
A STUDY OF BEN JONSON. Crown 8vo, 7s.
THE SISTERS: A Tragedy. Crown 8vo, 6s.
ASTROPHEL, &c. Crown 8vo, 7s.
STUDIES IN PROSE AND POETRY. Crown 8vo, 9s.

SYNTAX'S (DR.) THREE TOURS: In Search of the Picturesque, in Search of Consolation, and in Search of a Wife. With ROWLANDSON'S Coloured Illustrations, and Life of the Author by J. C. HOTTEN. Crown 8vo, cloth extra, **7s. 6d.**

TAINE'S HISTORY OF ENGLISH LITERATURE. Translated by HENRY VAN LAUN. Four Vols., small demy 8vo, cl. bds., **30s.**—POPULAR EDITION, Two Vols., large crown 8vo, cloth extra, **15s.**

TAYLOR (DR. J. E., F.L.S.), WORKS BY. Crown 8vo, cloth, **5s.** each.
THE SAGACITY AND MORALITY OF PLANTS: A Sketch of the Life and Conduct of the Vegetable Kingdom. With a Coloured Frontispiece and 100 Illustrations.
OUR COMMON BRITISH FOSSILS, and Where to Find Them. 331 Illustrations.
THE PLAYTIME NATURALIST. With 366 Illustrations.

TAYLOR (BAYARD).—DIVERSIONS OF THE ECHO CLUB : Burlesques of Modern Writers. Post 8vo, cloth limp, **2s.**

TAYLOR (TOM).—HISTORICAL DRAMAS. Containing "Clancarty," "Jeanne Darc," "'Twixt Axe and Crown," "The Fool's Revenge," "Arkwright's Wife," "Anne Boleyn," "Plot and Passion."   Crown 8vo, cloth extra, **7s. 6d.**
₊ The Plays may also be had separately, at **1s.** each.

TENNYSON (LORD) : A Biographical Sketch.   By H. J. JENNINGS.
Post 8vo, portrait cover, **1s.**; cloth, **1s. 6d.**

THACKERAYANA : Notes and Anecdotes. Illustrated by Hundreds of Sketches by WILLIAM MAKEPEACE THACKERAY. Crown 8vo, cloth extra, **7s. 6d.**

THAMES, A NEW PICTORIAL HISTORY OF THE. By A. S. KRAUSSE. With 340 Illustrations Post 8vo, **1s.**; cloth, **1s. 6d.**

THIERS (ADOLPHE).—HISTORY of the CONSULATE & EMPIRE of FRANCE UNDER NAPOLEON. Translated by D. FORBES CAMPBELL and JOHN STEBBING. With 36 Steel Plates. 12 vols., demy 8vo, cloth extra, **12s.** each.

THOMAS (BERTHA), NOVELS BY. Cr. 8vo, cl., **3s. 6d.** ea.; post 8vo, **2s.** ea.
THE VIOLIN-PLAYER. | PROUD MAISIE.
CRESSIDA. Post 8vo, illustrated boards, **2s.**

THOMSON'S SEASONS, and CASTLE OF INDOLENCE. With Introduction by ALLAN CUNNINGHAM, and 48 Illustrations. Post 8vo, half-bound, **2s.**

THORNBURY (WALTER), WORKS BY.
THE LIFE AND CORRESPONDENCE OF J. M. W. TURNER. With Illustrations in Colours. Crown 8vo, cloth extra, **7s. 6d.**
Post 8vo, illustrated boards, **2s.** each.
OLD STORIES RE-TOLD. | TALES FOR THE MARINES.

TIMBS (JOHN), WORKS BY. Crown 8vo, cloth extra, **7s. 6d.** each.
THE HISTORY OF CLUBS AND CLUB LIFE IN LONDON: Anecdotes of its Famous Coffee-houses, Hostelries, and Taverns. With 42 Illustrations.
ENGLISH ECCENTRICS AND ECCENTRICITIES: Stories of Delusions, Impostures, Sporting Scenes, Eccentric Artists, Theatrical Folk, &c. 48 Illustrations.

TROLLOPE (ANTHONY), NOVELS BY.
Crown 8vo, cloth extra, **3s. 6d.** each; post 8vo, illustrated boards, **2s.** each.
THE WAY WE LIVE NOW. | MR. SCARBOROUGH'S FAMILY.
FRAU FROHMANN. | THE LAND-LEAGUERS.
Post 8vo, illustrated boards, **2s.** each.
KEPT IN THE DARK. | THE AMERICAN SENATOR.
THE GOLDEN LION OF GRANPERE. | JOHN CALDIGATE. | MARION FAY.

TROLLOPE (FRANCES E.), NOVELS BY.
Crown 8vo, cloth extra, **3s. 6d.** each: post 8vo, illustrated boards, **2s.** each.
LIKE SHIPS UPON THE SEA. | MABEL'S PROGRESS. | ANNE FURNESS.

TROLLOPE (T. A.).—DIAMOND CUT DIAMOND. Post 8vo, illust. bds., **2s.**

TROWBRIDGE (J. T.).—FARNELL'S FOLLY. Post 8vo, boards, 2s.

TYTLER (C. C. FRASER-).—MISTRESS JUDITH : A Novel. Crown 8vo, cloth extra, **3s. 6d.**; post 8vo, illustrated boards, **2s.**

TYTLER (SARAH), NOVELS BY.
Crown 8vo, cloth extra, **3s. 6d.** each; post 8vo, illustrated boards, **2s.** each.
THE BRIDE'S PASS. | BURIED DIAMONDS.
LADY BELL. | THE BLACKHALL GHOSTS.
Post 8vo, illustrated boards, **2s.** each.
WHAT SHE CAME THROUGH | BEAUTY AND THE BEAST.
CITOYENNE JACQUELINE | DISAPPEARED. | NOBLESSE OBLIGE.
SAINT MUNGO'S CITY. | THE HUGUENOT FAMILY.
THE MACDONALD LASS. With Frontispiece. Cr. 8vo, cloth, **3s. 6d.**

UPWARD (ALLEN), NOVELS BY.
THE QUEEN AGAINST OWEN. Crown 8vo, cloth, **3s. 6d.**: post 8vo, bds., **2s.**
THE PRINCE OF BALKISTAN. Crown 8vo, cloth extra, **3s. 6d.**

VASHTI AND ESTHER. By the Writer of "Belle's" Letters in *The World*. Crown 8vo, cloth extra, **3s. 6d.**

VILLARI (LINDA).—A DOUBLE BOND : A Story. Fcap. 8vo, 1s.

VIZETELLY (ERNEST A.).—THE SCORPION : A Romance of Spain. With a Frontispiece. Crown 8vo, cloth extra, **3s. 6d.**

WALFORD (EDWARD, M.A.), WORKS BY.
WALFORD'S COUNTY FAMILIES OF THE UNITED KINGDOM (1895). Containing the Descent, Birth, Marriage, Education, &c., of 12,000 Heads of Families, their Heirs, Offices, Addresses, Clubs, &c. Royal 8vo, cloth gilt, 50s.
WALFORD'S SHILLING PEERAGE (1895). Containing a List of the House of Lords, Scotch and Irish Peers, &c. 32mo, cloth, 1s.
WALFORD'S SHILLING BARONETAGE (1895). Containing a List of the Baronets of the United Kingdom, Biographical Notices, Addresses, &c. 32mo, cloth, 1s.
WALFORD'S SHILLING KNIGHTAGE (1895). Containing a List of the Knights of the United Kingdom, Biographical Notices, Addresses, &c. 32mo, cloth, 1s.
WALFORD'S SHILLING HOUSE OF COMMONS (1895). Containing a List of all the Members of the New Parliament, their Addresses, Clubs, &c. 32mo, cloth, 1s.
WALFORD'S COMPLETE PEERAGE, BARONETAGE, KNIGHTAGE, AND HOUSE OF COMMONS (1895) Royal 32mo, cloth, gilt edges, 5s.
TALES OF OUR GREAT FAMILIES. Crown 8vo, cloth extra, 3s. 6d.

WALTON AND COTTON'S COMPLETE ANGLER ; or, The Contemplative Man's Recreation, by IZAAK WALTON ; and Instructions how to Angle for a Trout or Grayling in a clear Stream, by CHARLES COTTON. With Memoirs and Notes by Sir HARRIS NICOLAS, and 61 Illustrations. Crown 8vo, cloth antique, **7s. 6d.**

WALT WHITMAN, POEMS BY. Edited, with Introduction, by WILLIAM M. ROSSETTI. With Portrait. Cr. 8vo, hand-made paper and buckram, **6s.**

WARD (HERBERT).—MY LIFE WITH STANLEY'S REAR GUARD. With a Map by F. S. WELLER. Post 8vo, **1s.** ; cloth, **1s. 6d.**

WARNER (CHARLES DUDLEY).—A ROUNDABOUT JOURNEY. Crown 8vo, cloth extra, **6s.**

WARRANT TO EXECUTE CHARLES I. A Facsimile, with the 59 Signatures and Seals. Printed on paper 22 in. by 14 in. **2s.**
WARRANT TO EXECUTE MARY QUEEN OF SCOTS. A Facsimile, including Queen Elizabeth's Signature and the Great Seal. **2s.**

WASSERMANN (LILLIAS), NOVELS BY.
THE DAFFODILS. Crown 8vo, **1s.** ; cloth, **1s. 6d.**
THE MARQUIS OF CARABAS. By AARON WATSON and LILLIAS WASSERMANN. Post 8vo. illustrated boards, **2s.**

WEATHER, HOW TO FORETELL THE, WITH THE POCKET SPECTROSCOPE. By F. W. CORY. With 10 Illustrations. Cr. 8vo. **1s.** ; cloth, **1s. 6d.**

WEBBER (BYRON).—FUN, FROLIC, AND FANCY. With 43 Illustrations by PHIL MAY and CHARLES MAY. Fcap. 4to, picture cover, **1s.**

WESTALL (WILLIAM). — TRUST-MONEY. Post 8vo, illustrated boards, **2s.** ; cloth limp, **2s. 6d.**

WHIST, HOW TO PLAY SOLO. By ABRAHAM S. WILKS and CHARLES F. PARDON. Post 8vo, cloth limp, **2s.**

WHITE (GILBERT).— THE NATURAL HISTORY OF SELBORNE. Post 8vo, printed on laid paper and half-bound, **2s.**

WILLIAMS (W. MATTIEU, F.R.A.S.), WORKS BY.
SCIENCE IN SHORT CHAPTERS. Crown 8vo, cloth extra, **7s. 6d.**
A SIMPLE TREATISE ON HEAT. With Illustrations. Crown 8vo, cloth, **2s. 6d.**
THE CHEMISTRY OF COOKERY. Crown 8vo, cloth extra, **6s.**
THE CHEMISTRY OF IRON AND STEEL MAKING. Crown 8vo, cloth extra, **9s.**
A VINDICATION OF PHRENOLOGY. With Portrait and 43 Illustrations. Demy 8vo, cloth extra, **12s. 6d.**

WILLIAMSON (MRS. F. H.).—A CHILD WIDOW. Post 8vo, bds., **2s.**

WILSON (DR. ANDREW, F.R.S.E.), WORKS BY.
CHAPTERS ON EVOLUTION. With 259 Illustrations. Cr. 8vo, cloth extra, **7s. 6d.**
LEAVES FROM A NATURALIST'S NOTE-BOOK. Post 8vo, cloth limp, **2s. 6d.**
LEISURE-TIME STUDIES. With Illustrations. Crown 8vo, cloth extra, **6s.**
STUDIES IN LIFE AND SENSE. With numerous Illusts. Cr. 8vo, cl. ex., **6s.**
COMMON ACCIDENTS: HOW TO TREAT THEM. Illusts. Cr. 8vo, **1s.** ; cl., **1s. 6d.**
GLIMPSES OF NATURE. With 35 Illustrations. Crown 8vo, cloth extra, **3s. 6d.**

WISSMANN (HERMANN VON).—MY SECOND JOURNEY THROUGH EQUATORIAL AFRICA. With 92 Illustrations. Demy 8vo, **16s.**

WINTER (J. S.), STORIES BY. Post 8vo, illustrated boards, **2s.** each; clo h limp. **2s. 6d.** each.
CAVALRY LIFE. | REGIMENTAL LEGENDS.
A SOLDIER'S CHILDREN. With 34 Illustrations by E. G. Thomson and E. Stuart Hardy. Crown 8vo, cloth extra, **3s. 6d.**

WOOD (H. F.), DETECTIVE STORIES BY. Post 8vo, boards, **2s.** each.
PASSENGER FROM SCOTLAND YARD. | ENGLISHMAN OF THE RUE CAIN.

WOOD (LADY).—SABINA : A Novel. Post 8vo, illust. boards, **2s.**

WOOLLEY (CELIA PARKER).—RACHEL ARMSTRONG ; or, Love and Theology. Post 8vo, illustrated boards. **2s. :** cloth, **2s. 6d.**

WRIGHT (THOMAS), WORKS BY. Crown 8vo, cloth extra, **7s. 6d.** each.
CARICATURE HISTORY OF THE GEORGES. With 400 Caricatures, Squibs, &c.
HISTORY OF CARICATURE AND OF THE GROTESQUE IN ART, LITERA-TURE, SCULPTURE, AND PAINTING. Illustrated by F. W. Fairholt, F.S.A.

WYNMAN (MARGARET).—MY FLIRTATIONS. With 13 Illustra-tions by J. Bernard Partridge. Crown 8vo, cloth extra, **3s. 6d.**

YATES (EDMUND), NOVELS BY. Post 8vo. illustrated boards, **2s.** each.
LAND AT LAST. | THE FORLORN HOPE. | CASTAWAY.

ZANGWILL (I.)—GHETTO TRAGEDIES. With Three Illustrations by A. S. Boyd. Fcap. 8vo, picture cover, **1s.** net.

ZOLA (EMILE), NOVELS BY. Crown 8vo, cloth extra. **3s. 6d.** each.
THE DOWNFALL. Translated by E. A. Vizetelly. Fourth Edition, Revised.
THE DREAM. Translated by Eliza Chase. With 8 Illustrations by Jeanniot.
DOCTOR PASCAL. Translated by E. A. Vizetelly. With Portrait of the Author.
MONEY. Translated by Ernest A. Vizetelly.
LOURDES. Translated by Ernest A. Vizetelly.
EMILE ZOLA: A Biography. By R. H. Sherard. With Portraits, Illustrations. and Facsimile Letter. Demy 8vo, cloth extra, **12s.**

SOME BOOKS CLASSIFIED IN SERIES.

, *For fuller cataloguing, see alphabetical arrangement, pp. 1-26.*

THE MAYFAIR LIBRARY.   Post 8vo, cloth extra, **2s. 6d.** per Volume.

A Journey Round My Room. By X. De Maistre. Translated by Sir Henry Attwell.
Quips and Quiddities. By W. D. Adams.
The Agony Column of "The Times."
Melancholy Anatomised : Abridgment of Burton.
Poetical Ingenuities. By W. T. Dobson.
The Cupboard Papers. By Fin-Bec.
W. S. Gilbert's Plays. Three Series.
Songs of Irish Wit and Humour.
Animals and their Masters. By Sir A. Helps.
Social Pressure. By Sir A. Helps.
Curiosities of Criticism. By H. J. Jennings.
The Autocrat of the Breakfast-Table. By Oliver Wendell Holmes.
Pencil and Palette. By R. Kempt.
Little Essays : from Lamb's Letters.
Forensic Anecdotes. By Jacob Larwood.

Theatrical Anecdotes. By Jacob Larwood.
Jeux d'Esprit. Edited by Henry S. Leigh.
Witch Stories. By E. Lynn Linton.
Ourselves. By E. Lynn Linton.
Pastimes and Players. By R. Macgregor.
New Paul and Virginia. By W. H. Mallock.
The New Republic. By W. H. Mallock.
Puck on Pegasus. By H. C. Pennell.
Pegasus Re-saddled. By H. C. Pennell.
Muses of Mayfair. Edited by H. C. Pennell.
Thoreau : His Life and Aims. By H. A. Page.
Puniana. By Hon. Hugh Rowley.
More Puniana. By Hon. Hugh Rowley.
The Philosophy of Handwriting.
By Stream and Sea. By Wm. Senior.
Leaves from a Naturalist's Note-Book. By Dr. Andrew Wilson.

THE GOLDEN LIBRARY.   Post 8vo, cloth limp, **2s.** per Volume.

Diversions of the Echo Club. Bayard Taylor.
Songs for Sailors. By W. C. Bennett.
Lives of the Necromancers. By W. Godwin.
The Poetical Works of Alexander Pope.
Scenes of Country Life. By Edward Jesse.
Tale for a Chimney Corner. By Leigh Hunt.

The Autocrat of the Breakfast Table. By Oliver Wendell Holmes.
La Mort d'Arthur : Selections from Mallory.
Provincial Letters of Blaise Pascal.
Maxims and Reflections of Rochefoucauld.

THE WANDERER'S LIBRARY.   Crown 8vo, cloth extra, **3s. 6d.** each.

Wanderings in Patagonia. By Julius Beer-bohm. Illustrated.
Camp Notes. By Frederick Boyle.
Savage Life. By Frederick Boyle.
Merrie England in the Olden Time. By G. Daniel. Illustrated by Cruikshank.
Circus Life. By Thomas Frost.
Lives of the Conjurers. By Thomas Fros..
The Old Showmen and the Old London Fairs. By Thomas Frost.
Low-Life Deeps. By James Greenwood.

Wilds of London. By James Greenwood.
Tunis. By Chev. Hesse-Wartegg. 22 Illusts.
Life and Adventures of a Cheap Jack
World Behind the Scenes. By P. Fitzgerald.
Tavern Anecdotes and Sayings.
The Genial Showman. By E. P. Hingston.
Story of London Parks. By Jacob Larwood.
London Characters. By Henry Mayhew.
Seven Generations of Executioners.
Summer Cruising in the South Seas. By C. Warren Stoddard. Illustrated.

THE PICCADILLY (3/6) NOVELS—*continued.*

By Mrs. CAMPBELL PRAED.
Outlaw and Lawmaker. | Christina Chard.

By E. C. PRICE.
Valentina. | Mrs. Lancaster's Rival.
The Foreigners.

By RICHARD PRYCE.
Miss Maxwell's Affections.

By CHARLES READE.
It is Never Too Late to | Singleheart and Double-
Mend. | face.
The Double Marriage. | Good Stories of Men
Love Me Little, Love | and other Animals.
Me Long. | Hard Cash.
The Cloister and the | Peg Woffington.
Hearth. | Christie Johnstone.
The Course of True | Griffith Gaunt.
Love. | Foul Play.
The Autobiography of | The Wandering Heir.
a Thief. | A Woman-Hater.
Put Yourself in His | A Simpleton.
Place. | A Perilous Secret.
A Terrible Temptation. | Readiana.
The Jilt.

By Mrs. J. H. RIDDELL.
Weird Stories.

By AMELIE RIVES.
Barbara Dering.

By F. W. ROBINSON.
The Hands of Justice.

By DORA RUSSELL.
A Country Sweetheart.

By W. CLARK RUSSELL.
Ocean Tragedy. | The Phantom Death.
My Shipmate Louise. | Is He the Man ?
Alone on Wide Wide Sea. |

By JOHN SAUNDERS.
Guy Waterman. | The Two Dreamers.
Bound to the Wheel. | The Lion in the Path.

By KATHARINE SAUNDERS.
Margaret and Elizabeth | Heart Salvage.
Gideon's Rock. | Sebastian.
The High Mills.

By HAWLEY SMART.
Without Love or Licence.

By T. W. SPEIGHT.
A Secret of the Sea.

By R. A. STERNDALE.
The Afghan Knife.

By BERTHA THOMAS.
Proud Maisie. | The Violin-Player.

By ANTHONY TROLLOPE.
The Way we Live Now. | Scarborough's Family.
Frau Frohmann. | The Land-Leaguers.

By FRANCES E. TROLLOPE.
Like Ships upon the | Anne Furness.
Sea. | Mabel's Progress.

By IVAN TURGENIEFF, &c.
Stories from Foreign Novelists.

By MARK TWAIN.
The American Claimant. | Tom Sawyer Abroad.
The £1,000,000 Bank-note. | Pudd'nhead Wilson.

By C. C. FRASER-TYTLER.
Mistress Judith.

By SARAH TYTLER.
Lady Bell. | The Blackhall Ghosts.
The Bride's Pass. | The Macdonald Lass.
Buried Diamonds.

By ALLEN UPWARD.
The Queen against Owen.
The Prince of Balkistan.

By E. A. VIZETELLY.
The Scorpion : A Romance of Spain.

By J. S. WINTER.
A Soldier's Children.

By MARGARET WYNMAN.
My Flirtations.

By E. ZOLA.
The Downfall. | Dr. Pascal.
The Dream. | Money. | Lourdes.

CHEAP EDITIONS OF POPULAR NOVELS.
Post 8vo, illustrated boards, **2s.** each.

By ARTEMUS WARD.
Artemus Ward Complete.

By EDMOND ABOUT.
The Fellah.

By HAMILTON AIDE.
Carr of Carrlyon. | Confidences.

By MARY ALBERT.
Brooke Finchley's Daughter.

By Mrs. ALEXANDER.
Maid, Wife or Widow? | Valerie's Fate.

By GRANT ALLEN.
Strange Stories. | For Maimie's Sake.
Philistia. | The Tents of Shem.
Babylon. | The Great Taboo.
The Devil's Die. | Dumaresq's Daughter.
This Mortal Coil. | The Duchess of Powys-
In all Shades. | land.
The Beckoning Hand. | Ivan Greet's Masterpiece.
Blood Royal. | The Scallywag.

By E. LESTER ARNOLD.
Phra the Phœnician.

By ALAN ST. AUBYN.
A Fellow of Trinity. | Master of St.Benedict's
The Junior Dean. | To His Own Master.

By Rev. S. BARING GOULD.
Red Spider. | Eve.

By FRANK BARRETT.
Fettered for Life. | Honest Davie.
Little Lady Linton. | A Prodigal's Progress.
Between Life & Death. | Found Guilty.
The Sin of Olga Zassou- | A Recoiling Vengeance
lich. | For Love and Honour.
Folly Morrison. | John Ford ; and His
Lieut. Barnabas | Helpmate.

SHELSLEY BEAUCHAMP.
Grantley Grange.

By Sir WALTER BESANT.
Dorothy Forster. | For Faith and Freedom.
Children of Gibeon. | To Call Her Mine.
Uncle Jack. | The Bell of St. Paul's.
Herr Paulus. | Armorel of Lyonesse.
All Sorts and Condi- | The Holy Rose.
tions of Men. | The Ivory Gate.
The Captains' Room. | St. Katherine's by the
All in a Garden Fair. | Tower.
The World Went Very | Verbena Camellia.
Well Then. | The Rebel Queen.

Sir W. BESANT & J. RICE.
This Son of Vulcan. | The Ten Years' Tenant.
My Little Girl. | Ready-Money Mortiboy
The Case of Mr. Lucraft. | With Harp and Crown.
The Golden Butterfly. | 'Twas in Trafalgar's
By Celia's Arbour. | Bay.
The Monks of Thelema. | The Chaplain of the
The Seamy Side. | Fleet.

Two-Shilling Novels—*continued.*

By AMBROSE BIERCE.
In the Midst of Life.

By FREDERICK BOYLE.

Camp Notes.	Chronicles of No-man's
Savage Life.	Land.

By BRET HARTE.

Californian Stories.	Flip.	Maruja.
Gabriel Conroy.	A Phyllis of the Sierras.
The Luck of Roaring	A Waif of the Plains.
Camp.	A Ward of the Golden
An Heiress of Red Dog.	Gate.

By HAROLD BRYDGES.
Uncle Sam at Home.

By ROBERT BUCHANAN.

Shadow of the Sword.	The Martyrdom of Ma-
A Child of Nature.	deline.
God and the Man.	Annan Water.
Love Me for Ever.	The New Abelard.
Foxglove Manor.	Matt.
The Master of the Mine	The Heir of Linne.

By HALL CAINE.

The Shadow of a Crime.	The Deemster.
A Son of Hagar.	

By Commander CAMERON.
The Cruise of the "Black Prince."

By Mrs. LOVETT CAMERON.

Deceivers Ever.	Juliet's Guardian.

By HAYDEN CARRUTH.
The Adventures of Jones.

By AUSTIN CLARE.
For the Love of a Lass.

By Mrs. ARCHER CLIVE.
Paul Ferroll.
Why Paul Ferroll Killed his Wife.

By MACLAREN COBBAN.

The Cure of Souls.	The Red Sultan.

By C. ALLSTON COLLINS.
The Bar Sinister.

MORT. & FRANCES COLLINS.

Sweet Anne Page.	Sweet and Twenty.
Transmigration.	The Village Comedy.
From Midnight to Mid-	You Play me False.
night.	Blacksmith and Scholar
A Fight with Fortune.	Frances.

By WILKIE COLLINS.

Armadale.	My Miscellanies.
After Dark.	The Woman in White.
No Name.	The Moonstone.
Antonina.	Man and Wife.
Basil.	Poor Miss Finch.
Hide and Seek.	The Fallen Leaves.
The Dead Secret.	Jezebel's Daughter
Queen of Hearts.	The Black Robe.
Miss or Mrs.?	Heart and Science.
The New Magdalen.	"I Say No!"
The Frozen Deep.	The Evil Genius.
The Law and the Lady.	Little Novels.
The Two Destinies.	Legacy of Cain.
The Haunted Hotel.	Blind Love.
A Rogue's Life.	

By M. J. COLQUHOUN.
Every Inch a Soldier.

By DUTTON COOK.

Leo.	Paul Foster's Daughter.

By C. EGBERT CRADDOCK.
The Prophet of the Great Smoky Mountains.

By MATT CRIM.
Adventures of a Fair Rebel.

By B. M. CROKER.

Pretty Miss Nevill.	Bird of Passage.
Diana Barrington.	Proper Pride.
"To Let."	A Family Likeness.

By W. CYPLES.
Hearts of Gold.

By ALPHONSE DAUDET.
The Evangelist; or, Port Salvation.

By ERASMUS DAWSON.
The Fountain of Youth.

Two-Shilling Novels—*continued.*

By JAMES DE MILLE.
A Castle in Spain.

By J. LEITH DERWENT.

Our Lady of Tears.	Circe's Lovers.

By CHARLES DICKENS.

Sketches by Boz.	Nicholas Nickleby.
Oliver Twist.	

By DICK DONOVAN.

The Man-Hunter.	From Information Re-
Tracked and Taken.	ceived.
Caught at Last!	Tracked to Doom.
Wanted!	Link by Link
Who Poisoned Hetty	Suspicion Aroused.
Duncan?	Dark Deeds.
Man from Manchester.	The Long Arm of the
A Detective's Triumphs	Law.
In the Grip of the Law.	

By Mrs. ANNIE EDWARDES.

A Point of Honour.	Archie Lovell.

By M. BETHAM-EDWARDS.

Felicia.	Kitty.

By EDW. EGGLESTON.
Roxy.

By G. MANVILLE FENN.

The New Mistress.	Witness to the Deed.

By PERCY FITZGERALD.

Bella Donna.	Second Mrs. Tillotson.
Never Forgotten.	Seventy - five Brooke
Polly.	Street.
Fatal Zero.	The Lady of Brantome.

By P. FITZGERALD and others.
Strange Secrets.

ALBANY DE FONBLANQUE.
Filthy Lucre.

By R. E. FRANCILLON.

Olympia.	King or Knave?
One by One.	Romances of the Law.
A Real Queen.	Ropes of Sand.
Queen Cophetua.	A Dog and his Shadow

By HAROLD FREDERICK.

Seth's Brother's Wife.	The Lawton Girl.

Pref. by Sir BARTLE FRERE.
Pandurang Hari.

By HAIN FRISWELL.
One of Two.

By EDWARD GARRETT.
The Capel Girls.

By GILBERT GAUL.
A Strange Manuscript.

By CHARLES GIBBON.

Robin Gray.	In Honour Bound.
Fancy Free.	Flower of the Forest.
For Lack of Gold.	The Braes of Yarrow.
What will the World	The Golden Shaft.
Say?	Of High Degree.
In Love and War.	By Mead and Stream.
For the King.	Loving a Dream.
In Pastures Green.	A Hard Knot.
Queen of the Meadow.	Heart's Delight.
A Heart's Problem.	Blood-Money.
The Dead Heart.	

By WILLIAM GILBERT.

Dr. Austin's Guests.	The Wizard of the
James Duke.	Mountain.

By ERNEST GLANVILLE.

The Lost Heiress.	The Fossicker.
A Fair Colonist.	

By HENRY GREVILLE.

A Noble Woman.	Nikanor.

By CECIL GRIFFITH.
Corinthia Marazion.

By SYDNEY GRUNDY.
The Days of his Vanity.

By JOHN HABBERTON.

Brueton's Bayou	Country Luck.

By ANDREW HALLIDAY.
Every-day Papers.

By Lady DUFFUS HARDY.
Paul Wynter's Sacrifice.

Two-Shilling Novels—*continued.*

By THOMAS HARDY.
Under the Greenwood Tree.

By J. BERWICK HARWOOD.
The Tenth Earl.

By JULIAN HAWTHORNE.

Garth.	Beatrix Randolph.
Ellice Quentin.	Love—or a Name.
Fortune's Fool.	David Poindexter's Dis-
Miss Cadogna.	appearance.
Sebastian Strome.	The Spectre of the
Dust.	Camera.

By Sir ARTHUR HELPS.
Ivan de Biron.

By HENRY HERMAN.
A Leading Lady.

By HEADON HILL.
Zambra the Detective.

By JOHN HILL.
Treason Felony.

By Mrs. CASHEL HOEY.
The Lover's Creed.

By Mrs. GEORGE HOOPER.
The House of Raby.

By TIGHE HOPKINS.
Twixt Love and Duty.

By Mrs. HUNGERFORD.

A Maiden all Forlorn.	A Mental Struggle.
In Durance Vile.	A Modern Circe.
Marvel.	Lady Verner's Flight.

By Mrs. ALFRED HUNT.

Thornicroft's Model.	Self-Condemned.
That Other Person.	The Leaden Casket.

By JEAN INGELOW.
Fated to be Free.

By WM. JAMESON.
My Dead Self.

By HARRIETT JAY.
The Dark Colleen. | Queen of Connaught.

By MARK KERSHAW.
Colonial Facts and Fictions.

By R. ASHE KING.

A Drawn Game.	Passion's Slave
"The Wearing of the	Bell Barry.
Green."	

By JOHN LEYS.
The Lindsays.

By E. LYNN LINTON.

Patricia Kemball.	The Atonement of Leam
The World Well Lost.	Dundas.
Under which Lord?	With a Silken Thread.
Paston Carew.	The Rebel of the
"My Love!"	Family.
Ione.	Sowing the Wind.

By HENRY W. LUCY.
Gideon Fleyce.

By JUSTIN McCARTHY.

Dear Lady Disdain.	Camiola.
Waterdale Neighbours.	Donna Quixote.
My Enemy's Daughter.	Maid of Athens.
A Fair Saxon.	The Comet of a Season.
Linley Rochford.	The Dictator.
Miss Misanthrope.	Red Diamonds.

By HUGH MACCOLL.
Mr. Stranger's Sealed Packet.

By AGNES MACDONELL.
Quaker Cousins.

KATHARINE S. MACQUOID.
The Evil Eye. | Lost Rose.

By W. H. MALLOCK.
A Romance of the Nine- | The New Republic.
teenth Century. |

Two-Shilling Novels—*continued.*

By FLORENCE MARRYAT.

Open! Sesame!	A Harvest of Wild Oats.
Fighting the Air.	Written in Fire.

By J. MASTERMAN.
Half-a-dozen Daughters.

By BRANDER MATTHEWS.
A Secret of the Sea.

By LEONARD MERRICK.
The Man who was Good.

By JEAN MIDDLEMASS.
Touch and Go. | Mr. Dorillion.

By Mrs. MOLESWORTH.
Hathercourt Rectory.

By J. E. MUDDOCK.

Stories Weird and Won-	From the Bosom of the
derful.	Deep.
The Dead Man's Secret.	

By MURRAY and HERMAN.

One Traveller Returns.	The Bishops' Bible.
Paul Jones's Alias.	

By D. CHRISTIE MURRAY.

A Model Father.	A Life's Atonement.
Joseph's Coat.	By the Gate of the Sea.
Coals of Fire.	A Bit of Human Nature.
Val Strange.	First Person Singular.
Old Blazer's Hero.	Bob Martin's Little
Hearts.	Girl.
The Way of the World.	Time's Revenges.
Cynic Fortune.	A Wasted Crime.

By HENRY MURRAY.
A Game of Bluff. | A Song of Sixpence.

By HUME NISBET.
"Bail Up!" | Dr. Bernard St. Vincent.

By ALICE O'HANLON.
The Unforeseen. | Chance? or Fate?

By GEORGES OHNET.

Dr. Rameau.	A Weird Gift.
A Last Love.	

By Mrs. OLIPHANT.

Whiteladies.	The Greatest Heiress in
The Primrose Path.	England.

By Mrs. ROBERT O'REILLY.
Phœbe's Fortunes.

By OUIDA.

Held in Bondage.	Two Little Wooden
Strathmore.	Shoes.
Chandos.	Moths.
Idalia.	Bimbi.
Under Two Flags.	Pipistrello.
Cecil Castlemaine's Gage	A Village Commune.
Tricotrin.	Wanda.
Puck.	Othmar.
Folle Farine.	Frescoes.
A Dog of Flanders.	In Maremma.
Pascarel.	Guilderoy.
Signa.	Ruffino.
Princess Napraxine.	Syrlin.
In a Winter City.	Santa Barbara.
Ariadne.	Ouida's Wisdom, Wit,
Friendship.	and Pathos.

MARGARET AGNES PAUL.
Gentle and Simple.

By C. L. PIRKIS.
Lady Lovelace.

By EDGAR A. POE.
The Mystery of Marie Roget.

By Mrs. CAMPBELL PRAED.
The Romance of a Station.
The Soul of Countess Adrian.
Outlaw and Lawmaker.

By E. C. PRICE.

Valentina.	Mrs. Lancaster's Rival
The Foreigners.	Gerald.

By RICHARD PRYCE.
Miss Maxwell's Affections.

TWO-SHILLING NOVELS—*continued.*

By JAMES PAYN.

Bentinck's Tutor.	Talk of the Town.
Murphy's Master.	Holiday Tasks.
A County Family.	A Perfect Treasure.
At Her Mercy.	What He Cost Her.
Cecil's Tryst.	A Confidential Agent.
The Clyffards of Clyffe.	Glow-worm Tales.
The Foster Brothers.	The Burnt Million.
Found Dead.	Sunny Stories.
The Best of Husbands.	Lost Sir Massingberd.
Walter's Word.	A Woman's Vengeance.
Halves.	The Family Scapegrace.
Fallen Fortunes.	Like Father, Like Son.
Humorous Stories.	Married Beneath Him.
£200 Reward.	Not Wooed, but Won.
A Marine Residence.	Less Black than We're
Mirk Abbey.	Painted.
By Proxy.	Some Private Views.
Under One Roof.	A Grape from a Thorn.
High Spirits.	The Mystery of Mir-
Carlyon's Year.	bridge.
From Exile.	The Word and the Will.
For Cash Only.	A Prince of the Blood.
Kit.	A Trying Patient.
The Canon's Ward.	

By CHARLES READE.

It is Never Too Late to	A Terrible Temptation.
Mend.	Foul Play.
Christie Johnstone.	The Wandering Heir.
The Double Marriage.	Hard Cash.
Put Yourself in His	Singleheart and Double-
Place.	face.
Love Me Little, Love	Good Stories of Men and
Me Long.	other Animals.
The Cloister and the	Peg Woffington.
Hearth.	Griffith Gaunt.
The Course of True	A Perilous Secret.
Love.	A Simpleton.
The Jilt.	Readiana.
The Autobiography of	A Woman-Hater.
a Thief.	

By Mrs. J. H. RIDDELL.

Weird Stories.	The Uninhabited House
Fairy Water.	The Mystery in Palace
Her Mother's Darling.	Gardens.
The Prince of Wales's	The Nun's Curse.
Garden Party.	Idle Tales.

By AMELIE RIVES.
Barbara Dering.

By F. W. ROBINSON.
Women are Strange. | The Hands of Justice.

By JAMES RUNCIMAN.
Skippers and Shellbacks.
Grace Balmaigne's Sweetheart.
Schools and Scholars.

By W. CLARK RUSSELL.

Round the Galley Fire.	The Romance of Jenny
On the Fo'k'sle Head.	Harlowe.
In the Middle Watch.	An Ocean Tragedy.
A Voyage to the Cape.	My Shipmate Louise.
A Book for the Ham-	Alone on a Wide Wide
mock.	Sea.
The Mystery of the	
"Ocean Star."	

GEORGE AUGUSTUS SALA.
Gaslight and Daylight.

By JOHN SAUNDERS.
Guy Waterman.
The Two Dreamers. | The Lion in the Path.

By KATHARINE SAUNDERS.

Joan Merryweather.	Sebastian.
The High Mills.	Margaret and Eliza-
Heart Salvage.	beth.

By GEORGE R. SIMS.

Rogues and Vagabonds.	Tinkletop's Crime.
The Ring o' Bells.	Zeph.
Mary Jane's Memoirs.	My Two Wives.
Mary Jane Married.	Memoirs of a Landlady.
Tales of To-day.	Scenes from the Show.
Dramas of Life.	

TWO-SHILLING NOVELS—*continued.*

By ARTHUR SKETCHLEY.
A Match in the Dark.

By HAWLEY SMART.
Without Love or Licence.

By T. W. SPEIGHT.

The Mysteries of Heron	Back to Life.
Dyke.	The Loudwater Tragedy.
The Golden Hoop.	Burgo's Romance.
Hoodwinked.	Quittance in Full.
By Devious Ways.	

By R. A. STERNDALE.
The Afghan Knife.

By R. LOUIS STEVENSON.
New Arabian Nights. | Prince Otto.

By BERTHA THOMAS.
Cressida. | The Violin-Player.
Proud Maisie.

By WALTER THORNBURY.
Tales for the Marines. | Old Stories Retold.

T. ADOLPHUS TROLLOPE.
Diamond Cut Diamond.

By F. ELEANOR TROLLOPE.

Like Ships upon the	Anne Furness.
Sea.	Mabel's Progress.

By ANTHONY TROLLOPE.

Frau Frohmann.	The American Senator.
Marion Fay.	Mr. Scarborough's
Kept in the Dark.	Family.
John Caldigate.	The Golden Lion of
The Way We Live Now.	Granpere.
The Land-Leaguers.	

By J. T. TROWBRIDGE.
Farnell's Folly.

By IVAN TURGENIEFF, &c.
Stories from Foreign Novelists.

By MARK TWAIN.

A Pleasure Trip on the	Life on the Mississippi.
Continent.	The Prince and the
The Gilded Age.	Pauper.
Huckleberry Finn.	A Yankee at the Court
Mark Twain's Sketches.	of King Arthur.
Tom Sawyer.	The £1,000,000 Bank-
A Tramp Abroad.	Note.
Stolen White Elephant.	

By C. C. FRASER-TYTLER.
Mistress Judith.

By SARAH TYTLER.

The Bride's Pass.	The Huguenot Fami'y.
Buried Diamonds.	The Blackhall Ghosts.
St. Mungo's City.	What She Came Through
Lady Bell.	Beauty and the Beast.
Noblesse Oblige.	Citoyenne Jaqueline.
Disappeared.	

By ALLEN UPWARD.
The Queen against Owen.

By AARON WATSON and LILLIAS WASSERMANN.
The Marquis of Carabas.

By WILLIAM WESTALL.
Trust-Money.

By Mrs. F. H. WILLIAMSON.
A Child Widow.

By J. S. WINTER.
Cavalry Life. | Regimental Legends.

By H. F. WOOD.
The Passenger from Scotland Yard.
The Englishman of the Rue Cain.

By Lady WOOD.
Sabina.

CELIA PARKER WOOLLEY.
Rachel Armstrong ; or, Love and Theology.

By EDMUND YATES.
The Forlorn Hope. | Castaway.
Land at Last.

OGDEN, SMALE AND CO., LIMITED, PRINTERS, GREAT SAFFRON HILL, E.C.